The Sufism of Rumi

K. Khosla was born in India in 1910. After taking a
degree in Economics at Cambridge he followed a
career in the Indian steel industry. He has written
articles on a wide variety of topics and was the co-
author of *Jamsetji Tata* a biography of the founder of
modern industrial India. An acknowledged authority
on Sufism he has had a passion for mystical poetry
since early youth and he describes this book as 'a work
of love'.

The Sufism
of Rumi

K. Khosla

Element Books

© K. Khosla 1987
First published in Great Britain in 1987 by
Element Books Ltd.
Longmead, Shaftesbury, Dorset

Printed in Great Britain by
Billings, Hylton Road, Worcester

Designed by Humphrey Stone

Cover illustration: an early portrait
of Mevlana Jalalu'd-Din Rumi

British Library Cataloguing in Publication Data
Khosla, K.
The Sufism of Rumi.
1. Jalal al al-Din Rumi
I. Title
297'.4'0924   PK6482

ISBN 0-906540-93-3

Contents

Acknowledgements

For permission to use extracts and general ideas, grateful thanks are extended to the following copyright holders, authors and publishers:

Gibb Memorial Trust and Messrs Luzac and Company:
The Mathnawi of Jalalu'd-Din Rumi, edited by Dr R.A. Nicholson;
The Mathnawi of Jalalu'd-Din Rumi, translated by Dr R.A. Nicholson;
The Mathnawi of Jalalu'd-Din Rumi, commentary by Dr R.A. Nicholson;
The Kashf al-Mahjub of 'Ali B. 'Uthman al-Jullabi al-Hujwiri (the oldest Persian treatise on Sufism), translated by Dr R.A. Nicholson.

George Allen and Unwin:
Rumi: Poet and Mystic, translated by Dr R.A. Nicholson;
The Meaning of the Glorious Koran, an explanatory translation by Muhammad Marmaduke Pickthall.

John Murray:
Discourses of Rumi, A.J. Arberry (a translation of Rumi's *Fihi ma fihi*, (meaning 'In it what is in it').

Cambridge University Press:
Studies in Islamic Mysticism, Dr R.A. Nicholson.

Bell and Hyman:
The Mystics of Islam, Dr R.A. Nicholson.

The Theosophy Company, Los Angeles, California:
Isis Unveiled, by Madame H.P. Blavatsky, centenary anniversary edition – a photographic facsimile reproduction of the original edition of 1877;

The Secret Doctrine, Madame H.P. Blavatsky – a photographic facsimile reproduction of the original edition of 1888.

The Theosophical Publishing House, Adyar, Madras, India:
The Voice of the Silence, Madame H.P. Blavatsky.

Oxford University Press:
The Tibetan Book of the Dead, edited by Dr W.Y. Evans-Wentz (3rd edition, 1956);
The Sufi Orders in Islam, J. Spencer Trimingham.

Faber and Faber:
The Enneads of Plotinus, translated by Stephen McKenna.

Routledge and Kegan Paul:
The Mesnevi of Mevlana Jelalu'd-Din Muhammad er-Rumi, Book the First, together with some account of the life and acts of the author, of his ancestors, and of his descendants, illustrated by a selection of characteristic anecdotes, as collected by their historian, Mevlana Shemsu'd-Din el Aflaki. Translated and the poetry versified by James W. Redhouse (London, 1881);
The Book of the Dead, A.E. Wallis Budge (an English translation of the chapters, hymns, etc., of the Theban Recension, 1956 edition).

Routledge and Kegan Paul, London; and Harcourt Brace Jovanovich Inc., New York:
The Secret of The Golden Flower, translated and explained by Richard Wilhelm, and translated into English by Cary F. Baynes.

Watkins Books:
The Yoga of the Bhagawat Gita, Sri Krishna Prem;
The Yoga of the Kathopanishad, Sri Krishna Prem.

The Publishers:
Special mention must be made of my publishers, Element Books. I know of their personal interest in Sufism and kindred subjects, and am gratefully appreciative of the sympathetic care and understanding with which they have published my humble effort.

Introduction

Persia's greatest mystical poet, Jalalu'd-Din Rumi, was born at Balkh in Persia in AD 1207. He came of a family of renowned jurists and divines who claimed descent from the first Caliph Abu Bakr. His father Baha'u'd-Din Walad was a highly venerated instructor and preacher, and was also well versed in Sufism. His learned work, the *Ma'arif* ('Gnoses'), was to be later a source of delight and instruction to his son Walad.

In 1219, when Jalal was twelve years old, his father left Balkh and took his family to Nishapur, where he went to see the famous mystical poet Shaykh Faridu'd-Din 'Attar, who predicted Jalal's spiritual greatness, blessed him and gave him a copy of his mystical poem, the *Asrar Nama* ('Book of Mysteries').

Persia has produced three great mystical *mathnawi* writers, that is, writers of poems with rhyming couplets. Of them, the first was Sana'i, whose best-known work is the *Hadiqatu'l-Haqiqat* ('Garden of Truth'); the second was the afore-mentioned 'Attar, who was a prolific writer and to whose well-known allegorical poem, the *Mantiqu't-Tair* ('Conference of the Birds'), we shall have occasion to refer in chapter 6; and the third and by far the greatest was Rumi. In the following couplet, Rumi acknowledges his debt to the first two:

> 'Attar was the spirit and Sana'i its two eyes,
> We came after Sana'i and 'Attar.

Thus, according to Rumi, 'Attar was the spirit and Sana'i the two eyes of Sufism.

From Nishapur, the family journeyed to Baghdad, and then

to Mecca, where Baha performed the pilgrimage. They then proceeded to Damascus and, finally, settled in Rum, as Asiatic Turkey was then called. The reason for this migration was the dread of the Mongol hordes which, under Chingiz Khan, were sweeping down from the north-east, carrying death and destruction before them, and were already nearing Balkh.

Laranda, not far from Konya (Iconium), was their first home in Turkey. Here, Rumi married Gawhar ('Pearl'), daughter of one Lala of Samarkand, and in 1226, his eldest son Sultan Walad was born. Walad wrote poetry and has left us interesting biographical material concerning his father. Rumi's own works also give some information about him.[1]

From Laranda, on the invitation of the Seljuq king 'Ala'u'd-Din Kaiqubad I, or rather of his vizier, the Parwana Mu'inu'd-Din, Baha moved with his family to Konya, the capital of the Seljuqs of Rum, where he taught and preached till his death in 1230. His pedagogic excellence earned him the title of *Sultanu'l-'Ulama* ('King of the learned').

A year or so after Baha's death one of his old pupils, Burhanu'd-Din Muhaqqiq of Tirmidh, came to Konya looking for refuge under the Seljuq king, who was known for his piety and patronage of men of letters. He could not meet Baha, as he was already dead; but meeting his son Jalal, he took his spiritual training in hand and formally initiated him into the doctrines and practices of Sufism. The training continued for a period of about nine years until the death of Burhan in 1240, whereafter Jalal himself assumed the rank of Shaykh and began to teach and preach, attracting a large number of disciples. At the same time, for four or five years till he met Shamsu'd-Din of Tabriz — his Socratic spiritual director — he continued to practise austerities in seclusion, attaining increasingly higher degrees of perfection.

Much of Rumi's theosophy centres round the Perfect Man, who is a mirror of all the attributes of God. God made him in his own image and the world in the image of his spirit. To be united with such a man is to be united with the Light of God. The degree of perfection, of course, is not the same in all cases.

There is no repetition in life. In Rumi's case, three Perfect Men appeared, dividing his life into three distinct phases.

The first of the trio was Shamsu'd-Din of Tabriz, who has just been mentioned. He came to Konya in a coarse black felt hat and wide cloak in 1244 — four or five years after the death of Burhan. In the words of Redhouse, he was 'exceedingly aggressive and domineering in his manner', and he flouted Islamic tenets. Because of his flighty wanderings, he was nicknamed *Paranda* ('The Flier').[2] Jalal met him and, recognising in him the image of God, took him to his house.

Shams's company wrought a miraculous change in Rumi. The latter was so struck by the light of this spiritual sun that he became utterly heedless of whatever he had learnt and practised. His traditional knowledge, gnosis, theosophical doctrines and pedagogics all lay neglected. Nothing existed for him but Shams, with whom he would remain closeted in spiritual communion, completely dead to the outside world. As his son Sultan Walad says about him, the man of exoteric knowledge who was also well versed in Sufism had now become a lover, the adept a novice, the *Shaykh* a learner.

Rumi had written hardly any poetry before and he was now in his late thirties, generally a little late to attract the Muse of poetry. But love has wonderful powers. It made Rumi a poet and the Muse laurelled his brow. Shams had touched the triggers in him.

Rumi's disciples, however, cut off from their beloved master, who had taken to the dervish cloak and stopped teaching, believed that Shams was having a bad influence on Rumi, and resented his association with him. They abused Shams and threatened him with violence. Shams decided to leave Konya and went and took refuge in Damascus.

Deeply pained by this separation from his spiritual master, Rumi became heedless of everything and even more indifferent to his disciples. Seeing his anguish, they became repentant. He forgave them, and sent his son Walad to Damascus to bring Shams back. On the latter's return, they were kind to him at first, but soon jealousy seized them afresh and they again took to abusing him and became thirsty for his blood. Again, Shams left and took asylum in Damascus. Around 1247, he mysteriously disappeared. Some said that he was killed by Rumi's disciples. Others, citing the authority of Sultan Walad, said that Shams had told the latter in advance of his intended mysterious disappearance, and so, when he suddenly disappeared, none knew his whereabouts or found any trace of him.

The broken-hearted Rumi himself twice visited Damascus in search of Shams, but to no purpose. After suffering agony for three or four years, Rumi chose for his companion one Salahu'd-Din, surnamed Zarkub ('gold-beater') after his profession. He said that the Shams he was seeking had arrived in the form of Zarkub, and the two, Shams and Zarkub, were one spirit in two bodies, and he appointed him as his deputy.

His disciples resented this fresh intrusion and complained that Zarkub was illiterate, with no idea of pedagogics. But Rumi and Zarkub had been Burhan's fellow-pupils, and Rumi knew that Zarkub was held in high esteem by Burhan, and was able to prevail upon his disciples to accept Zarkub as their instructor.

Rumi got his son Walad married to Zarkub's daughter Fatima, and taught her 'to read the Koran and other books'.

Salah acted as instructor for nine or ten years, and died around 1261.

The third Perfect Man in Rumi's life was his disciple Husamu'd-Din, whom he appointed as his deputy in place of Zarkub. Husam continued in this capacity till Jalal's death in 1273, when he stepped into the latter's shoes, becoming the Chief of the Mevlevi Order of Dervishes which had been founded by Rumi. He carried on in this position till his death in 1284, when Sultan Walad stepped into the breach as the Chief of the Order.

Husam was the inspirer of the *Mathnawi*, and Rumi describes him as 'the key of the treasuries of the empyrean', 'the trustee of the treasures on earth', 'the Abu Yazid (Bayazid) ... and the Junayd[3] of the age'. In Book VI of the *Mathnawi*,

Rumi calls the *Mathnawi* the *Husami Nama* ('Book of Husam'). In Book II, he says that there was delay in starting it, as Husam was not available. According to some, Husam had lost his wife and was too grief-stricken to attend to the *Mathnawi*. But for Rumi and his followers, death was an occasion not for sorrow, but for rejoicing. The real reason for the delay, as appears from the Preface to Book II and its opening verses, was, firstly, that Divine Wisdom is sent down gradually and 'not without calculation', as too much of it at a time would destroy one's understanding; and, secondly, and perhaps mainly, that Husam was observing seclusion and carrying out other Sufi practices at this time, and, without him, without his spring-tide, the buds of Divine Knowledge remained unburst in Rumi's heart.

Rumi was of the view that there was nothing worse than poetry, and he says that when he thought of rhymed couplets for communion with God, He told him that 'I will throw word, sound and speech into chaos, so that, without these three, I may converse with you' (M.I, 1727–30).[4] This might be the reason why Rumi wrote no poetry until his late thirties, when the intoxicating company of Shams changed him from a jurist and divine into the greatest mystical poet that Islam has known.

THE WHIRLING DERVISHES

Rumi instituted *sama* (which literally means 'audition', but here includes music, singing and dancing) as part of the religious service. Though strictly speaking Islam does not approve of music and dancing, in Rumi they have a spiritual significance. Because of the peculiar gyrations performed by his followers, the latter came to be known in the West as 'The Whirling Dervishes'.

RUMI'S LITERARY OUTPUT

Rumi's literary work is of staggering dimensions. Of his two major works, both poetical, one is the *Diwan* ('Collection of Poems'), which contains over 3,000 mystical odes, followed by some 2,000 quatrains — altogether 35,000 verses or more. It is named after Shams and is dedicated to his memory. It is known as the *Diwan-i-Shams-i-Tabrizi*. His other and more serious work is the *Mathnawi*, which is in six volumes and, according to Dr Nicholson's edited Text, contains 25,632 verses. It is a later work than the *Diwan*, except that a small portion of the latter was written concurrently with the *Mathnawi*.

Of his prose works — three in number — the *Fihi ma fihi* ('In it what is in it') may be singled out for mention, as, like the *Mathnawi*, it is didactic in nature, covering common ground with it at times, and is more relevant in our context.[5] It contains discourses addressed to his disciples, and has been translated into English by A. J. Arberry under the title of *Discourses of Rumi*.

There are three eminent men to whom Rumi is mainly indebted. Of these, Sana'i and Attar have already been mentioned. The third was the great Andalusian Arab mystic Ibnu'l-'Arabi, who is said to be the father of Islamic Pantheism. Rumi himself has been described as a 'Monist Pantheist'.

The odes of Rumi, though at times didactic, are mainly concerned with individual mystical states. They are love, vision and rapture, and represent the outpourings of a spirit reeling in divine madness, jubilating in union, crying in separation. Spiritual in content, rich in beauty and melody, erotic and Bacchanalian in symbolism, they are like 'enchanted wine poured from the Holy Grail'.

The *Mathnawi*, on the other hand, is sober and serious. It is a rich amalgam of knowledge (*ilm*), gnosis (*ma'rifat*) and love (*ishq*). It is often described as 'the Koran in the Pahlawi (Persian) tongue'. It expounds verses from the Koran, and explains the sayings and traditions of prophets, particularly of the Prophet Muhammad, and narrates incidents from the lives of saints and dervishes. It explains mystical themes through the medium of beast fables, stories and anecdotes drawn from various sources, some religious, some general, a few even

14

crude. Parables and homely analogies abound. Ribaldry also is found in the *Mathnawi*, as it incurred no odium in those days.

Although Rumi's stories and fables are entertaining, they are essentially didactic in purpose. As he himself says, the *Mathnawi* is 'the shop for Unity' and anything other than God that is found in it is just an idol, that is, a means of attraction (M.VI, 1528).

The style of the *Mathnawi* is terse and cryptic, even ambiguous at times, except in the stories and anecdotes where it is generally plain and simple. Rumi does not believe in divulging the Divine mysteries to all and sundry. As he says: 'Of a hundred esoteric mysteries, I speak only of one and that too not in full, but in hair-form, so that the subject does not reach every ear,' (M.I, 1762; M.II, 3505). On the whole, however, his language is not very involved or intricate. No artificial devices mar the flow of his work. The metaphors and flowers of speech that break the seriousness of the text every now and then are charmingly inwoven. Rumi's style is all his own — original and not without melody.

If the *Mathnawi* is difficult to understand, it is because of its abstruse subject matter, and the loose and rambling manner in which it is presented. It is not systematic or methodical; it ignores sequence and cohesion. Often, more is concealed than revealed. Themes generally overlap. Even the stories are interrupted by long digressions. Rumi's *Mathnawi*, as Whinfield[6] says, is not 'doctrinal', but 'experimental'. He speaks of what he has experienced or felt in his heart, and what is inwardly experienced has its own logic.

Basically, the *Mathnawi* is instructional. It speaks of moral and mystical truths as Rumi sees them, and gives guidance to the spiritual wayfarer, pointing out sign-posts and danger-signals on the Way. Each reader derives instruction and delight from it, according to his taste and capacity. There is food for all in the *Mathnawi*.

Speaking of the *Mathnawi* in the Preface to the First Book, Rumi says: it is the Greatest Science of God, the Clearest Way of God, and the most manifest Proof of God. The like of its Light is 'as a niche wherein is a candle' shining with an effulgence brighter than the dawn. It is the Heart's Paradise, with fountains and foliage.... Like the Nile of Egypt, it is a drink to the patient, but a sorrow to the House of Pharaoh and unbelievers.

Both the *Diwan* and the *Mathnawi* are great works, and both are rooted in mystical love and gnosis in different ways. Describing the difference between them, Dr Nicholson says: 'The one is a majestic river, calm and deep, meandering through many a rich and varied landscape to the immeasurable ocean; the other a foaming torrent that leaps and plunges in the ethereal solitude of the hills.'

A glimpse of some of the themes from Rumi discussed in this book is given below:

i God said: 'I was a hidden treasure, and I desired to be known, so I created this creation in order that I might be known.' That 'hidden treasure' was the totality of His countless attributes inherent in His Essence. As the creation is a reflection of all His attributes, it is really God's outward Self-manifestation rather than creation.

ii God's Essence is the Self whereby He exists, and it is beyond knowing. It is manifested through His names and attributes which inhere in it. It is the source of life on all levels of being.

iii All is God. He is transcendent as well as immanent, and yet is beyond description. The world is an objectification of His countless attributes, and is permeated by His Essence. It is beautiful and real, if its outwardness is not mistaken for its inward reality.

iv The purpose of the creation is Divine worship, which includes
  a) the ritual worship which makes one's intentions manifest;
  b) performance of our assigned tasks to keep this God-created world going on a co-operative basis, and

constantly manifesting His attributes; and

c) constant striving after self-perfection as the necessary means of return to Him.

v The process of evolution does not end with man. He can rise to angelhood, and to countless still loftier stations, and become perfect. The Perfect Man alone reflects all the Divine attributes. God made him in His own image, and He made the creation in his spirit. The Perfect Man is not only the origin of the creation, but also its object. It is through him alone that God can see His Self-manifestation, as no other created thing reflects His attributes in full as does the Perfect Man.

vi Predestination is a fact, as all action is willed and decreed by God. Free will also is a fact, as man reflects the attributes of God and one of them is free will. What is predestined is hidden from us. It is only by use of free will and exertion that we can come to know what is predestined.

vii Evil is relative. It exists because good exists. Heedlessness of God is evil, but is necessary to keep this world going. Lust is evil, but is necessary for procreation. Even the producer of the counterfeit coin is not wholly evil. The coin has the semblance of genuineness; it is not wholly false.

Wealth is commonly said to be the root of evil. 'How good is righteous wealth,' said the Prophet, provided it is acquired by fair means and spent on right ends.

Woman is evil. But she is also a ray of God. It is through her that God performs the creative function.

viii As in Christian mysticism, the Sufi Path may be conveniently described as a three-staged Path. The first stage is that of self-purification. It involves the killing of the 'appetitive soul', that is, the flesh and the devil. Self-mortification leads to the second stage, the stage of ecstasy and illumination, of contemplation of God and His attributes. Intense contemplation leads to the third stage, which is the unitive state. This stage involves union with the Divine attributes, and, in its highest reaches, with the Divine Essence.

The Prophet Muhammad was the chiefest of the prophets, the best creature that God ever created. He was the Perfect Man *par excellence*, the Logos, the origin and object of creation.

In Rumi's view, one's individuality is not lost in the unitive state. One may not taste any part of the ounce of vinegar dropped in an ocean of honey, but it is there; its essence is inviolate.

ix Death is not the end. It is the birth of a new form of spiritual life. Rumi believes in Resurrection, though some — an insignificant minority — have thought that he was a Reincarnationist.

x Death is no occasion for sorrow; it is an occasion for rejoicing. For it is the spirit's Homeward flight. Hence, Rumi introduced joyous hymn-singing into the burial service.

xi Rumi speaks of Heaven and Hell in the manner of the orthodox, and also, speaking on another level, he describes them as spiritual states.

xii The torments of Hell are terrible, but they bring remembrance of God and are purifying.

xiii Eventually, the Lord's eternally precedent Mercy will prevail and save us all, Satan not excluded.

Rumi's material is rich and wide-ranging, and his 'experimental' Sufism is concerned with truths of universal interest. But he is no breaker of idols. He rejects no faith as false. According to him, the aim of all creeds is God, and, in this sense, they all are one. In any case, when the end is reached, the means become redundant. His catholicity is exceptional.

In his Commentary[7] on *The Secret of the Golden Flower*, a Chinese Book of Life, Dr Jung says that the psyche possesses a common sub-stratum. He calls it the Collective Unconscious.

As a common heritage, it ... does not consist merely of contents capable of becoming conscious, but of latent dispositions towards identical reactions. Thus the fact of the Collective Unconscious is simply the psychic expression of identity of brain structure, irrespective of all racial differences.

It is strange that, in the same Commentary, he should also say that it would be a mistake for the West to imitate the East — theosophy, according to him, is the West's best example of this mistake — but must develop from its nature what the East has developed from its inner being. On the contrary, one would think that the identity of instincts and brain structure would lead the human nature everywhere to raise similar questions and find similar answers, regardless of racial and cultural variations. It is because of such identity that Rumi's relevance is universal.

But what Dr Jung says of the background of *The Tibetan Book of the Dead* is true of Sufism also. Here, it 'is not the niggardly European "either or", but a magnificently affirmative "both and"', except that in the higher reaches of Sufism, both affirmation and negation stand transcended, and the One remains and naught beside Him.

THE METHOD OF APPROACH

Rumi, as already stated, is not orderly or systematic; he does not pre-plan; and he assumes much as known, though unknown to many; he is deliberately reticent. In order to understand him, a basic knowledge of Sufism is essential. I have, therefore, sought to provide some kind of framework within which Rumi's spiritual experiences might be better appreciated. Basic and interpretative material has been included where felt necessary, in the hope that it might prove helpful.

I have consulted with profit several English, Persian and Urdu commentaries on the *Mathnawi*. But the one author I would like to single out for mention is Dr Nicholson. I have leaned heavily on his works, especially those listed in the Acknowledgements, and they have been of great help to me. My gratefulness to him is profound.

I have made relatively restricted use of the sonorous *Diwan*, as its individual mystical odes are generally descriptive of individual mystical states and these receive fuller treatment in the *Mathnawi*, and I intended to keep the book restricted in size. It was a self-denying ordinance for reasons of space.

Though no long passages have been quoted from Rumi, his language has been woven into the text, in order to reproduce some of the spirit and flavour of the original.

I have also drawn on other faiths and thought-systems, as they might give one a better understanding of Rumi's Sufism and a better appreciation of his universality. Though over 700 years old, his teachings are still valid; time has not reduced their relevance.

While I hope that this slender book will give the reader an intelligible, overall picture of Rumi's Sufism — 'the precious life-blood of a master spirit' — I wish it to be understood that all that is good in this book is Rumi's, and all its imperfections are mine.

K. KHOSLA
Dehra Dun,
India

1

God and the Creation

'I was a hidden treasure, and I desired to be known, so I created this creation in order that I might be known,' God is reported to have said to the Prophet Muhammad.

This refers to God's Self-manifestation to Himself within Himself. He was the 'treasure' of all His attributes in His own Essence, which are not separate from each other, nor from the Essence. No duality or plurality was involved; all was One.

Rumi tells us that when we say that 'God is One', it is to be understood as a denial of duality, not as an expression of the real nature of Unity (M.VI, 2714, heading). His Unity transcends definition and description.

THE DIVINE ESSENCE, NAMES AND ATTRIBUTES

God is Self-subsistent. His Essence is the Self whereby He exists and is beyond knowing. It is manifested through His names and attributes which inhere in it.

In His essence, which has no outwardness and is utterly inward, God has no form or colour. For that which has no outwardness does not exist, that is, does not stand forth as a separate entity, and can have no form. And that which has no form can have no colour. The Formless is thus Colourless. Rumi often uses the terms 'Formlessness' and 'Colourlessness' when referring to the Divine Essence.

God is hidden, says Rumi, as things are made manifest by their opposites and He has no like or opposite (M.I, 1131). He cannot enter the imagination. Do not seek to investigate the Essence of God, said the Prophet, as in itself it is unknowable. It is only through His names and attributes, which are its

21

individualisations and forms, that its knowledge can be sought. Earlier, Plotinus[1] also said: 'Seeking Him, seek nothing of Him outside; within is to be sought what follows upon Him; Himself do not attempt' (*Enneads*, vi, viii, 18).

In reference to the Divine Essence, Rumi uses the symbol of the sun, the Central Spiritual Sun. Unlike our visible sun, the Spiritual Sun has nothing even dimly comparable in the mind or externally. It is everlasting and has no yesterday (M.I, 119–21). The Divine Essence, which is the Self of God, neither rises nor sets. It is only in relation to His motes, that is, His attributes, which appear only when He manifests Himself, that He can be said to have a rising place. Himself, the Absolute is beyond all rising places (M.II, 1107–8).

The Spiritual Sun, the Divine Essence, is the source of life and light. It was at its ray, says Plato, that God lighted a fire which we call the sun (*Timaeus*).[2]

There is a tradition that God sprinkled of His Light upon mankind. That Light is one, just as the sun's orb is one. The human spirits that received that Light are, therefore, one in essence, possessing the same Light.

In spiritual matters, there is no division, no numbers or units. Plurality and differentiation arise when the Light shines and is fragmented in the windows of the body, that is, in the animal spirit or soul, which is the medium of sense-perception, and which sees each self as separate and independent (M.I, 681; M.II, 186–9).

Plurality is essential, as the One created the creation for Self-manifestation and He cannot manifest Himself and make known His names and attributes without becoming the Many.

The Divine names are not mere proper names, with no meaning, but denote eternal ideas or attributes[3] (M.IV, 218–19). If the One represented one or a specific number of attributes, one or a specific number of names would have sufficed. But as the vast, multitudinous creation is a reflection of all His attributes, thus completing His desire for Self-manifestation, His names and attributes are countless. No matter how many names we gave Him, He would remain undefined. As Rumi says, even all the atoms in the world could not adequately proclaim His qualities of Beauty, Majesty and Perfection in their infinite forms.

Speaking of His Names, the orthodox allow the application of only such names as are found in the Koran or in any Apostolic Tradition. It is aptly said that He is 'the Nameless of the hundred names'.

It is a common Sufi belief that the name reveals the named it objectifies, as there can be no real name without the named, no subject without the object. Every name in reality is one of the names of God. But only he can understand the meaning of the original Divine name who has tasted the cup of *Hu* (God), and whom the fantasy born of that name and attribute shows the way to union with Him (M.I, 3453–4). Thus, if he becomes one with the name Allah, which comprises all His names and attributes, he realises that there is nothing apart from Him. As Rumi says, in that unitive state, one's petition to God is like God's petition to Himself (M.V, 2242, heading).

Rumi has no room for the externalist, who is content with the formal recitation of a divine name, without understanding or seeking its meaning, and asks him:

> Do you know a name without a thing answering to it?
> Have you ever plucked a rose from R,O,S,E?
>
> (M.I, 3456 tr. Nicholson)

It is the kernel that matters, not the husk as such; the named, not just the name we have recited or spelt.

If we are unable to understand the reality of the object named it is because, with us, the name of a thing is descriptive of its outward appearance, which is a changing state and is only a step in its evolution towards its final state. With God, it is the last state of an object which determines its name, and is its reality towards which it evolves. Thus, the Caliph Umar was nicknamed 'idolater' at first, but in pre-existence his name was believer, as he was a believer in the end. What we call 'seed' was before God a potential form in non-existence, exactly as it appeared in the external world. No name He gave ever changed. It was these names reflecting the final state of the things named which God taught Adam, the father of mankind, giving him knowledge of particulars (M.I, 1234 etc.). This is the meaning of the Koranic text: 'He taught the Names', and it was this knowledge that Adam communicated to the angels.

Rumi says that God calls Himself by different names for our benefit. He calls Himself *Basir* (Seeing), *Sami'* (Hearing), and *'Alim* (Knowing), so that out of fear of Him or to please Him, we may do no evil, speak no evil, think no evil (M.IV, 21517). His name *Jabbar* (Almighty) is meant to inspire us with humility (M.I, 617). God calls Himself *Kafi* (All-sufficing), and says: I will give you satiety without bread, roses without the spring, healing without medicine, and all good without the mediation of any secondary cause or another's help (M.IV, 3516–20), and so one should not be impatient, greedy or concupiscent.

But God also has what appear to us conflicting names. Thus, He is not only *Hadi* (Guide), but also *Mudhill* (Misguide). Pharaoh and Moses both worshipped God, executing His Will, as decreed by Him. But whereas Moses was guided aright by Him, Pharaoh lost the way. The Divine Will that illumined Moses darkened Pharaoh (M.I, 2447–50). Iblis, who was predestined to lead men astray, invokes God by the name *Mudhill*, and manifests this predestined trait in all His actions (M.V, 953).

In essence, the soul belongs to the realm of unity. Whatever names the different souls possess derive their essential meaning from what God decreed for them in pre-existence (M.I, 296). He has eternally known and decreed who will be a true believer (*mumin*) and who a hypocrite (*munafiq*). As the Tradition has it, 'verily, God created man in darkness, and then He sprinkled upon them [mankind] of His Light, and he to whom that Light attained was guided, and he whom it missed went astray'.

Faith and unbelief, obedience and disobedience, sorrow and joy, all are the effects of predispositions which God created in the souls. The latter acquire nothing new in their earthly existence. On return to their original 'Colourlessness', there is no duality, no conflict (M.I, 2468). To quote Rumi, God is 'the coincidence of contraries' (*Diwan*).

THE DOCTRINE OF THE UNITY OF GOD

'There is no God except God' is the doctrine of the Unity of God; it is the Moslem faith formula. It means that God is One, with no sharer in His Essence, attributes and powers, no partner in His actions. He is utterly transcendent. He is beyond all spatio-temporal relations, wholly unlike any of His creatures, wholly apart from the creation, wholly unreachable by thought.

The Koran mentions His 'complementary' aspect also, namely, His Immanence, His Self-manifestation in the creation. He is the First and the Last, and the Outward and the Inward (Koran, lvii, 3). As the source of created beings, He is the First (*al-awwal*), and, as the end to whom we all shall ultimately return, He is the Last (*al-akhir*). As transcendent, He is the Inward (*al-batin*), and, as immanent, He is the Outward (*al-zahir*). 'He ever is at work, Himself being what He doeth. For did He separate Himself from it, all things would then collapse' (Hermes).

According to the Sufi interpretation of the doctrine of the Divine Unity (*tawhid*), not only is there no God except God, but there is nothing but God. Described thus, the doctrine is called that of the Unity of Being (*wahdatu'l-wujud*).

In Rumi, the *tawhid* is to burn oneself before the Beloved (God), to melt away one's existence in that Existent who nourishes and sustains existence, as copper melts away in the elixir (M.I, 3010–11), so that the One remains and naught besides Him.

The entire variegated universe is one with Him or is the external form of One Being; or the Reality is One and the different created beings are its manifestations; or Pure Being is One and all else is Not-being. (See *Islamic Mysticism*, Jili, pp.82, 83).[4] In the words of the eleventh-century dervish poet

Baba Kuhi of Shiraz:[5]

> In the market, in the cloister — only God I saw,
> In the valley and on the mountain — only God I saw.
> I passed away into nothingness, I vanished,
> And lo, I was the All-living — only God I saw.
>
> (tr. Dr Nicholson)

In Bacchanalian language, 'The whole universe is a tavern, and the heart of every atom is His wine-cup.' But the wine alone is real; without it, the tavern and the cup are as nothing; they are not-being.

But even the extreme form of the Sufi doctrine of the Unity of Being does not render irrelevant the immanent aspect of God. The text, 'Whithersoever you turn, there is the Face of *Allah*' (Koran, ii, 115) refers to this aspect. It is a Face that, in Rumi's words, 'runs infinitely and for ever' (*Discourses*, p.32). Whilst it is nowhere, nowhere is it not. It is the essential aspect or Self of God, whose attributes constitute all existence.

According to Jili, the Face refers to the Divine Holy Spirit (*ruhu'l-quds*) which constitutes the spirit of man and is individualised in every object of sense and thought (*Islamic Mysticism*, p.109).

According to Rumi, there is a union between the Lord of man and the spirit of man, but it transcends description and analogy (M.IV, 760).

With the Stoics, God is not separate from the world, but is its soul, and we all have a part of the Divine Fire. In Christianity, God incarnates in man. In Hinduism, 'Thou art That' (God or Spirit). 'The circle is infinite and the centre everywhere.'

How should He, then, be hidden from us?

The reference here is not to God throned in His solitary Transcendence, who, of course, is utterly unknowable, but to God in His Immanence — to God 'closer to us than our neck-veins' (Koran, 1, 16). His Light or Spirit is the ground of all our experience. His attributes are universally manifested. He is hidden because of His proximity, His immanence and unbroken presence everywhere, because 'Earth's crammed with heaven, And every common bush afire with God.'

The simple fact is that our outer organs are not fitted for sight of Him or of His Spirit. It is only the pure eye of spirit that can see the Spirit.

In Moslem theology, God is seen or known by what He created. The creation is the evidence of His existence. But for Rumi mere evidence is not enough. 'Nature, poor step-dame, cannot slake my drouth.' Nothing less than God would do for Rumi. The outward visible form is not the same as its original or inward reality. The pomp and splendour of the world is 'borrowed', unlike that of the Upper World of Command (*amr*), the spiritual world immediately following upon the Divine Utterance *kun* (Be), the world of Cosmic Ideation, which is essential and real (M.II, 1103). The borrowed must not be mistaken for the original.

Take the cloud. Its splendour and beauty are not original. The transfigured cloud must not be called the moon (M.II, 693). The moon itself is lit by the sun, just as the visible sun is lit by the Spiritual Sun, that is, by the Light of God.

Or take the wall that is illumined by sunbeams. It does not become identical with the sun or its beams. Nor does the reflection share in the nature of the original. It is entirely dependent on the original, and vanishes when the original withdraws itself. The original, on the other hand, is entirely independent of the reflection.

This is true of all the physical transcripts of the Divine archetypes. They are temporary reflections of the Light of God, and though real in the sense that they are the objectification of the Real, Rumi warns us against letting them veil His essential Transcendence; we must not mix Him with His creation. God alone is real and is transcendent, and Not-being remains Not-being, existing only to the extent to which the Divine attributes are reflected in it.

But the cosmological significance of Not-being must not be underrated. Just as Not-being is wholly dependent on Being, the Supreme Being manifests Himself only to the extent to which the Divine attributes are reflected in it. Being and Not-being are thus in mutual debt.

Referring to His Immanence, Rumi says that God cannot be separated from us who are His creatures. Nor can we endure to be separated from Him. How should the fish endure to be separated from the water? (M.II, 1113). There is no creature that is not connected with Him, though the connection is indescribable, as there is no separating or uniting in the spirit and our thought and intellect can only think of separating and uniting (M.IV, 3695-6).

The Sufi knows that God is both transcendent and immanent, though he may stress His transcendence at times and, at times, His immanence. He also knows that transcendence and immanence are limiting qualities, and God is above all limitation. These terms are used only for convenience; they do not describe His Essence, which is unknowable and, therefore, indescribable. 'Why dost thou prate of God? Whatsoever thou sayest of Him is untrue' (Meister Eckhart).

THE ORIGIN OF CREATION

It is stated in the Koran that creation is by God's Will and Choice, and that He is the Creator of the heavens and the earth and all that is therein. He just utters the command 'Be', and it is (Koran, xvi,40). This is similar to what is stated in Genesis: Let there be light; and there was light. God's fiat is absolute.

Before man's creation, this world lay latent in God's eternal Knowledge, which is the 'hidden treasure', and He was nursing the latent capacities of each object and preparing it for its destined role in the manifested universe. As Rumi says: Where were Moses and Jesus, when the sun was watering the sown fields of existing objects? Where were Adam and Eve, when God strung this bow? (M.III, 1275-6).

According to Moslem philosophers, everything, including our universe, proceeds by logical necessity from One First Cause. According to Rumi, God is not the First Cause. He is the absolute Knower, Willer, Seer, etc. He does not act from the necessity of His nature. He is independent of causality. He is not joined to any cause. He decrees and acts as He pleases, altering His custom when He wills, saying to the sea, for example, 'Be full of fire', or to the mountain, 'Be light as wool.' The duality of cause and effect, and how and why, does not apply to Him (M.II, 1625–9).

God is said to have created the world out of nothing, which means out of none of the things we know as things. He created them out of Himself, out of the 'hidden treasure' that He was.

Referring to God's creative command 'Be', Rumi says that when God desires a thing, He says to it, 'Be' (*kun*), and it is. That is the form His command takes. The entire creation is His speech — speech as the expression of thought; it is born of the Divine Voice — the creative 'Be'.[6]

The word 'Be' works like magic, as if God were a super-magician, says Rumi. He merely recites spells on the non-existences which have no eye or ear, no sense-perception, but are just ideas, and instantly they dance into existence; and when He recites a spell on the existent, they rush back into non-existence. God says something into the rose's ear and it laughs; something to the stone, and it turns into cornelian; something to the body, and it becomes spirit; something to the sun, and it becomes radiant; something into the ear of the cloud, and its eyes rain tears; chants something to the earth, and it becomes humble, silent and submissive like a Sufi (M.I, 1448–55). Nothing happens except at His command.

As the whole creation has come from a single source, one may wonder why this one has come sober, that one intoxicated? Why is this river honey and that one poison, when all rivers flow from a single Sea? Why did true and false dawns arise, when all light is from the everlasting Sun? Why did true sight and strabism come about, when every eye's blackness is from a single Collyrium? Why are the good and bad coins struck, when God is the Governor of the Mint? (M.VI, 1605–9). Whoever has ever seen unity with so many numbers, or so many motions surging from the essence of rest? (M.VI, 1612). How should this endless variety and the innumerable opposites spring from the One Real Being who transcends in essence all plurality and mutability?

Rumi's explanation is that in the essence and action of the Sea, there is no opposite or like, no howness or whatness, no conditionality. All that exists, all these opposites and likes, have been given existence by that Sea, but they are like a flake of foam on the surface of the Sea — the 'multi-headed foam'. They differ in appearance, but in their hidden essence they are one. How should God create His opposite or like? Instead of an opposite bestowing being and existence on its opposite, it flies from it. And if God made His own like — identical with Himself in essence, attributes and actions — that like might claim the title of creator like God. On what ground could it be considered different? All this conditionality tosses like foam on a Sea that has no like or opposite — a Sea whose every drop is beyond the reach of the intellect and the spirit, of Universal Reason, a Sea that is unfathomed and boundless (M.VI, 1617 etc.).

In Rumi, as among the Sufis in general, the reason for creation was God's desire[7] for Self-manifestation from which not He, who is Self-sufficient and needs nothing, but the creation would gain. Rumi refers to this reason in the following verse which is in reply to David's question as to why He created the two worlds:

> God said to him: O temporal man, I was a hidden treasure,
> I sought that that treasure of kindness and munificence
> should become manifest.
>
> (*Diwan*)

God sought to manifest the 'hidden treasure' — the 'treasure' of 'Kindness and Munificence', of eternal Knowledge, of absolute Wisdom, of infinite Thought. The Absolute is one Thought, says Rumi, going forth from itself and breaking into many forms of thought in the world; it is the origin and stuff of creation.[8]

As the Divine attributes which appear in the Divine Essence are, in their real nature, identical with the Essence, this manifested universe, as a reflection of His attributes, is an expression of God's idea of Himself, of His Essence in external

30

guise. Thought is at once the subject and object of creation.

In the words of Rumi, the wave of thought sped from the Sea of Wisdom. The Sea is only another name for the Divine Essence, which is the sole Agent of action, and its waves are only another name for its attributes, which are forms of the Essence. The Essence is manifested through its attributes when they appear in it. That Wisdom, that Thought, also produces the form of voice and speech for the waves of Thought, the concrete voice being the expression of abstract thought. All forms, sensible or ideal, spring from Formlessness, another name for Thought or Reality (M.I, 1137–41). They are entirely speech and are born of speech.

Rumi likens the Divine names and attributes inhering in the Essence to the stars that move in other heavens, immanent in the radiance of the Light of God, neither mutually joined, nor mutually separate (M.I, 755–6). The creation of the world is the manifestation of the Essence in the form of attributes which are one with the Essence and, yet, distinct from it. It is, as stated earlier, the manifestation of God as the object of Thought. Thought is the raw material of the universe. It is the foundation of God's Workshop. It is the material on which He works in Non-existence, which is the plane of potential existence. Not only the universe as a whole, but also the individuals and their past and future have their origin in Thought. This is like the Pythagorean doctrine that 'God is the Universal Mind diffused through all things' — a doctrine that underlies all ancient thinking.

If it be asked why God works in Non-existence, Rumi's answer is that He does so because Not-being is a mirror that reveals the existence of all crafts, because it is opposite that reveals the opposite. In our day-to-day life also, the builder seeks a virgin site if he is to build, and not a built-up site; the carpenter seeks a house which has no doors and windows if he is to exercise his craft; the tailor seeks untailored material if he is to display his tailoring excellence. Examples can be multiplied. Understandably, God, the Master Craftsman, works or uses His creative energy in Non-existence. Forms are born from Formlessness, instruments from non-instrumentality. Handlessness weaves hands; the Soul of the soul makes a full-formed Man. God's mine and treasury are nothing but non-existence being brought into manifestation (M.I, 3204–5; M.VI, 1367–71, 3712–15). In Buddhism, 'the Unbecome, the Unborn, the Unmade, the Unformed' is the source of all that is 'become, born, made, formed'.

Elsewhere, Rumi speaks of three stages of descent of the Absolute. The first is the spacious world of pure, abstract ideas, called the world of Non-existence ('adam) because of its abstractness. This world feeds another world, narrower in extent, the World of Similitudes ('alam-i-mithal), where the ideas are dressed in fantasy; it is the world of ideal forms, which know no materialisation. The World of Similitudes is the intermediate world that feeds our still narrower world of external existence (hasti-i-khariji), both spiritual and sensible, the sensible being the familiar world of scent and colour, narrower than the spiritual (M.I, 3092–7).

Divine Wisdom, says Rumi, flows through the orchard of souls into the phenomenal world, and permeates and feeds all grades of being. Whatever exists in the world has its roots above (M.II, 2452–5); it is a flow of ideas or essences from latency into external form or objective manifestation.

In the *Diwan*, Rumi tells us:

The earth and the skies receive aid from the World of Intellect,
For the Intellect is a luminous realm, pure and pearl-scattering.
To the World of shining Intellect come aids from the Attributes,
The Attributes of the Essence of the Creator, who is the King of
'Be' and it was.

According to Dr Nicholson, there is a close similarity between what Rumi says about the descent of the Absolute and the theory of Emanations of Plotinus[9], though nowhere in Rumi, and it is said that nowhere in Persian literature, is Plotinus mentioned by name, though Rumi mentions Plato several times.

Referring to the apparently beautiful forms, Rumi says:

Poor copies out of Heaven's original,

Pale earthly pictures moulder to decay,
What care although your beauties break and fall,
When that which gave them life endures for aye?

(Diwan, tr. Nicholson)

Though this world is a copy, God's beauty is displayed here in every beautiful form — in the beauty of the rose, in the stature of the cypress, in the charm of the narcissus. Only we must not regard these objects or their beauty as intrinsic or permanent. The verses quoted above therefore say that we must not lament the passing away of what is only a copy, of something that is ephemeral, however beautiful, as its reality, its source, everlastingly abides.

THE GOAL OF CREATION

The goal of creation is man — man who has attained spiritual perfection, the Perfect Man, also described as the Logos. While the Perfect Man will occupy us in detail in chapter 4, here we shall speak briefly of the Islamic Logos doctrine, which is wider in application than the Greek.

The Logos is variously rendered as the Word, Reason, Spirit or the World Soul. In Philo of Alexandria, the Logos was an intermediate being between 'It' and the pluralistic universe. The Logos is also rendered as Thought. The evangelist St John had already identified Christ with the Platonic-Stoic Logos. In Sufism, it was the archetypal Muhammad that was the Logos. As the Logos, he was 'the Heavenly Man', the creative origin of all things. He is the equivalent of the creative command 'Be', of the active principle of Universal Reason or Intellect.

The Logos doctrine is not an integral part of Islam. But it occurs in Sufism. It is said to have originated in the Islamic context in the ninth century AD, and it was developed by the great Arab mystic Ibnu'l-'Arabi (AD 1165–1240). It figures in Rumi. Muhammad, he says, is pure light fashioned by God from fire, that is, from the Majesty of His Essence (M.II, 909). In him, the eternal Word of God was revealed. He is the mirror of God and God is his mirror. He is the direct reflection of God's eternal Knowledge, the very first thing that God created. In Muhammad's words as ascribed to him by Sufis, 'I was a prophet, when Adam was yet water and clay', that is, he was the first prophet in eternity; 'I am the light of God and all things are of my light', which is the first manifestation of the Divine Essence. It was from that light that Adam gained his knowledge of God (M.II, 910). Not only the sensible world, but also its hidden ground, the spiritual world, derive their life from Muhammad. His light not only created the entire creation, but also sustains and governs all things, high and low, in both worlds. The reference is to the Logos doctrine, when Rumi says:

> We are the shadow of God, we are from the
> light of Mustafa (Muhammad),
> We are a precious pearl dropped in the oyster shell.
>
> (*Diwan*)

Muhammad is also described as the *Qutb* or the Axis on which all the spheres of existence revolve. Not only was he the cause of creation, but also its object in the sense that in him and through him alone does God see Himself, with all His Names and attributes. 'But for thee, I would not have created the heavens', God said to Muhammad, that is, Muhammad was the Thought that was the core of the heavens and, in the end, was the lord of *lawlak* ('But for thee'). All things were but preparations for his coming. It is like the boughs, leaves and roots that are sent first, but they are there only for the sake of the fruit (M.II, 970–4).

Rumi takes a broader view of the Logos doctrine than the Platonists and Christians. He does not identify the Logos exclusively with the name of Muhammad, but with every Perfect Man, prophet or saint, even if temporally his prior. Rumi's argument is that when many lamps are lighted from a single candle, it matters not whether you receive the light from the last lamp or from the candelabrum (M.I, 1947–9). He identifies with the Logos the tenth-century martyr-saint Hallaj who was executed for his utterance 'I am God', and also his own spiritual director Shams-i-Tabriz and his companion and deputy Zarkub and his disciple and the inspirer of the *Mathnawi*, Husamu'd-Din — three Perfect Men in whom he saw the manifestation of the Divine Consciousness (see Introduction). He himself, Rumi says, is addressed by God as 'the Consciousness of the world' (*asrar-i-jahan*) (M.I, 1731), that is, as the Logos. Although he considers himself inferior in rank to the prophets, he refers to himself as a sun without shadow in both worlds, or externally a mote revolving like a prophet round the Spiritual Sun, being like him one with the Essential Light. In other words, he has the saintliness of a prophet, but not the latter's exoteric mission from God (M.II, 1109–10).

In Sufism, election precedes succession. Muhammad's spiritual heirs are chosen by God in eternity to inherit his spiritual mantle. Through them — the Perfect Men — God becomes conscious of Himself in the creation.

The name Muhammad applies to the idea of Muhammad (*al-haqiqatu'l-Muhammadiya*), not to any particular person in flesh and blood. The Prophet can assume the forms of the most Perfect Men in any age, and though the forms may carry their own names, that is, other than Muhammad, the latter is their spiritual essence or reality.

In Rumi, as in Islam, the Prophet Muhammad remains a man, a supremely Perfect Man. He does not become God or the son of God. He himself is reported to have said that there were among his people some who were similar to him in nature and aspiration, and their spirit saw him by the same light by which he saw them (M.I, 3462–3).

The Prophet attached no worth to majesty or fame. He did not even wish to become a prophet. On returning to his former blissful life with God, he says: 'Would that I had never been a prophet and never come into the world, which, in comparison with that absolute union, is all burden and torment and suffering' (*Discourses*, p.212).

Islam unequivocally states that God begets not, nor was He begotten (Koran, cxii,3). He has neither father, nor son, nor uncle; He is not connected with lust (M.III, 1319–22).

Muhammad, as prophet and guide, knew that not mind-boggling theology or metaphysics, but a homely description of God and of His love for His creatures was required, if love and worship of Him was to be invoked in the heart of the common man. Hence, he said: 'The people are God's family.'

This world, says Rumi, looks after us like a nurse whose services have been borrowed for three or four days, that is, for a short time, and he beseeches God: O Mother, take us direct, with no nurse or intermediary (M.V, 698; 701–2).

Rumi also refers to the saints as His children in exile (M.III, 81). In the Koran, God is said to have breathed of His Spirit into Adam (Koran, xv, 29). All this makes God and His creatures one loving family. As Rumi says, we are the family of the Lord, and infant-like we crave for milk (M.I, 927).

The Spirit or Breath which the Lord breathed into Adam is believed to have a cosmological significance. It is the mighty out-going, creative Breath by which the creation is breathed out. As is said in the *Isha-Upanishad*, 'Out of Self comes the breath that is the life of all things.' Outbreathing His Breath, the Lord unites Himself with Adam or mankind as a whole, without any commingling (*imtizaj*) or incarnation (*hulul*). Jili identifies this Breath with the Holy Spirit (*ruhu'l-quds*) (*Islamic Mysticism*, p.109). It was the Breath of the Merciful (*nafasu'l-Rahman*). The Divine Breath can also be interpreted as His Light or Consciousness, which is the archetypal Muhammad; it then becomes the basis of the Islamic Logos doctrine.

If the Lord's Outbreath is the creation or manifestation of this universe, then His Inbreath, which it is natural to assume would follow His Outbreath, may be said to be the death of the universe and its withdrawal into latency.

THE CONSTANT RENEWAL OF THE UNIVERSE

Rumi says that the form rolled forth from Formlessness and rolled back into it. Every moment we are dying and returning to Him. Every moment, the world is renewed, though, to us, because of the swiftness of its renewal, it appears continuous.

It is like a dexterously whirled firebrand which appears as a long line of fire (M.I, 1141-7). If we are not aware of the constant renewal of the world, it is because the renewal is of like by like (*tajaddud-i-mithal*), and the change is too rapid for our perception.

Rumi says in the *Diwan*:

> The world is like a rivulet that appears congealed, but
> Is going and arriving again and again — whence is this?

An ancient prayer in the Jewish daily morning service says of God that 'He reneweth every day continually the work of creation.' The doctrine of constant creation was also held by the Dead Sea Brotherhood.

It is the law of evolution that death preludes a new life. Without death, there could be no transformation into a newer form of existence.

Rumi says that God creates even man anew every moment, sending something new into his heart, in no way like its prior or successor, though man is not aware of it (*Discourses*, p.200; M.V, 3641-3).

According to Heraclitus, 'This world ... was ever, is now, and ever shall be an everlasting fire, with measures kindling and measures going out.' In such a world, as Heraclitus believed, perpetual flux was only to be expected, a doctrine which science does not refute. 'All is flowing'; 'nothing ever is' (Heraclitus). 'The one [is] living the other's death and dying the other's life.'

To a Sufi, the whole creative process is but a single, timeless moment or flash of Divine revelation. Constantly and simultaneously, outside Time's framework, life and its renewal are displaying God's attributes of Mercy (*rahmat*) and Beauty (*jamal*) and death His attributes of Majesty (*jalal*) and Wrath (*qahr*). His Self-revealing acts are simply countless, each virginal and different, but all indivisibly co-existent. It is a perpetual revelation of the One in the Many and the Many in the One.

'The entire circle of existence begins and ends in a single

point', the Divine Essence. Its appearance as an extension in time is an illusion that arises because the immediacy and simultaneity of death and renewal is beyond our perception. To us, they appear as separate events occurring within the framework of Time, and so we regard the world as enduring. We are prisoners of time and space, and not in timeless union with God, where alone can the truth be learnt (M.I, 1145-9).

HOW LONG DID CREATION TAKE?

In the Koran, as in Genesis, it is said that God created this creation in six days, a day being the equivalent of our one thousand years. In the context of the ascension of the angels and the Spirit to God in a day, the Koran mentions the span of a day as fifty thousand years (Koran, lxx,4). In Rumi, every day in the life of an adept also is equal to fifty thousand years — the reference being to the Lord's timeless epiphanies (M.V, 2182). Whatever span is assigned to a day is meant to convey the unimaginably long time that creation took, according to our reckoning.

According to Manu (who lived before the beginning of the Christian era and whose code is a principal source of Hindu law), 1,000 divine ages compose one creative Day of Brahma, one Night of Repose being of the same duration as the creative Day, and 1,000 divine days are equal to 4,320,000,000 human years, which covered the period of creation.

The Dahriyya (materialists) regard the world as eternal, not attributable to any beneficent Lord, but arising out of the clashes and combinations of atoms. Rumi rejects the view that the world is not the creation of God, and holds with the orthodox that the universe originated in time, though how long the process took he does not mention, except that it took aeons. In the spiritual world itself, according to him, the spirit was flying involuntarily for hundreds of thousands of years before its descent into matter (M.VI, 220).

Rumi also speaks of the non-temporal aspect of the world and says specifically of the soul in pre-existence that it 'neither grew nor came to birth', that is, it knows no beginning, growth or end (M.I, 1927). It was in God's eternal Knowledge; it was one with God.[10]

Elsewhere, referring to the soul's pre-existence — particularly to that of the Prophet's soul — Rumi says:

> I was when the Names were not,
> There was no sign of existence bearing a name,
> From us, Names and Named became manifest
> That day when I and we were not.
>
> *(Diwan)*

Also:

> We were boasting in the Baghdad of Eternity that 'I am God',
> Before there was this uproar and mystery about Mansur[11].
>
> *(Diwan)*

The same may be said of the universe and of every part of it, if this distinction between latency and externality is borne in mind. The archetypal universe has always been held in the Divine Mind, and is, therefore, identical with it, and hence eternal, while its offspring, the objective universe, is temporal, a creation in time. In other words, what is known as creation is really a manifestation of His Self, both when He brings it into being within Himself, and when He gives it the vesture of externality.

IS THIS WORLD EVIL?

There are passages in Rumi describing the world as a wicked place, which is contrary to what he says about the beauty and orderliness of the universe. Thus, he says that this world is but 'foam full of floating jetsam', 'a decrepit old hag'; 'an enchantress' that is fair to men with objects of lust, 'women, children ... gold and silver', not really beautiful; it is a false coin that is not gold, but a coin 'only decked out fair' with gilding (*Discourses*, p.22).

But Rumi does not spurn the world as such. The world is a true copy of the beauteous eternal original. The world he spurns is the world in which one is attached to wealth, to things that enchant the senses; in which one is a slave of the flesh and the devil, and oblivious of God. The world, in his own words, 'is not goods, silver, weighing-scales and women', but is 'heedlessness of God' (M.I, 983). And as such heedlessness is a common phenomenon, the world becomes almost synonymous with it, and, in this sense, evil. Man has used his free will in great measure to make it evil, but the good he has done must also not be forgotten.

Elsewhere, justifying the ways of God to man, Rumi explains that even heedlessness of God serves a positive purpose. Without it, with everyone full of God, who would run the affairs of the world and display His attributes? Besides, there would be no good and evil for the soul of man to choose between. God has created both worlds, and both must be kept going. He has, therefore, appointed two sheriffs, heedfulness and heedlessness — the former for the next world and the latter as the support of this world. (*Discourses*, p.120; M.I, 2065–6).

Nor is wealth evil. Like everything else, it belongs to God, and nothing that is His is evil. 'How excellent is righteous wealth', said the Prophet (M.I, 984), referring to wealth that is lawfully earned and is used for religious or righteous purposes. It is not enough that it is used aright; the means of its acquisition must also be right. Noble ends do not justify ignoble means.

God says in the Koran: Spend in the way of the Lord (Koran, ii, 195). Now, how can one spend unless one earns, and can one earn unless one works? This means that one must work and earn.

In distinguishing lawful from unlawful food, Rumi does not go by the religious Law (*shari'at*). According to him, one should know that a morsel is lawful or unlawful according as knowledge and wisdom, love and tenderness and heedfulness of God are born from it, or malice, envy and guile, ignorance and heedlessness of God. Its means of acquisition also would be right, if it brings increase of light and perfection. The morsel that is lawful by this test may not always conform with the provisions of the religious Law.

Wealth becomes evil when it captivates the heart, making

one oblivious of ethics and morality; it, then, becomes the heart's ruin. But nobly used, it becomes the heart's support; it fulfils worldly needs, and can serve the cause of righteousness and social good. If wealth were evil, King Solomon would not have been blessed with riches and honour. Nor did he have any craving for them; they meant nothing to him. He called himself 'poor'. His wealth lay in knowledge and wisdom (M.I, 984–6). He was a prophet, a man of God.

WHAT A WONDERFUL WORLD

This world is not to be denigrated, but understood in its reality. To denigrate it would be to denigrate its Creator. Evil is evil only in relation to us, not in the absolute sense. God has uttered 'Earth and moon like syllables of light'. He has drawn lovely forms, like eye and profile, cheek and mole, on the tablet of fantasy in the ideal world. He has shaped beautiful, pictured images in that Non-existence, suitable for every thought. The forms we see in this world are copies of their divine archetypes. They are 'poor' copies, as described in Nicholson's verse-rendering quoted earlier, but poor only in the sense that symbol and reality, copy and original, are not identical; the symbol or copy is inferior.

But no true symbol or copy is wholly without reality. A gazing soul can espy in these weaker glories some shadows of eternity; it can see the Tigris in a drop of water. It may be mentioned, in passing, that in Rumi's verse, the adjective 'poor' does not appear, though implied in a sense. Plato also held that though the sensible world was inferior to the eternal, it was 'the fairest and the best'. In Plotinus, it is beautiful, because Soul has created it from Divine memory.

Not only beautiful, but being the outward form of the Divine attributes and pervaded and animated by the Divine Essence, and, therefore, a Self-manifestation of God to Himself, this universe is also real. It is 'the living, visible garment of God', woven in the 'roaring loom of Time', and it serves as His manifest evidence to us. He cannot reveal Himself without it, and it, the universe, cannot exist without

Him. It is phenomenal in the sense that it is the external expression of that Reality. It becomes illusory only if seen with the sensual eye and its outwardness is mistaken for its inward Reality; otherwise, it is no illusion. It is phenomena that have concealed God from us, and tend to make us heedless of Him.

But the Sufi gnostic (*arif*) has his spiritual eye open. Knowing that what is Below is in exact accordance with what is Above, he, by contemplation of experience on earth, ascends to an understanding of the archetypal pattern of experience Above. In Plato, one ascends from the beauty of one to the beauty of many, and, eventually, attains to the science of beauty. In contemplating the beautiful phenomenal copies, the gnostic perceives the ever-changing, never-repeating epiphanies of Divine Beauty. In his case, 'the phenomenal is the bridge to the Real'. Human love also, if it purifies the soul, is a ladder to Divine love (M.I, III).

The Sufi is no mere introvert. He does not belittle extroversion. He looks within and beholds the inner archetypes of beings, and then looks without and sees them in their objective form. Whether he looks within or without, above or below, he is firmly balanced on the threshold, and sees the light within or up, and its reflection without or below. There is no confrontation between the inner and the outer or between the upper and the lower world. In Orphic language, he is 'a child of Earth and Starry Heaven'.

Rumi lends meaning and dignity to this world. Everything here, if seen with the eye of spirit, he says, is brimful of Divine Wisdom; it is a Tigris of His over-flowing Beauty. It was a 'hidden treasure' that burst forth and manifested its splendour in Adam. Appearance or fantasy is not nothing, not without reality hidden in it. This phantasmagoria, this world of appearance, the last in the series, is a form of Divine Thought (M.I, 2860–3); it is the outward form of Universal Intellect. The underlying essence or spirit that animates or governs it is Divine Knowledge and Wisdom (M.IV, 3259; M.I, 1030).

This creation, as stated earlier, is an outflow of God's Kindness or Munificence, or what may be called His Mercy.

He, as the All-Merciful (*al-rahman*), gave temporal existence and form to non-existence, and He also endowed it with the necessary temporal receptivity. This gift was no less valuable, as, without receptivity, no form of existence is possible (M.V, 1537-8).

God says that there is nothing whose store-houses are not with Him; but He sends down His gifts in a known measure, according to need. Any excess or superfluity would only be a burden on the recipient. What good, for example, would fragrant musk be to one with no sense of smell, or things of beauty to the blind, or music to the deaf? (M.I, 2383-5). God provides relief; Hedoes not impose unnecessary burdens.

God also takes into account the recipient's power of reception. Even in the case of Muhammad, the Koran did not come down chapter by chapter, but word by word. The gradualness of its descent was not without reason. Muhammad himself is reported to have said: 'If it were to come down upon me all at once, I would dissolve and vanish away' (*Discourses*, p.41).

THE ORDERLINESS AND HARMONY OF THE UNIVERSE

This vast universe, with its bewildering variety, operates, as one can see, in an orderly and harmonious manner. The view held by some philosophers that this wonderful fabric owes its origin and functioning to nothing other than 'accidental collocations of atoms', and that man is doomed to extinction in the death of the solar system, so that our life is only a few noisy years in the being of the eternal Silence, is too mechanistic and depressing a view to appeal to man's deeper instincts. Life is more than mere mechanics. One of the greatest scientists of all time, Dr Albert Einstein, speaks with inner conviction when he says: 'I refuse to believe that God plays dice with the cosmos'; and that 'Everyone who is seriously involved in the pursuit of science becomes convinced that a spirit is manifest in the laws of the universe — a spirit vastly superior to that of man, and one in the face of which we with our modest powers must feel humble.'

This universe is not random or patternless; it is orderly and purposeful. The formative Divine command 'Be' gives it order and pattern, 'tones and numbers'. In the words of Shakespeare:

> The heavens themselves, the planets and this centre
> Observe degree, priority and place,
> Insisture, course, proportion, season, form
> Office and custom, in all line of order.

Rumi says that it is because of order and discipline that heaven became full of light, and the angels became pure and holy. But when the sun, in its 'irreverence', deviates from its fixed course, it is divinely punished with an eclipse (M.I, 91–2). Cosmic justice, like human justice, rewarding good and punishing evil, operates inexorably. Hence, when Satan sought to deviate from his allotted rank and rise above his peers and equal God Himself, he was thrown back and hurled to 'bottomless perdition'. All created things must suffer from some imperfection and go off the path at times, and they must pay for the deviation. God alone is absolutely Perfect.

Referring to this universe at large, Rumi says that the outwardness of its form which alone is visible to the naked eye is not without purpose. In his words:

> [God said:] I revealed a mirror whose face was the Soul, and whose back was the world;
> The back becomes better than the face, if you know not the face.
> *(Diwan)*

Rumi's point is that but for the back of the mirror, which here stands for the objective universe which is Not-being, the face of the mirror, symbolising the heart or soul of the universe, would not reflect the Divine attributes. Not-being thus reflects the attributes of Being. The phenomenal universe is necessary for Him to manifest Himself to Himself (M.I, 3201–2), but it is only a reflector.

THE COSMOLOGY AND RESOLUTION OF STRIFE

If this world is the creation of God, and it operates in an

orderly fashion and is purposeful, why should it be strife-ridden? Why should not there be peace and harmony everywhere?

The reason is that God desired to be known and His Self-manifestation could not be complete without the display of contraries. And where contraries exist, strife is inevitable. As Rumi says, the whole universe is stricken with a terrible conflict. There is war of nature, war of action, war of speech. The four elements are the four pillars by which the world is upheld, and each pillar seeks to destroy the other. My own mental and bodily states are in mutual opposition, and I am always fighting with myself. How can I act in harmony with another? You have the same terrible war within you. We are in opposition both within ourselves and with others, because we are the branch, and the four warring elements are the stock, and the stock has reproduced its own nature in the branch (M.VI, 46 etc.).

We are not personally responsible for the creation of strife whether it is the strife of venom with antidote, or of mote with mote, or of religion with unbelief. All our strife and peace is in the light of the Essence. The strife is from our original nature which we did not create; it is between the fingers of God; it is determined by the diversity and contrariety of the Divine attributes and thoughts and ideas, which are reflected in the universe. Our life is only a peace of contraries, and there is no escape from this world of strife, unless we are blessed with the innate capacity to effect the escape, or unless God redeems us and guides us to the uni-coloured spiritual world of everlasting peace (M.I, 1293; M.VI, 35 etc.).

Opposites may lead to strife, but strife is not wholly evil. It fulfils a function in the evolutionary process. Rumi says that the whole world is eating and is eaten (M.III, 30). But this does not destroy the world. On the contrary, when one kind devours and entombs another kind, the kind that is devoured is assimilated to a higher kind, and it provides nourishment and strength to the latter. In this way, the higher forms live on the lower, and the lower, when swallowed by the higher, are elevated to higher forms. Death is the portal to higher forms of existence.

Strife, however, is only one aspect of the creation. The other aspect is love, which is one with strife in the Essence, and harmonises all discord, and preserves the continuity of the manifested universe. All opposites are mutually linked by the original unity from which they take their rise and to which they seek to return.

Speaking of the mutual attractiveness of opposites, Rumi says that God's Wisdom in destiny and decree has paired all the particles of the world as mates, and made each mate the lover of its mate. Love is all-pervading. Take heaven and earth. When earth is left with no heat or with no freshness or moisture, heaven supplies the deficiency (M.III, 4400–5).

Similarly, God puts desire for each other in man and woman, so that by their union children may be born and the human world kept going.

Night and day may be contraries or enemies in appearance, but they are in mutual embrace to a common end. Night refreshes man, preparing him for the next day's task. Without night — without sleep — he would have little energy to carry him through the day (M.III, 4415–20).

The entire creation is pervaded by well-balanced contraries, by strife as well as by love. Duality divides, and it is love that makes one out of two.

But what is it in others that we love? Is it cheek and mole, or stature and build? No, says Rumi, it is not the form or the face, whether it be love of earthly things or spiritual. If you loved a person for her form, why abandon her when she is dead? Her form still is there, though frozen and motionless. Why, then, this revulsion from her? Again, if the form really mattered, which is the object of sense-perception, every one alive with the senses would love her in equal measure. But love is blind. Lovers have separate beloveds, each rating his beloved as the best. One sees Helen's beauty in a brow of Egypt; another like Titania, the queen of the fairies, finds Bottom, the ass, both wise and beautiful. Does the beloved's constancy or love alter her form or face? No! How is it, then, that her fidelity increases the lover's love for her, or her love increases his fidelity to her? No, it is not her form or physical beauty that inspires love, but something besides, something spiritual and divine in her.

Physical beauty in mankind is passing and decays. Why, then, says Rumi, set your heart on skin and bones, on fleeting earthly beauty, which is only a temporary reflection of the Divine Beauty? Why seek the shadow, and not the real? Why not seek the spirit, whose beauty is lasting and whose lips give of the Water of Life to drink? (M.II, 703 etc.). Why not set your love on the One Eternal, who gives the life-increasing wine? Do not say that He is inaccessible. It is not difficult to deal with the generous, and He is All-bountiful (M.I, 219–21).

Explaining the unifying influence of love, Rumi says that love manifests as 'lordship' in the beloved, and as 'servitude' in the lover. They are contrary qualities, but only in appearance; in reality, they are the same. They issue from the same source — the Divine Essence, which, in Sufism, is another name for love. Love is gnosis; love is simple essence, uncompounded. Hence, Rumi exhorts us to give ourselves body and soul to God, lose ourselves in Him, and, like Bayazid (see Introduction, p.12; also n.3), become 'the wine-drinker and the wine-cup and the cup-bearer' in one.

Referring to opposites like Paradise and Hell, light and darkness, good and evil, Rumi says that it should not be forgotten that they are only different names for different aspects of a single Reality, being the reflections of the Divine attributes, which are one in the Essence. They appear diverse only in their outwardness, and this diversity is relative. 'There is no position without its negation'; 'High stands on low' (Lao-Tzu). The opposites condition one another. A thing appears evil only in relation to parts; it appears evil, because our partial vision is unable to see the soul of goodness in it; because we only consider ourselves, forgetting that we all are hiddenly inter-linked. In relation to the Whole, there is no good or evil. Both are involved in one another; both are an undifferentiated unity.

Rumi refers to the story of Moses and Pharaoh. In the unity of Colourlessness, both of them worshipped Reality and were at perfect peace. But in this phenomenal world, they were in conflict — Moses representing faith and Pharaoh infidelity. Equally in accord with God's Will and Knowledge, both were running like balls, both here and above, running in obedience to the strokes of His bat's decree 'Be', and it was. When we return to the world of Colourlessness, Moses and Pharaoh are again in harmony. For colours originate from Colourlessness and wars from peace. In that formless spiritual realm, there is absolute unity (M.I, 2460–8).

What is true of Moses and Pharaoh is true of mankind in general. The bitter and the sweet sea are divided in this world. The righteous are divided from the wicked, and animality from divinity in man. They cannot mingle, for there is a barrier (*barzakh*) between them which they do not seek to cross. Both kinds flow from the same source, where they are the same; it is only on objectification that they are kept apart by their original nature or predestined character (M.I, 297–8). Every parting and separation originates from union (M.VI, 60).

The Peerless One, says Rumi, expelled contraries from Paradise. And where there is no contrary, there is nothing but peace and everlastingness (M.VI, 56–8). Compare Nicholas of Cusa, a fifteenth-century Christian mystic: 'The place wherein Thou art found unveiled is girt round with the coincidence of contraries, and this is the wall of Paradise wherein Thou dost abide.'

Elsewhere, Rumi traces the origin of the opposites back to the Primal Covenant. In that Covenant, God said to the pre-existent human souls: 'Am I not your Lord?' (*a-lastu rabbikum*). The word *alast* is a case of the mingling of negation and affirmation, because *alast* is an affirmative question, meaning 'I am', but the word *laysa*, meaning 'is not', is also contained in it. Opposites have their roots above, going right back to the Covenant of *alast* (M.V, 2124–6).

DIVINE WORSHIP IS THE PURPOSE OF CREATION

God says in the Koran: 'I have not created the jinn and mankind except to worship Me' (Koran, li,56). Was God, then, a mere seeker of sycophants, of lovers and worshippers?

God Himself answers this question in the Koran, when, as Rumi narrates, He tells Moses that He did not ordain worship for His own profit; He ordained it as a kindness to His creatures, so that by worship of Him they might purify and perfect themselves. He is not sanctified by our praise; it is we who are sanctified (M.II, 1755–8).

Among the countless attributes of God, there are groups which involve a complementary relationship. Love belongs to one such group. There can be no love without a lover and no lover without a beloved. According to a well-known tradition, before creation, 'God was and there was naught besides Him', and, according to the Sufi doctrine of 'the Unity of Being', all is God; there is no 'otherness' anywhere. He has the attributes of both lover and beloved, sycophant and the object of sycophancy. He is the One in the Many. The illusion of 'thou's' and 'I's' arises from the creation of two opposites, essence and form. The visible creation is only His external form, 'the time-vesture of the Eternal', and whether He loves it, His outward form, or loves the inward Reality, He is only loving Himself. His purpose is that all 'thou's' and 'I's' should become one soul and be sunk in Him (M.I, 1787–8). He knew exactly what the creation would be like. If He did not love it, He need not have created it. He is subject to no compulsion. His Choice and Will are wholly free.

Elsewhere, Rumi explains that lover and beloved are two attributes of the single essence of love, and, as attributes, they cannot become one. The terms union and separation apply to them as attributes, not to the essence of love, where there can be no duality.

Also, Rumi says that love is uncalculated affection, and is wholly the attribute of God. It is related to man only metaphorically. Which of His creatures can be said to love Him, when He is the uncalculated totality of love, and there is and can be no sharer in this or in any other of His countless attributes? (M.II, Preface, para.3.)

Earlier, the Absolute was referred to as one Thought going forth from itself and breaking into many forms of thought in the world. Without such Self-sundering, there would have been no creation. But the one Thought cannot remain broken. The outward form of Reality, which is this universe, and its inward Reality, which is the Divine Essence, must be united; the Many must return to the One. This is possible through the Perfect Man, 'the crown and pattern of the eternal Plan', who reflects all the Divine attributes, and is steeped in His Essence. He is dead to self. This is the real profession of the Divine Unity (*sirr-i-tawhid*).

The process of evolution of the World-Spirit is from the lowest form of soul-life to the highest. The aim of the entire creation is gradually to move towards 'Perfection', that is, to return to Him. The homing instinct is natural. But the interior journey that the return involves can only be performed by means of love and worship of God. There is no other way.

In Rumi, the worship of God is not limited to ritual worship, which, of course, it includes, and whose inner significance will be dealt with in chapter 8. Here, we shall be concerned with worship, first, in a general way, and then in the context of the Primal Covenant between God and man.

Our original nature consists of certain God-given predispositions. If we act according to them, we shall be serving His purpose. In fact, He brings such actions into manifestation in us in order to display His attributes.

God desired to keep the world in good order, and to this end He set certain people to occupy themselves with its affairs. He has ordained a separate prayer for each worker. Work is worship, as is commonly said. To perform worldly tasks conscientiously is to worship Him.

Also, God has created a suitable place of worship for everyone both in this world and the next. As the vile are purified by cruelty, that is, by punishment for their vileness, and are only made cruel by kindness, prison is their cloister in this world, and Hell-fire their place of worship in the next world. By means of suffering, both prison and Hell remind their dwellers of God, of His Existence as well as Omnipotence, and of their own servitude. Suffering thus helps them to fulfil the final purpose for which man has been created, namely, to serve God. Similarly, for those who are noble and walk after righteousness, God has created another mosque where they are kindly treated. That mosque is Paradise. Man has been given the power of action in everything, and is accorded a place of worship suited to his need (M.III, 2983–7). Even a thief who is hung on the gallows, says Rumi, is a preacher to the Moslems that such is the fate of anyone who commits a theft (*Discourses*, p.214).[12]

As prisons are man-made, we know something about the effects of prison life upon prisoners. But Hell belongs to the unseen realm of faith. While this concept will be discussed at length in the last chapter on 'Death and After', it should suffice for the present to state that, according to Rumi, Hell-dwellers should not be thought to be unhappier than they were in this world — a view not conventionally held, but which finds mention in Sufism, and which may be said to represent one aspect of the truth of Hell. There, in Hell, its dwellers are aware of God, which they were not in this world, and awareness of God which comes with self-awareness is sweeter than awareness of any 'otherness'. There, the infidels also come to long for union with God, being unable to suffer separation any longer, and they wish they were dust (Koran, lxxviii,40), in order that, back on earth, they might perform devotional works and become aware of the grace of God (M.III, 408; *Discourses*, p.236).

According to a tradition, while the Perfect Man, who has overcome carnality and become pure light, is higher than the angels, the man whose intelligence is overcome by lust is lower than the beasts. The angels occupy the middle rank, as they are free from lust and carnality, and worship and service of God is their sustenance. Their praise of God is spontaneous, requiring no effort on their part. God values exertion.

WORSHIP AND THE PRIMAL COVENANT

In the context of worship, Rumi refers to the Primal Covenant between God and the pre-existent human souls, when to His 'Am I not your Lord?', they said: 'Yes verily. We testify' (Koran, vii,172). Man thus stands pledged to obey the Lord. The Lord loves him, and he loves the Lord, His love manifesting itself as Lordship, and man's love as servitude.

This pledge is generally referred to as the 'Trust', 'the burden of Trust' (*bar-i-amanat*), which is variously interpreted. To the orthodox, it is the essence of the Faith, with its commands and prohibitions, and to the Sufi, the inspiration of Divine love and gnosis. It is also the burden of free will — which free will is operative in subordination to the Divine Will.

It is stated in the Koran that God offered the Trust to the earth and the heavens and the mountains, but they shrank from it, as it involved the exercise of choice and free will; it involved decision-making, and this they considered an unbearable burden. They preferred to function involuntarily as God willed and decreed, expecting no reward and fearing no punishment, now or later.

Rumi takes the instance of earth, air, water and fire, and says that they are aware of God, though we may not know it, whereas we, with our freedom of choice, are aware of things other than God, but are unaware of Him. They all, the heavens included, shrank from the Trust, saying that they disfavoured our kind of life in which man was alive to things created by God, but dead in relation to Him (Koran, xxxiii, 72; M.II, 2370-4).

But man accepted the Trust, and lo, he has proved sinful and foolish.

God has set high worth on man and says that He has bought his life and possessions, and if he expends them on Him and gives them to Him, He would reward him with everlasting Paradise (Koran, ix, III).

It is just not enough for man to say that even if he does not serve God in utter devotion in terms of the Covenant, he performs so many other useful worldly tasks. This is rank folly. He was not created for those other tasks. It is like using a sword of priceless Indian steel for cutting up putrid meat, or a gold bowl for cooking turnips. What a senseless waste of precious steel and gold. Man was created for a high purpose and he must seek to fulfil that purpose.

God says in the Koran: 'And We honoured the children of Adam' (Koran, xvii,70), and not 'And We honoured heaven and earth', so that it has fallen to man to perform the task which even the heaven and the earth do not perform. When he performs it, sin and folly are expelled from him and he becomes heavenly (*Discourses*, pp. 27–8).

But individuals differ; their souls have different essential natures. The character of their affirmation (*bala*) at the Primal Covenant was, therefore, also different. Rumi takes three broad classes of souls: those of the infidels, the orthodox, and of the prophets and saints, and says that the affirmation of the infidels came with reluctance, as if it were forcibly wrung from a slave. They bow down only for fear of damnation, not for the sake of God. They remember nothing of their pledge or of their former state, when all souls were fed and sustained by the Speech of God without letter and sound, and so they do not recognise His Speech when they hear it. Lust-blinded and disinherited of soul, they heed the promptings of the world, the flesh and the devil, and are heedless of God. They sell themselves to Hell as Faust sold himself to Mephistopheles for a few years of sensual pleasure.

The affirmation of the orthodox was based on faith and it meant: You are the one Lord we worship. Their idea of fulfilment of the Trust is to bear the burden of the Faith and be good Moslems in every way, so that they may gain peace and happiness here and spiritual delights in the other world. They remember something of the Divine Voice they heard on the day of *alast*, and when they hear it here in their hearts, their yearning for Paradise increases.

The third category, the prophets and saints, does not seek Paradise. Paradise and Hell are only another duality which, like every other duality, must be transcended. These Perfect Men seek God Himself and nothing else. Their affirmation came from their inmost souls and it meant: You are the one Lord we love and adore. Their ears are pre-attuned in heaven to God's Speech, so that when they hear it in their hearts, their pre-existent state becomes manifest before them and they are united with God. Further, they carry the obligation to display the Divine attributes for the enlightenment of others, just as God has displayed them in their hearts. The 'White Hand' of Moses one reads about is the manifestation of such attributes — or Divine illumination — by Moses.

Elsewhere, Rumi says that he who has not dreamt of *alast*, that is, of the vision and knowledge of God promised to the elect, His loving devotees in this life, and has no ear for God's Speech, cannot become His true servant and seeker in this world, as his worship of God must of necessity be uncertain and with a hundred vacillations; it cannot but be deficient. In the case of the true believer, on the other hand, the sweet savour of *alast* stays in his heart till the Resurrection, giving his soul peace and strength, so that he does not complain of tribulation, nor shrink from His commands and prohibitions. Anyone who has dreamt of the day of *alast*, of His vision and knowledge, walks in the path of righteousness, unvacillating, full of God (M.III, 2344–55).

That every object in the creation has heard God's Voice — *alast* — and has been given speech by Him is a basic Sufi doctrine. It is based on the authority of the Koran, and figures in Rumi. He says that not only to man has God given speech, but to every single thing, even 'to door and wall, stone and clod'. He has also given light, sight and discernment to all that is. It is said in the Koran that, at the Resurrection, hands and feet will speak like the tongue and give evidence. If the tongue, a mere piece of flesh, can speak, when commanded by the spirit, and man's own hands and feet exemplify matter's obedience to spirit, there is no reason why everything under the sun, be it animate or inanimate, should not be able to speak, if only God or Spirit commands it to speak (*Discourses*, p.119; Koran, xli,21), except that the nature of the speech will not be human.

What is true of speech is true of hearing also. Not only the Turk, the Kurd, and the Persian and the Arab heard the Voice of God with their spirit, without any mediation of ear and lip — not only man, but even wood and stone have heard and understood it. The sound of *alast* is coming from God at every moment, and non-existences are constantly springing into existence. Even if the response 'Yes' (*bala*) does not come from them, their emergence into existence is nothing but 'Yes' (M.I, 2107–11). God has only to say 'Be', and it is. This is proof enough that all existing things hear and understand God, for commands have to be heard and understood, before they can be obeyed. We can think of God's glorification by the inanimate, because of their hearing and understanding capacity.

According to Ibnu'l-'Arabi, the mineral, the lowest form of creation in our eyes, is the highest form of creation, as, lacking external sensibility and consciousness, it implicitly acknowledges and glorifies God, according to its original nature (Nicholson, *Commentary*, M.I, 512–13). The earth itself is humbly silent and prayerfully prostrate.

Next come the plants. They are not wholly without sensibility or consciousness. Their acknowledgement and glorification of God is not wholly implicit. In fact, they are said to respond to music and bring forth bigger blooms under its influence. It is, therefore, possible to conceive that, according to their nature, they also would praise God. In the words of Rumi, God's earth is wide and every leaf and bough on every tree growing out of it offers thanks to Him, exclaiming: Oh, what an excellent kingdom! What a spacious expanse! (M.V, 2560–1.) It is their thank-offering to Him for giving them existence, greenery and growth.

As for the animals, they live and move and are instinctual. They can be trained, and are grateful for any kindness received from man. And for one creature to be grateful to another is to be grateful to their Creator. It is praise of God. Rumi even goes further and says that just as man can rise above the angels, the dog, which is considered unclean by orthodox Moslems, and because of its uncleanliness, is seen as abhorrent, can, like the dog of the Companions of the Cave,[13] acquire gnosis (*ma'rifat*) in the company of gnostics and qualify for Paradise. What did the dog lose by its abhorred appearance, when it had acquired man's moral nature by companionship with those gnostics and become a seeker of God, with its spirit sunk in the Sea of Light? (Koran, xviii,10, etc.; M.I, 1022–3; M.II, 1425.) Majnun would fondle and kiss the dog of his beloved Layla[14] and compare him with the dog of the Companions of the Cave. The principle is that any dog that loves its master and is his guardian and shares his grief is blessed by God with stores of love and knowledge, and can justly be called the dog of the cave. Let not forms deceive us (M.VI, 2916; M.III, 567–76.)

With Ibnu'l-'Arabi, man comes last. His consciousness of self, his egoism, reason, intellect and even religion veil him from God. Be that as it may, he has to prove by words and actions that he has carried out the Trust. He may do so now or in a hundred years, but till it is discharged, he will remain under detention (M.V, 174–5, 180–2).

There is the all-comprehending statement in the Koran that the seven heavens and the earth and all that is therein praise Him (Koran, xvii,44), and, also, the stars and trees worship Him (Koran, lv,6). But the Mu'tazilites (see p.22, also n.3) deny that minerals and plants glorify God; at the most, according to them, they move him who contemplates them to hymn His praise. Rejecting this view, Rumi affirms as a fact of mystical experience that God has made everything His glorifier, and each praises Him in its own way, and is unaware of how others praise Him. Even the seventy-two sects of Islam are ignorant of one another's feelings and methods of adoration. The Sunni (the orthodox Moslem who equally reveres the first four successors of the Prophet) has one way of glorification, the Necessitarian another, and each believes the other to be astray and lost. When two persons speaking the same language cannot understand each other's utterance of praise, how can they understand the mute adoration performed by the plants and minerals, the master glorifiers, though possessing no fleshly tongue, no knee, no waist? (M.III, 1495–1504.)

The reason why one is ignorant of the other's way of glorification is that each praises God in a different fashion by displaying some of His attributes and its way is known only to it and to God. The Sufi knows the truth in a general way, but not the common man who is lost in worldliness, nor the rationalist seeking demonstrative proof. They cannot understand the spiritual life of the 'inanimate'. It lies outside their self-defined realm. But if we turn from the phenomenal to the spiritual world, we shall hear the tumult of the atoms of the world and their way of glorification will stand revealed (M.III, 1021–2). In fact, all things reveal their names and attributes to the Perfect Man. Thus, every new medicinal herb that grew in the Farther Mosque (*masjid-i-aqsa*) would tell Solomon its name and also to whom it was poison and to whom antidote (M.IV, 1287–91), and every star would tell Idris (Enoch) its name and circumstances and expound astronomy (M.VI, 2991). The music of the prophet David, who was known for his golden voice, would charm both the animate and the 'inanimate', and the mountains would chant psalms with him like master reciters of the Koran (M.III, 2499).

To the Sufi, as stated earlier, the entire creation is God's speech. Every sound, be it the hum of men or the noise of machine, the strains of the reed-flute or the rebeck, or the grand chime and symphony of Nature, every sound awakens in his soul memories of that First Melody heard on the day of *alast*, the Divine archetype of all subsequent sounds, and throws him into ecstasy. Trailing clouds of glory, we come from God, and by love and worship of Him we should seek to become perfect, and return to Him, our Origin and Home. In the lovely lines of Browning:

Look not thou down but up!
To uses of a cup
The festal Board, the lamp's flash and trumpet's peal,
The new wine's foaming flow,

The Master's lips aglow!
Thou heaven's consummate cup, what need'st thou with earth's wheel?

(*Rabbi Ben Ezra*)

2
Creative Evolution[1]

As the World-Spirit or Soul is all-pervading, it must cover not only the animate, but also the inanimate creation. What is understood as individual souls issue from the Universal Soul (M.III, 3080); they are its forms or individualisations. The entire universe is an aggregate of interlinked phenomena. It is the One playing the Many, the same essence appearing in different forms.

While nothing is soul-less in this world, and life is diffused through all, leaving no insulated spot anywhere, there are grades of living, some quiescent, some moving. If a thing is not self-moving in appearance, it is generally regarded as lifeless, though like us, it has its own life and is created and sustained by Divine Wisdom. At one time, we also were inanimate. Man has not been in his present state from the beginning. To quote Rumi:

> I have seen seven hundred and seventy bodies;
> Like greenery, I have repeatedly grown.

According to Rumi, man has taken aeons and undergone myriads of transformations before evolving as man.

The process of evolution is not without a purpose. With the creation of the universe, the One became the Many. The whole purpose of evolution is that the Many should return to the One.

Describing the broad stages of evolution, that is, the movement of the World-Spirit, Rumi says that from non-existence, God brought man into existence, and from the pen of existence, He transferred him into the world of matter, of stone and mineral. Dying to mineral, he became plant, and dying to plant, he became animal, and dying to animal, he became man. When did he become less by dying?

The will to live a higher life urges him on incessantly. Another step and he will die to man and rise to winged angelhood. Angelhood, also, he must leave behind and become that which transcends the imagination. He must eventually leave the realm of existence and return to non-existence, to God Himself, who is the First and the Last (M.III, 3901-6).

Death is thus a prelude to another life. Every new existence needs a new death. For without new deaths, new existences cannot arise. Progress is only another name for death, for it is only after its death that the old form progresses into the new. If the same form persisted for ever, progress would cease.

Cosmologically, Rumi speaks of 'nine Fathers' and 'nine Heavens'. His reference is to nine celestial spheres of ancient legends, each with a ruling intelligence, and all with the centre of the earth or universe as centre.[2] But he does not elaborate.

The spirit descends from God, and goes through the spiritual world, into the manifested universe, and circling 'awhile with the nine Fathers in each Heaven' (Rumi), that is, in each celestial sphere, it appears as each of the four elements, and, then, as mineral, plant, animal and man, and ultimately returns Home the same way by which it came.[3]

If man had remained permanently in the state of elements, he would not have progressed to the state of man as we know him. Myriads of existences have come to him, each better than its prior. He has received these existences from previous deaths. Why should he then turn away from the loss of self and union with God? Why this desperate clinging to the life of the present body? (M.V, 789, etc.)

ALL ELEMENTS ARE ALIVE BEFORE GOD

No form can be changed into another form, unless there is an affinity or homogeneity between the two forms. That affinity is provided by the all-pervading Divine Wisdom, by the All-

Soul of which nothing is void, by the One Life that runs in all. Nothing is dead. The inanimate not only possesses life, but rich living virtues; otherwise, the soil, for example, would not be receptive to the seed, and, keeping her trust, bring forth the true kind of what you sow therein. If you sow barley, you do not reap wheat. This is because soil and clay have been given the qualities of discrimination, trust and righteousness by God; because the Sun of Divine Wisdom and Justice have shone on them, making them wise and just (M.I, 508–12).

Not only the earth, but the other elements also, indeed all objects, are alive before God, and may be said to act according to their nature. Strike stone on iron and see how living fire leaps forth. How should this happen if the stone were dead, or if the fire that was latent were dead? Would fire, if lifeless, give heat and light, without which our own life would be impossible? Can wind be said to be dead, when it can produce ripples in the water, set leaves and flowers a-dancing, uproot trees? (*Discourses*, p.35.) Can anything dead impart motion to the motionless? Does not our own life hang on an airy breath which continuing it continues, which stopping it stops?

Again, can one live without water? Its price is above gold to a thirsty soul. Also, it is cleansing and purifying. It is hence that the expression 'the Water of Life' meaning the Elixir of Immortality has come into use. Water is life in more senses than one.[4]

The Koran narrates many miracles, some of which find mention in Rumi, investing all the four elements not only with life, but with powers of discernment and discrimination. It is not fair to say that because the truth of a thing cannot be logically established, it must of necessity be false. Just as everything has its own grade of living which we may not always understand, it can also have its own way of discernment, which, in our present state of knowledge, is profounder than our comprehension.

Many of the miracles are interpreted allegorically; but even if they are interpreted literally, they may serve a useful purpose. To believe in the truth of miracles, which are a breach of the customary order, we have to overcome our incredulity in matters beyond our perception, and if we are able to do so, we may also abandon our scepticism, if any, and begin to believe in the truth of the Unseen World.

With Hermetists, it is worthy of note, the four elements are 'forces relatively "blind" or "intelligent" according to which of the principles in them [one] deals with' (Blavatsky, *The Secret Doctrine*, Vol.I, p.461).

THE PLANT STATE

In the story of Daquqi, a relatively unknown saint, Rumi says that the saint saw seven trees at prayer, all lined up like a regular Moslem congregation behind a leader, and, without waist or knee, standing, kneeling and bowing, reminding the saint of what God says of the trees: They bow down (M.III, 2048–52; Koran, lv, 6).

Each blade of grass is a breathing lyre. Not only have the plants life, but also feelings of pleasure and pain, and, perhaps, a memory similar to ours, and possess an effective will to produce bigger blooms or fruit on exposure to music.

Rumi says that the whole creation is proclaiming: We have speech, hearing and sight, but are silent with you, as your spiritual ear and eye are closed. Turn from the phenomenal to the spiritual realm and you will hear in trumpet tones the God-given speech of every atom in the world (M.III, 1019–22).

We said earlier that all things disclose their names and attributes to the Perfect Man, as every new medicinal herb did to Solomon (M.IV, 1290). The reason is that the Perfect Man is the Logos, the very origin and cause of creation. No object in the vast creation, leave alone the medicinal herbs, can hide its name or attribute from him.

THE ANIMAL STATE

The next plane of being is the animal. The inward has expanded out more than in the plant state. There is life and movement which the human eye can effortlessly see. If the Divine Essence or Spirit is all-pervading, how should the dog be left without it? Can we, in all fairness, consider the cold-blooded human criminal as endowed with an immortal spirit, and a faithful, loving dog devoid of it? The dog of the Companions of the Cave is said to have attained moral excellence in their company, and will, it is believed, enter Paradise in the shape of man.

Again, Layla's dog which Majnun would fondle and kiss was the dog of his cave, and so is every other similar dog, though not similarly celebrated.

According to Rumi, wisdom and knowledge, excellence and volition can pass from man into the ox and ass and dog. The horse can be trained to become docile and smooth-paced, and the bear to dance and the goat to salaam (M.II, 1422–25).

Also, the animals have a vein of love and know what love is; otherwise, there could be no mating and reproduction amongst them. It was because of their knowledge of Majnun's love for Layla that wild animals like lions, wolves and bears would, as the legend goes, roam the desert in company with Majnun in daytime and guard him while he slept at night (M.V, 2006). It is but fair to admit that a good animal, loving and faithful, is higher than a man who is bestial and lustful.

THE HUMAN STATE

Man's next migration is from the animal state to man. As the universe was created in order that man should be evolved, as the tree is planted for the sake of foliage, fruit or flowers, with his emergence, the emergence of the Perfect Man, the process of creation may be said to have fulfilled its purpose. The objects created before him reflected only some of God's attributes. It is man alone who reflects them in their entirety.

Rumi's thinking on creative evolution or soul-development goes back to the distant past. Anaximenes held in the sixth century before Christ that animals developed out of frogs that came to land, and man developed out of animals. Hinduism, in the *Puranas*, mentions 8,400,000 grades of birth in seven stages: as plants, aquatic animals, reptiles, birds, quadrupeds, simian forms and man.[5] The relative closeness of the simian forms to man was thus known to the ancients. In *The Egyptian Book of the Dead*, in the Judgement scene, it is generally the ape-headed Thoth, god of Wisdom, and, in the Tibetan scene, it is the monkey-headed deity Shinje that supervise the weighing of the good and evil acts of the dead.

OUR BIRTH IS A FORGETTING

Ancient Wisdom and modern science are, in their own ways, in broad agreement about the evolutionary process that has culminated in man. Nor are they so apart now, as in the past, regarding the age of man. According to occultism, man existed some 18 million years ago, with the two sexes already separated, and the 'Races' that preceded such separation may have lived 300,000,000 years ago.[6] Modern anthropology takes man's family tree back to a primate called dryopithecus, a true ape that appeared some 20 million years ago. It split some 14 million years ago into three branches, of which one branch, the Ramapithecus, is believed by many anthropologists to be man's distant ancestor, the second branch evolved into the ancestors of today's great apes, his closest living cousins, and the third branch has become extinct.

Leave alone remembering his previous births, man does not even remember his recent human birth. If one were to tell the embryo in the womb that, outside, there is a marvellous world, with lovely sown fields, fruitful orchards, green hills and mountains, seas, rivers and lakes, and a beautiful blue sky lit by the sun at day and by the moon and stars at night, the embryo, blind and unimaginative, and knowing no food except blood, would turn away in disbelief. Similarly, the worldling refuses to believe in the existence of any world after this (M.III, 50 etc.).

Rumi cites for comparison the instance of a man who has lived in a city for many years, and goes to sleep and dreams of another city. He totally forgets the city of his birth and domicile, and thinks that he was born and has always lived in the city which has no real existence.

The spirit has traversed many planes of being, and lived on

each plane for aeons in the course of its descent from the world of spirit to the world of matter. Its perceptive faculty has been clouded by the journey, and it has quaffed deep of the poppied portion of earthly life and made no earnest effort that the heart should become pure and plainly see both the beginning and the end (M.IV, 3632–6).

THE GRADUALNESS OF MAN'S EVOLUTION

The evolutionary process is inevitably slow. For the evolving life-essence or life-flux or spirit cannot be bound up with a form foreign to its evolutionary state. Spiritual evolution must go hand in hand with the physical. A change in state requires countless transformations, each taking ages. In the spiritual world itself, the spirit was flying for hundreds of thousands of years before its descent into matter (M.VI, 220).[7]

In the progress from one state into another, which is gradual and continuous, the pattern is fixed. No state can be skipped, though all the states may co-exist. An ape, for example, cannot be suddenly lifted into the spiritual state, bypassing the human state. Animals have only the germ of the immortal spirit. This germ will develop through a series of countless evolutions before attaining to the state of man.

It is from ignorance that man has progressed to reason and fine discrimination. He never thought that he would take this route of progression and pass these stations. God manifested them in order that he may not disbelieve and say there was nothing more, but realise that countless loftier stations lie ahead. As in the past, so in the future, man will be brought to a hundred other different worlds (*Discourses*, p.129), and he will behold a hundred thousand other most wonderful intelligences (M.IV, 3649), immeasurably higher than our own.

While the earlier journey can be broadly mapped stage by stage, the final journey is beyond these five senses, beyond the infinitudes of space, to the shore of the Sea — the Sea of the Divine Essence. The Sea has no floor, no roof to shelter the voyager, no visible beacon, no name or sign to indicate the stage of the journey. In order to give some idea of its boundlessness, Rumi says that every two stages there are a hundred times as far apart as the Essential Spirit is from the plant state (M.V, 800–6). That Sea is our final destination; it was also our original point of start.

THE PRINCIPLE AND PURPOSE OF EVOLUTION

We said in the first chapter that the purpose of creation is Divine worship, and we discussed this worship in the context of fulfilment of one's assigned duties and functions in life, and also, in the light of the Primal Covenant. Here, we shall discuss it in the context of the creative evolutionary process.

The process is not without a purpose, nor without a guiding principle. 'As Above, so Below.' All our parts, all living creatures, the world itself, have been sent down as samples of the other world. It is only natural that to that other world, their home, all should seek to return. In the words of the Koran, 'Lo, we belong to God and to Him we are returning' (Koran, ii,156) — returning from ourselves. Again, 'Did you think that We created you for nothing, and that you would not be returned to Us?' (Koran, xxiii,115).

Every part of the creation was created with a purpose. In the words of St Paul, 'All things were created by Him and for Him.' If they undergo countless evolutions in myriads of years, it is only to attain union with Him, thus mingling their last state with the first.

If the purpose of evolution is union with God, the one grand principle that guides the evolutionary process is love. Love created this creation. If God had no love for the creation, He would not have created it. It is love now that is acting as the impelling force in the soul and calling it back. Every progression, every transmutation on the Way is the work of love. In this ascending process, love has three main ministers — humility, sacrifice of the lower form to the higher, and acceptance and assimilation of the lower by the higher.

In a sense, all things are humble, having come down as samples from a high estate. But that original humility is not

66

enough. Love demands something dynamic; it needs the dynamism of the sacrifice of self. As the way up is the same as the way down, involving stages, every created thing must die to each stage, before it can be assimilated into the next higher. 'Thou fool, that which thou sowest is not quickened except it die' (St Paul, *Corinthians*, xv,36). Dynamic humility culminating in the loss of self-hood, and assimilation of the lower by the higher, hold the key to progressive evolution.

Expounding the role of love, Rumi says that it is waves of love that turn the circling heavens. But for love, the world would be frozen dead. But for love, the animal spirit would not sacrifice itself for the Divine Breath that impregnated Mary (M.V, 3854-6). This body is like Mary, and everyone has a Jesus within him, but he is not born until the pangs of love arise in us, impelling us to strive for his birth. Without such pangs, there can be no such striving (*Discourses*, p.33). As Rumi explains, it is only when the Universal Soul touches the bosom of the striving individual soul that the latter is impregnated with a Messiah, a Perfect Child or a Perfect Man; it is the soul's spiritual birth or transmutation, the birth of one's True or Perfect self (M.II, 1183-4). Every mote loves that Perfection, and is hustling up like a sapling, as if chanting 'Glory to God', and is purifying itself for the waft of the Divine Spirit (M.V, 3858-9).

Rumi takes the instance of a corn seed. It is first cast into the earth. In due season, it shoots up from its humble subterranean abode and grows into ears of corn. It is then crushed in the mill and baked in the oven, and it emerges as bread, ready to be eaten by man and become his mind and spirit (M.I, 3165-7). It was not his congener, but by going through all this tribulation, it has negated itself and made itself homogeneous with him (M.I, 891-2). The animal spirit in the human body assimilated the inanimate bread and transmuted it into the spirit of life. Having become part of the living man, one day it also will soar with him to the Divine realm.

All this progression of the corn seed is the work of love. But love is not unilateral. Man also loves bread; otherwise, he would not eat it. It is love that transmutes the inanimate bread into the vital spirit, and makes the perishable thing imperishable.

What is true of the corn seed is true of the seed of every fruit and vegetable that goes into the earth. They all come up and become man's nutriment, and are raised with him above the empyrean.

Again, the essence of wax and firewood is dark, but when they sacrifice themselves in the fire, the essence becomes light (M.I, 1533).

The meanest form of soul-life in matter, whether at rest or in motion, will, in the fullness of time, make the loftiest spiritual ascent, and rightfully proclaim: Verily, unto Him we are returning (M.III, 464).

God loves all His creatures, particularly man, who alone in the creation reflects all His attributes. Coming from God, his soul longs to return to Him. The very origin of its love is in His love. 'He loves them, and they love Him', His love preceding man's (M.III, 4440). The burning intensity of Man's love for God is thus matched by God's love for him. If Man searches for God, it is because God searches for Man. As the great Hafiz says:

> If the light of the Beloved fell on the lover, what then?
> We were in need of Him, and He was longing for us.

3

Free Will and Predestination (and Good and Evil)

If all action is created by God, and nothing happens except at His Will and Decree, and nothing is outside His eternal Knowledge, does it mean that whatever man does is under compulsion or necessity, and he has no will of his own, no power of choice?

If that be the case, how does the problem of good and evil arise? How can man be held morally responsible for his actions? How can he hope to achieve perfection by personal striving and return to God, which is the ultimate goal of creative evolution?

According to Rumi, predestination is a fact, and man's free will also is a fact. The duality of free will and predestination is operative only in this world of plurality, and not in the spiritual world of unity where all that is to happen in the phenomenal world is foreknown, but which itself is free from all duality, from all distinction between compulsion and free will, and from every other pair of opposites.

The particular souls were differentiated by God in pre-existence as objects of His Knowledge, and each soul was imprinted in His 'dyeing vat' with its essential characteristics, like piety and faith, or ungratefulness and hypocrisy, and it will retain these characteristics for ever (M.VI, 4711-13). Hence, all our joys and all our pains in this world ultimately arise from predispositions which God has created in our souls (M.I, 834-5). We cannot escape from our predispositions. We cannot act differently from what is predestined. We cannot escape from self. Rumi tells the story of a free-born noble who begged King Solomon to command the wind to carry him to India, so that he might escape from Azrael, the Angel of Death, whose look of wrath and terror appeared to him to have set him up for a mark. No such escape was possible. He was destined to die in India (M.I, 956 etc.).

God says in the Koran about the plots of men that they might move the tops of mountains, but without His Will, they can accomplish nothing. Except for what was predestined, nothing can come out of their planning and exertion. Pharaoh himself had thousands of babes killed at birth, so that there would be no Moses, but it was to no purpose. Despite these wholesale killings, Moses came to birth, and was nurtured in the very house of Pharaoh (M.I, 951-4; Koran, xxviii,3 etc.).

The Divine destiny brings us not only what may seem evil; it also brings us good and proves a blessing in the end. If it veils the sun in a cloud, it also makes the sun shine and give heat and light to all. If it wraps us in night-black, it also gives a guiding hand at the last. If it goes after our life a hundred times, it also gives us life and healing. If it waylays us on numerous occasions, it also strikes our pavilion above the highest heaven. We should understand that the Lord's terrifying us in diverse ways is an act of His Kindness, for He does so in order to make us God-fearing, and, eventually, to establish us in the kingdom of security (M.I, 1255-61).

Nor is man a mere automaton. God has said: And We have honoured Man (Koran, xvii,70). Rumi explains that God has done this by placing in his hand the reins of free will. For as man reflects the attributes of God, his personal self must reflect in some measure the Divine Free will also — the free will to act or not to act in a certain manner in subordination to the Divine Will.

Man is not perfect. Half of him is honey-bee and half snake; half heavenly, half earthly; half good and half evil. In his soul resides the power of choice. That power, that instinct in man which enables him to choose between good and evil is moved to action when a desired object comes before it (M.V, 2975-6), i.e., when our sleeping angelic and devilish dispositions wake up and present good and evil objects before us (M.V, 2982–4). They do not force their views on us; they are only our brokers. They exist for the purpose of actualising the invisible, latent power of choice in us (M.V, 3004–5). We do good and earn praise; we do evil and earn blame. Action performed under compulsion cannot be the subject of praise or blame. If we cannot choose to become holy men or brigands, we cannot justly be rewarded with Paradise or condemned to Hell. Compulsory praise of God earns no wages. Why should we feel ashamed when we do something which we think is wrong, and happy and contented when we do something which we think is right, if we had no freedom of action? As the clay-eater, the worldling, has a desire for clay, and not for the sweet rose-conserve, God tells Moses to let the clay-eater be free to choose what he likes. The revolution of the heavens earns no merit or demerit, as their revolution is involuntary. It is free will that is the salt of devotion; it is our profit-earning capital (M.III, 3285 etc.).

Rumi's explanation of the law of cause and effect is relevant in this context. According to him, every phenomenal cause is secondary. It does not arise on its own, but is subject to the higher, essential or spiritual cause — the Divine attributes of Will, Power, etc. which is known to the Perfect Man, but not to the common individual. The essential cause not only creates the external cause, but also determines whether it will succeed or fail. Normally, however, the law of cause and effect is allowed to function according to expectation in order that it may furnish a basis for man's activity and facilitate the orderly functioning of the world.

The Arabic for cause is *sabab*, which means 'cord'. It is by God's device that this cord has come in this world. The turning of the water-wheel is the cause of the cord's movement, but we must not forget the real turner of the water-wheel, and believe that these cords of causation are manipulated by the spinning heaven above. The qualities of the planet under which we are born will, according to Rumi, influence our dispositions; for example, Mars will make us seek war and enmity, and Venus joyance, but they are not causative of action. The essential causes of all existences and of all actions are the Divine attributes which are also the sole determinants of the effectiveness or failure of each cause (M.I, 751–3, 843, etc.). Himself, God is above cause and causality, and is wholly independent, and is unbound by necessity (M.II, 1625–7).

It is through the secondary causes that God acts, and that makes them purposeful. In Rumi's story of the King and the Handmaiden, God, acting through the divine physician, cured the ailing, love-sick maiden and established the supremacy of His Will, when the finest of physicians, conceitedly relying on their skill and ignoring the power of God's Will, had failed.

Teleologically speaking, Rumi says that what is considered the effect of our action can also be viewed as its final cause. For man's retribution is already fixed in eternity, and his actions are designed to lead him towards the realisation of that retribution. Hence, retribution in the Hereafter is the effective or the final cause of his actions here, and not their final consequence. Thus, what is cause from one point of view is effect from another, and vice versa. The polarity of cause and effect is not only horizontal, as seen in this world, but also vertical as between the world below and the world above.

The extent of the applicability of the cause-and-effect phenomenon is not always fully appreciated. Rumi describes every cause as a mother, and every effect as a child. The Upper World, the essence, was the cause and this lower world, this form, is the effect, born as a child. The effect also becomes a cause, and gives birth to other effects (M.II, 1000–1). This interaction constitutes the whole circle of existence.

As all that happens Below is in full accordance with the eternal Originals or Divine Ideas Above, what we call causation is really correlation.

Like all our actions, our power of choice also is created by the Divine Omnipotence. We cannot escape His Power, His Knowledge, or any of His attributes reflected in us. Nor are we given knowledge of our destiny. If God had made known to us the defect and consequence of a particular action or desire, we would certainly recoil from it (M.IV, 1349–50).

Explaining in terms of universals and particulars or individuals, Rumi says that God's power of choice is universal, and it brings our individual power of choice into existence, and uses it, as He also uses the secondary causes as a means through which to manifest and fulfil His eternal Will and Command (M.V, 3087–8).

But this does not annihilate man's relative free will. In order to obviate any such misunderstanding, Rumi says that we humans can exercise power over the form that, according to us, has no free will. Thus, the carpenter has authority over wood, the ironsmith over iron, the builder over his tools. But the action in each case is the Lord's, performed, without instrumentality, through the free will of these men. Our exercise of authority over the inanimate objects cannot take away their 'inanimateness', as our free will is not absolute. We may change the secondary qualities which a thing acquires in the present life, but not the qualities inherent in its original nature. We cannot change an ordinary stone into a ruby. In the same way, God's power over our acts of free will which His creativity has created does not deprive them of the quality of free will (M.V, 3089–97).

We experience the operation of both compulsion and free will in our daily lives. Rumi takes the simple instance of the movement of the hand. There is the hand that shakes compulsively from palsy, and there is the hand that is voluntarily shaken from its position. In both cases, the movement is created by God, but we cannot conceive the two movements to be identically caused. The owner of the palsied hand has no cause to feel ashamed of its shaking, as his act is involuntary. But the other party has cause to feel ashamed of the impropriety of his act which is volitional (M.I, 1496–9).

The Koran itself is proof of the existence of free will in man. It says that even Heaven and earth would not accept the burden of free will except that they exercised their will to reject free will, as the moral responsibility entailed was considered dreadfully heavy. They preferred the simplicity of the one-way pull on the straight path to the perplexity of multi-directional pulls. But man accepted the 'Trust'; he accepted the burden of free will. He seeks freedom of will and its ministrants. As sickness reduces the practical operation of his free will, and health increases it, he seeks health. For the same reason, he seeks high office and affluence. Pharaoh was never destitute (M.VI, 210, heading).

The Koran lays down commands and prohibitions, and holds out promise of reward and threats of punishment. They can concern only those who have the power of choice. No reasonable man issues commands to a marble rock, or shows anger and hostility to brickbats and stones, or orders the pained figure of a cripple with palsied hands to take up arms and fight. To believe that God does what no reasonable man would do virtually amounts to regarding Him as ignorant and stupid (M.V, 3022–32).

Rumi refers to the Tradition, 'The Pen has dried concerning what shall be' from the beginning to the end of creation, and says that the purpose of this Tradition is that it should incite us to virtuous action. What the Pen wrote was that every act entails the appropriate consequence. He who does wrong here suffers wrong in the other world; he who does right tastes felicity. The portion of the unjust will be damnation, that of the just blessedness. The Tradition does not mean that, because of God's eternally prior decree which is unalterably fixed, His job is finished, and He might as well consider Himself dismissed from office. Foreordainment and predestination do not annul man's power of choice. The Pen has dried after inscribing that justice and injustice are not equal in His sight, that good and bad are distinct, that bad and worse are different; that obedience and disobedience of God, honesty and dishonesty, gratefulness and ingratitude, are not on the same plane. He would be a strange king if he treated his friend and foe alike, that is, those who follow and those who abandon the way that He in His Wisdom has laid down for us (M.V, 3131–9).

The Pen does not allow the reward of the righteous to be lost. How can acts of perfidy be equated with acts of fidelity? There may be pardon for the sinners, but there cannot be that illumination which is the hope of the pious. A robber may be pardoned, but not exalted to the high office of vizier or treasurer (M.V, 3151–4), unless sincerity and penitence have wholly purged him of evil and made him pure (M.V, 3160–1).

Recompense is inescapable. We eat and drink of the crop we sow. The pangs we suffer are the effect of our deeds. Good befalls the good and evil the evil (M.V, 3181–3). Rumi tells the story of a man, a Necessitarian, who was shaking down dates from a tree and eating them. Catching him red-handed, the owner of the orchard chidingly questioned him if he was not afraid of God. The thief said that there was no reason for such fear, as the tree belonged to God, and he was God's servant who had eaten God's property. For an answer, the owner had him tied to a tree with a rope and thrashed him hard. When the man asked the owner if he was not afraid of God, prompt came the reply that he, a servant of God, was only thrashing another servant of God with God's cudgel. The thief recanted from Necessitarianism and admitted the existence of free will (M.V, 3077–84; *Discourses*, p.160).

The obvious moral of the story is that one's action always recoils on one's own head. Even the Necessitarian, who considers himself exempt from responsibility, is not exempt from retribution for his wrong-doing. The Necessitarian Iblis could not save himself by saying to God: Thou hast made me to err (M.V, 3077, heading).

Rumi says that the existence of that which is imperceptible can be more reasonably denied than that which the outward or inward senses can perceive, and so, the Necessitarian who denies his manifest power of choice is worse than the infidel who denies the invisible Divine action, but not his own inward sense (M.V, 3009).

Even animals, says Rumi, are aware of man's free will. If a camel driver keeps striking a camel with a stick, the camel will try to strike the striker, not the stick. The Necessitarian should be ashamed that he has shut his eye to the light of his inward consciousness, that is, to his power of choice, which is known even to an animal (M.V, 3050–1).

Also, the way of the *Sunna* (the precepts and practices of the Prophet) is to work and earn, and not be a parasite on society. When a master places a spade in the hands of his servant, the object is known even without speech. Hands and feet, like spade, are signs of His Will. His meaning is that we should think of the end for which the object is created and seek to fulfil that end (M.I, 932–4). The carpenter, the water-carrier and the weaver all work and earn. Want impels everyone to choose some craft. As one man cannot do everything, different men take up different jobs and create a co-operative network which maintains the order of the world (M.V, 2420–4).

One may wonder how it is that while at times our resolutions and intentions are realised, at other times, they come to naught? Why should there be such thwarting at all?

Rumi explains that God's occasional annulment of man's desire and resolution is to make him aware of His Omnipotence and of his own humbleness.

Every seed of expectation he sows in his heart is wholly subservient to the Divine Will. But as with the external cause, He does not always deprive him of his heart's desire. For if He did, man would despair and never sow any hope; he may even feel that all action was futile. Also, if he nourished no hope, how could he, without hope's disappointment, realise its subordination to the Divine Will? (M.III, 4462–5).

Occasional failures serve another purpose also. Unsuccess, according to Rumi, can be the guide to Paradise. For while failure disappoints the common man, it also shatters his pride and makes him feel humble; it makes him a better man. The lover of God benefits in a different way. He resigns himself to the Divine Will with a hundredfold free will, and a hundred delights (M.III, 4467–70). What is failure to others is to him the fulfilment of God's Will, and hence an unmixed blessing. Failures test the sincerity of a man's devotion to God.

The Prophet said that what God wills comes to pass. Rumi explains that this does not mean that we should be inactive in our devotion to the Almighty. On the contrary, as His is the Will and the Power, we must perform the devotions due to Him with the will of a hundred men (M.V, 3111–6).

The absolute Necessitarian attributes every act to God and considers himself helpless. What will be will be. He argues that, before the spirits of created beings were 'embodied', without involving incarnation, and furnished with hands and feet, they were flying carefree in the spiritual realm, and were sustained by spiritual food from God. Effort or exertion had no existence then. They began to be in trouble when they were bound by the Divine Command: 'Down ye go', down to dusty earth, and Adam and Eve were expelled from Paradise (Koran, ii,36). In fact, even after their descent, their children remained carefree in their innocent infancy, when, unable to hold anything unaided, or run, they could only sit in their mother's lap or ride on their father's neck, and be fed and cared for. It was when they grew up and began to use their hands and feet and became men of affairs that the polarity of grief and contentment sundered their unity. The people are God's children, said the Prophet, and, to the Necessitarian, this means that His mercy wil look after them (M.I, 923–8). To bear the burden of exertion and acquisition is utterly futile.

Rumi is opposed to such desire-based interpretation (*ta'wil*) of the Koran and says that such interpreters should change themselves, instead of changing and debasing the meaning of the Koran (M.I, 1081).

The Necessitarian's belief in man's impotence can lead him to abdication of exertion and responsibility, of all sense of morality and goodness, reducing the story of man to a tale told by an idiot, not even sound and fury, just signifying nothing.

In practice, however, the Necessitarian is not wholly actionless. He fears predestined disappointment. But that fear does not generally weaken his effort to secure food which is vital to his survival. Even if it is brought free to him by someone, he has to exert himself to eat it. If no such charity is his lot, he knows that there is greater fear in indolence and greater hope in work. Why then, Rumi says, should we be held back by fear of disappointment in the matter of religion? Why must we be men of little faith? (M.III, 3096–9).

We also know that complete renunciation of exertion is impossible. Even if the external senses and actions are suppressed, mental activities would remain unchecked, and the suppressed outer senses would only break into all kinds of fantasy, more damaging to inner peace and psychic health than if they were left free.

Some renunciationists abandon themselves so utterly to God that they abstain from medicine even in grievous sickness, believing that its use is a negation of trust in God. This, however, is a personal code of certain Sufis. It was never enjoined by the Prophet, who would take medicine when ill, and commanded his companions to do likewise, in order to avoid unnecessary damage to their health. As Rumi says, exertion, medicine and disease all are realities, since they all are predestined. The use of medicine to cure disease is like using the necessary means to attain certain ends. Whether the ends are attained or not must be left to God.

In another reference to the impossibility of denying exertion, Rumi says that even the denier of exertion has to exert to deny exertion (M.I, 991).

Though the earlier Sufis believed in asceticism, scorning worldly delights, and regarding exertion as a negation of trust in God, in Rumi there is no ultimate confrontation between this world and the next. He advocates exertion for good ends. Righteous exertion is not a struggle with destiny. On the contrary, it is laid on us as a duty by destiny itself (M.I, 976), as it alone can lead us towards Perfection. As Blavatsky says in *The Two Paths*, 'Inaction in a deed of mercy becomes an action in a deadly sin.'

To use one's free will wisely not only conduces to the user's material and spiritual progress, but is also an attempt to thank God for this beneficent gift. Such thanksgiving has to be dynamic, expressing itself in righteous action.

Necessitarianism, leading to passivity and inaction, is a denial of that beneficence. Thanksgiving for this gift increases one's power of volitional action. Inaction born of Necessitarianism takes this gift away. Practice makes perfect, while inaction blunts whatever power or faculty one has (M.I, 938-9).

The earner, that is, the worker, is beloved of God, as the saying goes. It is only the indolent person who clings to Necessitarianism and is ungrateful for His gift of means. Using the analogy of the head, Rumi says: 'As my head is not broken, tell me why I should bandage it? When I am the world's physician, wherefore should I feign illness?' (*Diwan*). For anyone who takes Necessitarianism as his plea for idleness only pretends illness, and the pretender dies like a lamp (M.I, 1069-70). How can the pretender escape this fate? For abstention from righteous action can only render him incapable of such action and lead him to spiritual stagnation and death. In the material world also, his fate will be similar — material ruin.

Rumi says that we plainly see our power in affairs where our inclinations lie, but in matters which are against our inclination, we become Necessitarians. In carrying out the desires of the flesh, we happily exercise our free will, but what our reason desires we plead Necessity as an excuse for its rejection. Even if we bear the burden of religious obligations, we do so not as a matter of delight, but as a protection against the wrath of God. To the prophets and saints, on the contrary, the affairs of this world are matters of compulsion, while those of the other world are matters of free will (M.I, 635-8; M.IV, 1401).

Rumi's repeated emphasis on man's freedom of choice, and on his need for exertion and to earn, does not mean that he does not believe in the doctrine of 'Trust in God'. But one must work, along with trust in Providence. Sow the seed, and for the harvest rely on the Almighty (M.I, 947).

Here, Rumi is following the Prophet. He tells the story of a desert Arab who let his camel loose in the desert, saying that he trusted God to look after it. The Prophet, on hearing this, told the Arab: 'Along with trust in God, bind the knee of the animal', thus urging the use of means (M.I, 913–14).

Above all, God tells us to strive our utmost in His ways. Even a vain struggle is better than no struggle. Though king over all, lacking nothing, He is never idle. Every day, He is busy in an affair (Koran, lv,29). He has charged us to manifest His attributes, and that requires ceaseless exertion on our part. Until our last breath, we must not be idle, so that, at the last, He may take us to Himself. Whatever the soul in us strives to do, the eye and the ear of the soul's King is its witness (M.I, 1819–24; Koran, x,62). And we have the Prophet's Tradition that 'Earnest endeavour does not fail' (M.II, 1697).

If action were evil, God's action in creating this creation would be evil, and this cosmos a great, cosmic folly, and not purposeful and full of beauty and wisdom.

Rumi stresses not only the difficulty, but also the gradualness of the spiritual Path. Rooted in sense-life, we cannot withdraw ourselves from the outward world of form and colour and complete the steep spiral of ascent at one leap. The Path has stages, and one has to proceed step by step, toiling laboriously in a spirit of self-denial, experiencing 'spiritual states' or illuminative flashes which come as gifts from God (see p.129 *infra*). As Rumi says, the Lord has placed a ladder before us and given us hands and feet, so that, by degrees, we may climb to the roof (M.I, 929–31).

It must, however, be understood that the concept of free will and predestination does not have a fixed meaning. It means one thing to the Perfect Man and another to the common individual. The change in meaning is not uncommon, as the same thing can become different in a different environment. Thus, bread wrapped in a table-cloth is or seems inanimate, but when eaten and assimilated by man or by any other living creature, it becomes the life-giving spirit. What appear to us as raindrops are pearls in oyster-shells. Similarly, the common man's compulsion is the compulsion of the self-seeking soul which drives him to evil. He feels he is without choice in the matter, being completely subject to the compulsion of God's Will. The Sufi, on the other hand, finds the fulfilment of his free will in God's Will. He still acts, but only for the sake of God. Love harmonises the difference between free will and compulsion. His compulsion is not the compulsion of the ordinary man who is conscious of self, but is the effect of self-effacement and union with God. Dead to self, he has no will of his own. It is God's Will working through him (M.I, 1464-75).

Free will and compulsion mean one thing when applied to outward life, and another when applied to inward life. In the former case, they refer to one's subjection to or freedom from another man or from chance or misfortune. But when considered in the spiritual sense, compulsion is union with God, and, in this sense, there can be no compulsion in obeying the Divine Will. 'The good servant's will is the same as that of the good master' (Plotinus). This is all the truer when the servant has submerged his individuality in that of his master, that is, he has used his free will to surrender it to the Divine Will.[1]

But the debate between the Necessitarian and the holder of free will must go on. For if one disputant could refute and convert another in this and other controversial fields, it would mean that truth had become universally known, and everyone who was off the Path would recoil and, renouncing this strife-torn existence, rush headlong on the way that leads to the spiritual empyrean. There would, then, be perfect unity of mind and thought — no plurality, no multifarious manifestation of the One, which was the purpose of the creation.

Religious heresies and disputes between opposite schools of thought, moral, socio-economic or political, are reflections of the Maker's infinite attributes, and are divinely destined. It is by the Divine Destiny that the infidel disbelieves in destiny. Each warring faction is fed with irrefutable logical proofs. The worst heretic's argument will never fail, and all the seventy-two sects in Islam and different Sufi orders and every form of belief will remain in the world till the Resurrection (M.I, 1233; M.V, 3215-19).

81

As Adam discovered, the choice between two doubtful thoughts or alternatives is perplexing. Hence, Rumi seeks refuge from the wicked acts of the pillory of free will and begs God to favour him with one path, with its one-way pull, instead of leaving him perplexed with two paths. He likens himself to an emaciated camel whose back is bruised by his free will which, pulled by the senses, is like an ill-balanced load, sagging sometimes to this side, sometimes to that. He would rather recline and not roll, save like a ball that involuntarily turns over either to the right or to the left, following the Lord's Will (M.VI, 200–5, 214–19).

Necessitarianism is of different kinds. It is blameworthy (*jabr-i-madhmum*) when one rejects free will, means and righteous action, and believes that man is as helpless before the Maker as the fabric is before the needle, or the painting before the painter and the brush (M.I, 611–13). It is of medium kind (*jabr-i-awsat*) — which most people follow — when one carries out the religious obligations or ascetic practices more as a matter of form or for the sake of conformity or show than of his free will and volition. And it is laudable (*jabr-i-mahmud*) when, dead to self, one attributes all actions to God and none to oneself, so that the question of compulsion as ordinarily understood does not arise. Compulsion and free will cease to be distinct.

Rumi also speaks of the *hamil* (bearer) and the *mahmul* (borne). One who regards himself as a separate, independent entity and bears the burden of the senses, of exoteric knowledge, of external religious obligations purely as a matter of form, is a burden-bearer (*hamil*). But he who has gained mystical knowledge and illumination and regards all actions that proceed from him as being in accordance with God's Will and not his personal will is no burden-bearer. His 'Necessitarianism' is not a 'burden', not 'prison and chains'. It is of the laudable kind; it is his wings and pinions. He is now borne (*mahmul*) — borne heavenward by Divine love and power. As Rumi says, Necessitarianism is like the water of the Nile which is water to the true believer and blood to the infidel. Wings carry falcons to the King, but they carry crows to the grave-yard (M.VI, 1441-4).

Some Sufis hold that the best course is to believe in predestination, but to act as though one believed in free will (*Kashf*, p.17). But the Perfect Man is not content with this middle course. He knows that free will and predestination are one of the countless pairs of opposites, and neither in itself is true. Hence Rumi's exhortation: Behead selfhood and become naughted. The responsibility for all your actions will then rest on God. As God said to Muhammad: 'Thou didst not throw when thou threwest' (Koran, viii,17; M.II, 1306),[2] meaning that His action takes precedence over ours, and, in this case, as the Prophet was dead to self, it was obvious that the action was God's, the Prophet being an instrument through which He acted. The pull of the King of kings transcends the duality of compulsion and free will (M.V, 2196).

GOOD AND EVIL

Closely connected with the concept of predestination and free will is the concept of good and evil. From time immemorial, man has wondered why evil should at all exist? Does God ordain evil? What is its purpose, if any? Is it predetermined? If predetermined, of what avail is man's striving after good?

These questions have been discussed earlier in this chapter. Here, we shall deal with them in the specific context of good and evil, with some unavoidable repetition.

Rumi justifies the ways of God to man, but without denying the existence of evil. According to him, evil is relative, but is necessary; it serves a purpose, and has always some good hidden in it. Rumi's universal love, which is a reflection of God's love for man, does not leave the evil-doer without defence and hope.

God's ordainment, according to Rumi, is not the same as the thing ordained, and he cites two Traditions of the Prophet by way of illustration. The first is: 'Satisfaction with infidelity is infidelity'; and the second: 'The Moslem must be satisfied in every ordainment.' The two may appear contradictory. For while satisfaction with infidelity is opposition to God, dissatisfaction with it is dissatisfaction with something God has ordained. Rumi explains that the conflict is not real. Infidelity is not an ordainment or a decree; it is the effect of the ordainment; it is the thing ordained. Before God, infidelity is not infidelity, evil is not evil (M.III, 1363–8).

But why should any ordained thing be evil? Could it not be said that as God is the Creator of all that is, He must be the Creator of evil also and, therefore, Himself evil?

In answer, Rumi cites the analogy of the artist and says that ugliness in the painting is not the ugliness of the artist; it is only a display of the ugly by him. A versatile artist has the skill to produce both the ugly and the beautiful (M.III, 1372–3). If God could not display the ugly, He would not be the Super-artist that He is. It would be a reflection on His Omni-competence.

The Divine Spirit sees no fault (M.I, 1995). While the creative utterance brings all actions into existence, it is the religious command or the Law which designates them as good and evil. What is called sinful action is thus created by Him, but only as action, not as sin. The religious command or the Law which follows His creative utterance is designed to test our faith. God has given us the freedom to ignore or obey it. Also, the Law regulates the liberty of the individual in society, so that we do not fly at one another's throats, rendering life nasty, brutish and short.

All actions, whether good or evil, are in full accord with His Wisdom. In the realm of Colourlessness, there is no colour, no duality or conflict.

God made this world in order that the 'hidden treasure' might become plainly visible, and, to this end, He laid upon man the duty of manifesting His consciousness and qualities. Man is, therefore, always seeking action, in order to bring his inward consciousness into view. That is the purpose of his life. Inaction is like the agony of death to him (M.II, 994–9).

But it is not only good that he manifests, but also evil. This is so, as God's attributes are infinite, and include what appear as good and evil to us, the former being the reflection of His Mercy and Beauty and the latter the reflection of His Wrath and Majesty. If man did not display evil, the attributes of His Wrath and Majesty would remain unmanifested, and His desire for complete Self-manifestation would remain unfulfilled.

We often seek God's mercy, especially in times of trouble. If there were no vice, no evil, to forgive, how should Divine Mercy manifest itself? This again would mean that there was a deficiency in His Self-manifestation (M.IV, 1077–9).

Also, evil is necessary, as good would not be manifest unless there was evil. It is by their opposites that hidden things become manifest — happiness by pain and sorrow, white by black, light by darkness, good by evil. If the Lord is not manifest, it is because He has no opposite (M.I, 1130–5).

Evil, as Rumi says, is not absolute; it is relative. One's food can be another's poison. Snake poison is life to the snake, but is death to man. To the water creature, the sea is a garden, but to the land creature, it is agony and death. Zayd (or Smith) may be a devil to one, but a noble king to another; a true believer to one, but an infidel to another; a shield and saviour to one, but a source of pain and loss to another (M.IV, 65–73).

In fact, many of the faults we see in others are a reflection of our own faults. It is like seeing the world through blue glasses. Seen thus, the world appears blue. One who sees evil in others is the evil-doer, and when he curses others, he is only cursing himself (M.I, 1319–21, 1329).

Fault or evil arises only in relation to us in our ignorance, not in relation to the Lord. The Pure Spirit of the Lord sees no fault as such (M.I, 1995–6). In the *Gita*, the Pandavas and the Kauravas, symbolising good and evil respectively, are not strangers, but blood cousins, closely related.

Evil serves a positive purpose also. It is a necessary condition of moral life and progress, as there can be no triumph without an adversary. 'Why rushed the discords in but the harmony should be prized?'

In many cases which are common knowledge, some good is seen to arise out of the heart of evil. Is not lust one of the worst evils? And yet, without it, there would be no procreation. But for consideration of its procreative quality, Adam for shame of it would have made himself a eunuch (M.V, 941).

Another terrible evil is heedlessness of God. And yet this evil, as we have seen, is the prop of this world. As heedfulness of God is calamitous for this world, God has sent down a trickle of spiritual intelligence which keeps greed and other evils in check, and prevents people from destroying each other. If it were a heavier trickle, and there were more of heedfulness of God, neither virtue, nor vice would remain, and other-worldliness would overthrow this-worldliness. Hence, God has appointed two architects — heedfulness as architect of the other world, and heedlessness as architect of this world. Both good and evil are necessary to keep our world going and also provide the conditions for man's probation and his spiritual ascent (M.I, 2066–70; also, see p.40 *supra*).

The Prophet said that if one knew for sure that he would be recompensed tenfold on the Day of Judgement, an act of munificence would issue from him every moment. In general, munificence results from the sight of compensation. Similarly, miserliness consists in not seeing compensation. It results from ignorance (M.II, 895–8).

According to Socrates, no man sins wittingly; he sins out of ignorance of what is good. One cannot always be blamed for ignorance.

Rumi's charity is almost unparalleled. He says that no man is attracted to evil by love of evil. Man is attracted by love of good. Evil is there because good is there. Unless there be truth, no fantasy would exist in the world and nothing false would be shown. It is truth that lends value to falsehood. The fool buys the counterfeit coin because it is like the true in appearance and he mistakes it for a good coin. If no genuine coin were current, no false coin would be issued. If there were nothing defective in this world and all commodities were perfect, all fools would be perfect traders, for no competence would be required to assess the worth of goods. And if everything were defective, knowledge would be no advantage. All is not true in this world, nor is all false.

Nor is the producer of the counterfeit coin wholly evil. The coin he issues has the semblance of genuineness and is, therefore, not wholly false. And it serves to test the discriminating capacity of the buyer. The truth is hidden among a whole host of illusions, and it is only after careful examination that the soul can discover it (M.II, 2927 etc.).

As God told the Prophet, we should make trial of everything, even of the beautiful sky, and see if there are any flaws (Koran, lxvii,3). Good and evil are thrown together, so that after making trial we may choose the good. There is only one true dervish among the numerous wearers of the dervish mantle; it is only by making trial of them that we can find him (M.II, 2937).

The belief in the Unity of Being inevitably involves belief in predestination. All actions proceed essentially from Him and we are only the instrument through which He acts. We receive our portion of good and evil and of fantasies as predetermined by Him. One cannot change one's portion for another's. As Rumi says in the following quatrain, we quest after things according to our original nature and disposition, so that what we quest after that we are, and it has its roots above:

If you are in quest of a morsel of bread, you are bread,
And if you are in quest of the soul's essential nature, you are soul.
Listen to the secret from me if you would know,
Everything you seek after that you are, that you are.

The Lord weaves from one's good fancy the stuff of Paradise which is peace and blessedness, and from another's evil fancy the stuff of Hell, which is pain and misery (M.III, 3042–4).

Evil is born of ignorance. We who are immersed in the affairs of the world do not know the way to His roseries and furnaces. We do not know the class to which we belong, the good or the evil class. If the heart knew the way to the source of good and evil, would it not repel all evil thought? Would the cow follow the butcher to his shop, if she knew she was going to her doom? If the infidel knew that he was entering the mouth of destruction, would he not hastily recoil from infidelity and change to the Path of Faith? As it is, the blessed one wonders why the other one is in the fire of anguish and the unblessed one wonders why the blessed one is in the garden of felicity (M.III, 3045–52).

Briefly speaking, we cannot discern between good and evil, because the faultiness of our actions is hidden from us, because self-interest gives evil the appearance of good, and the Lord allows us to be deceived by appearances. It is because, this being a probationary existence, God, who is both a Guide (*hadi*) and a Misguide (*mudhill*), has ordained that the reason and the flesh shall pull us in contrary directions, and neither the cord that is pulling us, nor its Drawer, is visible to the outward eye (M.IV, 1322).

It is not without reason that the prophets are enjoined by God to deliver His message to all, regardless of what is predestined for us. His idea is that we should obey His commands, and keep striving in His ways, till we discover what we are. If we are timid and say that we shall not begin to strive until we know what He has predestined for us, we would only waste our lives, without gaining this knowledge or profiting in any other way. We would be like that merchant who would not embark on a sea voyage until he knew definitely that the journey was safe and he would not be drowned. Such a merchant can do no traffic, and will not only gain nothing, but may be deprived of fortune. Nothing ventured, nothing gained. All affairs turn upon 'may be', entailing both hope and fear, and, of them all, the affair of religion, of Truth and Goodness, is the worthiest and wholly worth the effort, as by means of it alone can we attain to liberation (M.III, 3081–91).

Besides, if the Lord made manifest the mystery of His eternal foreordainment, and the mark of religion or infidelity were visible on the forehead and not hidden, and evil's retribution were known, there would be a single harmonious creed, and not seventy-two fighting factions in Islam, and there would be no idols or idolaters in the world; all would be praising God and avoiding His Wrath. The world would be like the Resurrection, with none committing sin or evil (M.II, 984–8). It would cease to be the world of probation and the other world the world of recompense.

The requital of each act is a mystery to us, as the requital and the act are not of the same complexion. Thus, the labourer's work is toil and sweat, and his wage is 'gold and silver' (money). When a man prostrates in prayer, his prostration becomes Paradise — a garden of felicity — in the other world. His altruism and alms-giving here become date-palm and herbage there. The water of his renunciation becomes as a river of water in Paradise, his love of God as a river of milk, his joy in devotion as a river of honey, and his spiritual intoxication and longing as a river of wine. There is no resemblance between these causes and effects, and none knows how God has linked each cause and effect. But as these causes are under the control of man, that is, have shown obedience to him, the rivers of Paradise which are the fruits of one's dispositions, actions and attributes, as manifested in this world, may be said to be under his control, not by his might, but by the Lord's command (M.I, 3560; M.III, 3445–7, 3457–64).

Viewing the problem teleologically, retributive action in the other world is pre-existent in God's Knowledge, and is not only the final cause, but the real or substantive form of the action, while the human action is only its apparent or accidental form. The former is the substance and the latter the accident, and the two, like cause and effect, are dissimilar in complexion.

It may be asked whether human actions, like prayer and fasting, are carried forward to the other world, or they vanish in the inane.

Rumi says that they are not carried forward in the guise in which we see them. Their resurrection is in another form which is appropriate to their nature. God appoints a time, when an accident — thought, word or deed — should lose its outwardness and manifest itself in the hidden form of substance, or rather transmute itself into substance. What we take to God is not the temporary accidents of prayer and fasting, which become naught in no time, and so, cannot be carried forward. What we carry forward is our substance, human or asinine, as affected by our actions or accidents. Thus, good actions are accidents and their substance is faith in God, and evil actions are accidents, and heedlessness of God or unbelief is their real substance.

It is not enough to say before God: I have done this or that. God does not recompense actions as such. We must show the fruits of the accidents (M.II, 944–8).

Whether we talk of cause and effect or of substance and accident, no absolute dualism is involved. They are correlates, one being immanent in the other. They are like bird and egg. This is produced by that and that by this in succession (M.II, 982).

The mystery of good and evil is open only to the elect, whose spiritual eye is open, and who, transcending space and time, know the origin of every product, and can perceive from which cause, which lapse, our punishment has originated. Others do not know the origin of their suffering, especially, as no origin is like its product. No seed resembles the tree or the bough or the blossom that grows out of it (M.V, 3978, 3985).

Nor can we know evil till we know good, as only one contrary can reveal the other contrary. Although the Divine destiny is inexorable, we would do well to follow Rumi in his prayer: O Lord, deprive not the eye of true vision, so that our senses are not perverted, and non-existence does not appear as existence, sweet water as fire and fire as sweet water, an ordinary stone as a pearl or wool as a jasper (M.I, 1198–1201). Much earlier, did not the Prophet pray: 'O Lord show us things as they are'?

EVERYTHING HAS GOODNESS IN IT

Rumi sees the soul of goodness in everything that God has made. God has sprinkled of His Light upon them (humankind), and, having received that Light, the human spirit is one and indivisible. The Light of God never became separate. Plurality is only in the airy animal spirit, and it hides the underlying essential unity. To him who has knowledge of this unity, nothing is evil.[3] But such knowledge comes only through love — love that interlinks all in a harmonious whole. In fact, knowledge and love are one in spirit (M.II, 188–9; M.IV, 411).

Rumi tells the story of a king and two slaves. When the king asked one of the slaves in private what he thought of the other slave, he said that the other slave was evil in every way. But the other slave, when asked about the faults of the first slave, said that his faults were affection, loyalty, sincerity and generosity. The second slave, his heart purified, beheld by the Light of God and saw the soul of goodness even in the evil-minded slave, while the latter, his heart blackened by vice, saw the reflection of his evil self in the immaculate, mirror-like face of his associate (M.II, 887–90, 1013–14).

Evil is not permanent. Eventually, the truth dawns even on the soul of the worst evil-doer. It is said in the Koran, 'All are brought into Our Presence' (Koran, xxxvi, 32), where there is naught but bliss eternal. There is hope for all, even for Satan, for all are saved in the end (see p.242 *infra*).

Thus, evil has no real or absolute existence. It is relative and temporary; it has the semblance or soul of goodness in it; it is a necessary condition of man's probation on earth; and it is essential for the maintenance of this world of plurality as well as for the purpose of manifestation of the Lord's attributes. It is an essential part of the eternal Plan.

4

Man the Astrolabe of God

As stated in chapter 1, Rumi does not identify the Logos exclusively with the name of Muhammad, but with all the prophets and saints, whether his priors or successors. But the Prophet is supreme.

To follow Rumi, the Prophet said that he was 'the last and the foremost', that is, if in appearance he was born of Adam, in reality, he was 'the forefather of every forefather', the last prophet in time, but the first and the best creature that God created. All the other prophets and all the saints are born of his soul and substance; they are his spiritual successors; they have inherited the Idea of Muhammad. The angels also were created from his soul, and when they did homage to Adam at the Lord's command, it was for the sake of the Prophet (M.IV, 526–8). As our main concern in this chapter is with man, we may begin with Adam, who has been called the Logos, the World-Spirit, a saint, an angel, the father of mankind.

ADAM AND IBLIS

Moulded out of clay and the first in whom the light of Muhammad manifested itself, Adam is the astrolabe of the Lord's attributes of Sublimity, and his nature the theatre for His revelations. Nothing appears in him that is not the Lord's reflection (M.VI, 3138–9). He is God's vicar, and his true sons, his spiritual children, are the Perfect Men endowed with all the Divine names and attributes, which, in effect, comprise the whole universe. We may receive the Light of God either from Him or from Adam. It is like taking the wine from the jar or from the cup (M.I, 1944). It is the same wine, with the same fizz.

God taught Adam the Names, revealing to him their nature and reality, that is, the attributes of God they represented, displaying in his body all that is inscribed on the tablets of destiny and in the world of spirits. Being a saint, Adam, following the Lord's command, communicated this knowledge to the angels. They were simply bewildered. What he revealed to them was not contained in the wide expanse of their heavens, for it comprehended all that shall happen unto everlasting (M.I, 2648–51).

The angels were wholly reason and spirit, but in comparison with the spirit of Adam, they were like the body that is subordinate to the spirit. Adam is the rational soul of the cherubim. Even the most exalted angel received life and light from him. It was because of his superiority that God ordered the angels to do homage to him. The worship of a superior by an inferior was in keeping with His Justice. In obedience to His command, the angels — except Iblis (Satan) — made obeisance to Adam. It was an obeisance not to his form which is perishable, but to the Soul of the soul, to the imperishable Divine glory and beauty, to the light of Muhammad revealed in Adam (M.VI, 153–5).

Adam has also been described as the World-Spirit (*ruhu'l-'alam*), dwelling in the heaven of the world. God saw the existing things through him, and made them live by Adam's life in them. The universe is created in his image and will not perish, except with man's perishing (*Islamic Mysticism*, Jili, p.121, footnote 6).

The accursed Iblis, who for hundreds of thousands of years was a saint (*abdal*), the prince of believers (M.I, 3296), supreme among the angels, and who now disobeyed the Lord's command to bow to Adam, fell from grace and was expelled from Paradise. After his disobedience, God told Azazil, which was Satan's name before his fall: Go under the Seventh Earth … (M.II, 1623), where, according to some, Hell is located.

The traditional explanation for Iblis's disobedience is that he was envious of Adam and held him in disdain. Why should Adam be exalted above him in God's favour? He was better than Adam, he reasoned, as he was made of fire and Adam was made of clay (Koran, vii,12), and fire was better than clay.

God told him that pre-eminence was not hereditary; it did not depend on one's relationship with fire or clay; it was a spiritual heritage, not phenomenal, not of this passing world. Its inheritors were the spirits of the pious ones. Thus, Noah was a prophet, but his son went astray. Abu Jahl was the Prophet's enemy, but his son was a devout believer (M.I, 3399–402). Each is responsible for his own salvation or damnation.

But Iblis was stubbornly proud of his intellect. He did not listen to God. And that was his undoing. Unaware of Adam's reality, he scorned the latter's higher knowledge of God (M.I, 1012–13).

Iblis's disobedience has also been attributed to his ignorance of the fact that to worship another by the Lord's command is to worship God Himself, though this may not be in accord with His eternal Will that the creation should worship Him and naught besides Him. That God may will one thing and command another — an apparent inconsistency by common standards — was, it is said, not understood by Iblis, and so he went wrong.[1]

It is only fair that the accused should be given an opportunity to defend himself. Rumi affords him such opportunity in the story of Iblis and Mu'awia.[2] In this story, the former wakes up Mu'awia and asks him to arise, as it is prayer time. When Mu'awia refuses to believe that it could be the purpose of Iblis to be his guide to any good, Iblis advances arguments to prove his good intentions.

He says that he owes his origin to God's Mercy, not to any anti-God. It was He who in His mercy raised him from non-existence, rocked his cradle and nurtured him. An erstwhile angel and God's favourite, he was obedient to Him with all his soul. How could he now or ever cease to long for Him? (M.II, 2617–29). His refusal to bow to Adam was from envy, and not from any desire to disobey God, and this envy was from love

94

of God, and for fear lest Adam should displace him from His favour and become His favourite. No lover is free from envy (M.II, 264–23).

Besides, whether one is an infidel or a believer, one is only an instrument of God and belongs to Him. Even our dispositions are not our creation; they have been planted in us by God and we cannot alter or expel them (M.II, 2629). He, therefore, had no option, said Satan, except to act as he did, and it cast him in affliction. God led him astray and He alone can deliver him, being the sole Agent of action (M.II, 2645–51).

Satan regards himself as the equal of prophets and saints, charged, like them, with the mission to test the righteous and the wicked and help the former to salvation. He describes himself as the touchstone for the false and the true coin. The false coin is not false, because he has blackened its face; he is only the assayer of money. In other words, he does not make the good man bad, but only tests him. He is a mirror for the foul and the fair, and it is God who has made him the informer and the truth-teller. If he cuts down a sapless tree that is straight and guiltless, how is he to blame? It is hewn down, because the Lord did not bless it with sap. If it had sap, it would have been steeped in the Water of Life. Good works are unavailing without His blessing (M.II, 2686–97).

Thus, Satan views his fall from grace as something predestined by God, and he also considers the righteous and the wicked as subject to the compulsion of predestination.

Though driven from the Lord's presence, Satan does not give up hope. He does not look at His wrath which brought him anguish, for His wrath is secondary and temporal, and is no more than a speck on the alloy of His coin whose substance is Beauty, Grace and Favour. It may separate us from Him, but that separation is meant to chastise the soul and awaken it to the value of union with Him (M.II, 2630–4). Satan's hopeful reliance is on His eternally precedent Mercy, which will save all souls in the end, including his own (see p. 242 *infra*).

Satan fell, and, thereafter, he set about to bring Adam's fall.

God told Adam that he and Eve could eat of any fruit in the Garden, but they must not go near a particular tree. In Genesis, it is the fruit of the tree of the knowledge of good and evil that is forbidden; in Islam, it is wheat; according to others, it is grape, fig or camphor. The symbol may be different, but the implication is the same, namely, the obedience of the Lord's command is good and its disobedience evil. The Lord vouchsafed to them that they would not go hungry or naked (Koran, xx,118). He also warned them that Iblis was their enemy, and they should not let him tempt them to become wrong-doers, or they would be expelled from Paradise to a life of toil and tribulation on earth (Koran, xx,117).

But when the Divine destiny comes, no device can free us from its toils. As the Prophet said, when it comes, the widest expanse becomes narrow, and our eyes are veiled (M.III, 381). It came and threw Adam into a dilemma. He sought to interpret on his own what God had meant, instead of being effortlessly guided by the plain meaning of the prohibition. He did not feel sure whether this prohibition (*nahi*) was *tahrimi*, that is, its breach was unlawful and punishable as sin, or it was *tanzihi*, that is, its observance was meant to be purifying, but was optional and its breach involved no sin or punishment[3] (M.I, 1250–1).

Adam's dilemma was Satan's opportunity. He was able to tempt them to eat of the forbidden tree. One step towards sensual pleasure and his fate was sealed. When Adam realised his error, he cried: O Lord, we have done wrong (Koran, vii,23; M.I, 1252–4).

It was a small sin, but among the great, even a small fault is great. As Adam was the eye of the eternal Light, this hair-fine sin took on the dimensions of a mountain (M.II, 17–18). In punishment for their wrong-doing, the Lord expelled Adam and Eve from Paradise, saying: 'Fall ye down, one of you a foe to the other', and He added that if there came to them a guidance from Him, or a narration of His revelation through His Messengers and they followed it, they would not go astray, nor would any fear or grief come upon them; but if

96

they turned away from His remembrance, their abode would be the Fire (Koran, ii,359).

It is said that when God fashioned Adam's body out of earth and water and kneaded it for forty days, so that it was perfect, Adam remained on earth for some time, and then Satan came down and entered his body, and after examining his veins and sinews, exclaimed: If the Iblis I saw at the foot of the Throne was to be manifested, it must be this (*Discourses*, p. 39). Thus, Satan is no external entity separate from man.

Rumi ends up the story of Mu'awia and Iblis with the latter's confession that his work is malice and deceit, and he acted from envy. He knew that if Mu'awia missed his prayer, he would break into sighs and lamentations in penitence and they were worth more in the sight of the Lord than two hundred litanies and prayers. Hence, he sought to urge Mu'awia to a lesser good in order to keep him away from a greater good (M.II, 2780–5).

With Rumi, Satan is a symbol of evil. He describes him as fire and naptha whose nature is to burn; as an emblem of pride, envy and deceit (M.II, 2654–7), all plot and guile; the accursed one-eyed intellectualist; the arch-enemy of God. When you don the breastplate of knowledge and follow the way of light, he makes you cast off that breastplate and fly from that way (M.III, 4332–5). Rumi likens the carnal soul to a serpent, to a fiery dragon, and says: 'In the serpent see Iblis'[4] (M.II, 257).

Some commentators have invested the 'Fall' of Satan with a cosmological meaning. His rebellion against God, according to them, was simply an assertion of the Law of Evolution; of dynamic energy or active idea against static inertia or Pure Thought, which is entirely alien to the process of evolution. It was also an assertion of Satan's inherent free will against the Lord's command, though in conformity with His Will. As after his 'Fall', he says in Milton's *Paradise Lost*:

> Here we may reign secure; and in my choice,
> To reign is worth ambition, though in Hell.
> Better to reign in Hell than serve in heaven.

According to Rumi, God created Adam spiritually pure. But as opposite alone can manifest opposite, He created Adam's opposite in the form of Satan, so that the 'hidden treasure' of His attributes might become manifest.

All things in relation to God are good, says Rumi, and only in relation to us can anything be evil, and all of us, virtuous or vicious, are, each in his own way, doing God's service and are His obedient servants. Satan is no exception, except that his role is evil. He also fulfils God's purpose.

As a part of his role, Satan tempted Adam and Eve to eat of the forbidden tree — wheat in our — case and, as he had whispered to them, their hidden shameful parts became apparent to them (Koran, xx,121).

Adam and Eve were ignorant of good and evil before they tasted wheat. It was only when Satan caused them to disobey the Lord's command that they knew what wrong-doing or evil was. This knowledge of good and evil came to them before their 'Fall', but it was not in the quiet glades of Eden, but after their expulsion from Paradise that Adam 'knew' Eve as his wife and became the father of mankind.

Also, Satan is said to have opened the consciousness of Adam to his real nature, and, as Rumi says, became his mind and conscience.

Man is believed to be on probation in his earthly life. The righteous have, therefore, to be separated from the unrighteous, the good from the bad. This needs a tempter, a provoker (*Discourses*, p.58). Satan fills that role and makes trial of men. Subject to God's Will and Decree, they are free to choose between good and evil, of which two, God 'disapproves' the latter.[5]

It is man alone who has been endowed with free will, and is king over himself, unlike the instinctually governed beasts and angels and the entire will-less heavenly host.

It may have been noticed that in our text Adam went through the following stages before we came into being:

  i The pure Adam in whom the Divine glory is reflected, and who was created in the image of God's attributes, and corresponds to the Kabalistic Adam Kadmon, the Heavenly Man, the Logos;

ii Adam, with his wife Eve, but with their private parts hidden from them; they have no will or discernment at this stage;

iii Adam and Eve before their 'Fall', with their hidden parts apparent to them; and

iv The earthly Adam and Eve after their 'Fall' whose progeny we are.

Esoterically speaking, the 'Fall' of Satan and Adam, commonly regarded as a punishment for the sin of disobedience of the Lord's command, was from another angle a 'fall' into generation, into matter, which was necessary for the creation of mankind and the evolution of the Perfect Man in whom alone, according to His Will, He could see all His attributes and realise His desire for Self-manifestation. The 'fall' was also a punishment in the sense that it involved man's separation from the Lord and a soul-destroying struggle to reunite with Him.

THE PERFECT MAN

Referring to man's situation on earth, Rumi says that they took the feathers of an angel and tied them to the tail of an ass, so that, perchance, the ass in the radiant companionship of the angel, might become an angel (*Discourses*, p.118). The Perfect Man, as the Logos, 'is the consummation of this scheme of being, the completion of this sphere of life'.

The Perfect Man is a true king; for, with his kingly nature, his spiritual kingship, he is king in himself; he does not become king by treasuries and armies; his kingship abides for ever (M.II, 3208–9). His essence is Universal Reason or Intellect, which was created before the creation of the two worlds. His heart is a mirror that reflects the splendour of the Divine attributes. It is the secondary reflection from this mirror that penetrates and illumines the dark phenomena. Without such a mirror, neither heaven nor earth could bear the vision of the Lord's Beauty or endure the direct reflection of His Light. A filtering medium was necessary and it is the Perfect Man who is that medium (M.VI, 307–37).

The Perfect Man's spirit is oft depicted as a mole on the cheek of the Divine Beauty, which refers to the Divine Essence. The essential nature of the mole, that indivisible point of unity revealed from His Essence, comprehends all phenomena, and the temporal and the spiritual worlds are its reflection (M.II, 190–1). That single point 'is a centre from which circles a circumference'.

The Perfect Man's form is on earth, but his spirit is infinite and universal. The infinite spirit not only contains the entire finite universe, but transcends it, as he is its origin and cause, and the medium through which God fulfils His purpose of creation. The Macrocosm is within him, though philosophers, limiting themselves to his phenomenal form, regard him as the Microcosm. He is both Microcosm in his outward form, and the Macrocosm in his essence. The world is the jar, his spirit is the river. There is nothing in the jar that is not in the river (M.IV, 521, heading, 810–11). His heart is the substance of which the world is an accident. He is brimming with the Light of God, and his heart, his inward consciousness, is the real mosque in which He is worshipped.

The Perfect Man is not only the cause of creation, but also the sustaining principle of all that is. As God has made him in the image of His own attributes, his spirit has made the universe in the image of itself. Everything good and beautiful derives its quality from the Divine Goodness and Beauty reflected in the heart of the Perfect Man (M.III, 2265). Nothing is that does not derive its individual function and attribute through his medium. If wine in ferment begs of him for the intoxication of Divine Love, and the circling heavens for the Divine Consciousnes, it is because these and all other attributes are reflected in the Perfect Man, and, as the Logos, he is the creative and sustaining principle of all things, sensible or spiritual (M.I, 1811–12).

As the Microcosm, the Perfect Man sees the entire world within him; he does not have to look without. Rumi tells the story of a Sufi who was immersed in meditation in a garden and was asked by someone why he was sleeping and not beholding the vines, trees and green plants which were marks of the Lord's Mercy. The Sufi characteristically replied: the marks of the Lord's Mercy, the real orchards and fruit in subtle form, are within the heart. What is without is only the marks of the marks; only the reflection of their beauty falling upon the external world (M.IV, 1358–65).

This is similar to what the eighth-century saintly woman Rabi'a told her maid servant in reply to a similar suggestion. She said: Come in and see the Maker.

Addressing the Perfect Man, Rumi says: Thou art not a single thou, but a hundred thousand men hidden in one man; a sun hidden in a mote; the sky and a deep sea which is a drowning place of a hundred 'thou's'; a hundred thousand stacks in a handful; a hundred thousand Gabriels in the earthly frame of man, comprehending all realities, unifying all contraries (M.III, 1302–3; M.VI, 4578 etc.).

The Perfect Man is the cosmic thought and his essence manifests itself in all modes of individualisations. He is now the illuminating sun, now the vast sea, now the all-encircling Mount *Qaf*,[6] now the transcendental bird *Anqa*.[7] In his essence, he is neither this nor that, but greater. For every appearance reflects only some, not all of His attributes, while he reflects them all (M.II, 545). God is both One and Many, and the Perfect Man's nature reflects His attributes in both these aspects of Unity in Plurality (*Wahidiya*) and of absolute Oneness (*ahadiya*).

The Prophet said that God has said: 'I am not contained in spatial dimensions in the jar of high and low, nor in earth and heaven, nor in the empyrean, but I am contained in the true believer's heart. If you seek Me seek Me in those hearts.' God is contained (reflected) therein as a guest, without condition, howness, definition or description. 'Enter among My servants', He says, and 'thou wilt meet with a Paradise consisting of vision of Me.' The earth, heaven, the empyrean and the starry realm cannot reflect the infinite and boundless

Lord, for they are divided, bounded and numbered. The burnished heart of the Perfect Man has no bound; it is with Him; the heart is He (M.I, 2653–6, 3484–9; M.VI, 3072–3).

Again, speaking of the Perfect Man, God says: 'He is I and I Myself am he'; 'I was sick and you did not visit Me', meaning that when His friend is sick, God is sick (M.II, 1737–8), since the two are mystically one. There are frequent references in Rumi to God's oneness with His friends, but God makes it clear that whatever He says, He is the Sun that illuminates all (M.I, 1940), and is unique.

Elsewhere Rumi declares unequivocally that the Perfect Man cannot wholly become God; he is not His congener (M.II, 1170). He bears the imprint of His attributes, but is not the Reality.

The Perfect Man is the medium through which God sees Himself and His creatures. He has reasons to be grateful to the Perfect Man; the latter displays His attributes, thus serving the purpose for which God created this creation (M.IV, 1411–12). In reality, He is grateful to Himself, for emptying His lovers of their selfhood, He unites them with Himself, so that He is both lover and beloved (M.I, 1740).

The Perfect Man is a spiritual shepherd who guides mankind according to God's commandments. He dispenses spiritual sustenance to all and sundry, regardless of their desire or fitness to receive it (M.III, 3611–12). He bestows a life that is real gold, exempt from depreciation; it is a life precious and enduring (M.VI, 3277–8). Not that receptivity is of no account. As Rumi says, the Perfect Man displaying the Lord's Bounty has every kind of food on his table, so that no guest remains unprovided, and each receives his portion according to his need and capacity (M.III, 1895–6). The Sufi's bounty is lavish. The limitation is in the recipient.

Referring to the *pirs* who have become Perfect, Rumi says that they are God's elect in pre-eternity, and their spirits existed in the Sea of Divine Omnipotence, in the Nous, in the Divine Mind before the creation of form. The world and mankind still lay cradled in latency. These Perfect Men, the *pirs*, saw things potentially as they existed in God, and as every soul existed potentially as an idea in the Divine Mind or Nous — an idea is related to a particular object — they had foreknowledge of the creation, of all that is or will be. In other words, in the utter absence of objectivity, they have seen the object. They have known intuitively, without brain and mind, the material form of every existent being before its emergence into objectivity. Their spirit knew Adam's divine nature before its creation, and they scoffed at the ignorant angels, the terrestrial angels, who disapproved the creation of mankind, saying that man would only do evil and shed blood on earth (Koran, ii,30). Past or future does not exist for them. The *pirs* have beheld, Rumi says, entity in non-entity, every unconditioned being as conditioned, bread before the seeds of wheat, cold December in hot July. In the heart of the grape, they have beheld the wine, or rather, even before the creation of grapes, their spirit has quaffed the wine of Divine Love and shown signs of drunkenness (M.II, 168–82).

The Perfect Man is said to be a slave of God, but he is a slave only in form; in essence, he is the king of kings. He is the king-maker rather, for he manifests the Divine attributes in full, including His essential attributes, like unity and eternity, and displays His Kingship (M.V, 1882). In fact, lord and slave, lover and beloved, are correlates, one necessitating the other (M.I, 1736–40).

His gaze purified of sin and self, the Perfect Man sees by the all-seeing Light of God. He sees the empyrean, with its dwellers; he sees the paradises and the hells, and knows the essences and destinies of all things. In this world, he can tell the righteous from the unrighteous, and who is for Paradise and who is not; one by one, he can sift people like wheat from barley in the mill (M.I, 3507–10). He is the 'crown and pattern of the eternal Plan'.

PROPHETS AND SAINTS

While some of the prophets, like Muhammad and Moses, have been transmitters of the Law, the prophets, generally speaking, have a message to deliver to the people; they are preachers and instructors of mankind.

Rumi calls them God's vicars, and, according to him, the vicar and God are not two. In soul and essence, the prophets are one. They are like ten lamps of which each has a separate form. But one lamp's light cannot be distinguished with certainty from another's. It is like the light of our own eyes, which are two in number, but whose light is of a like nature, difficult to tell apart (M.I, 673–9).

Sufism has made a significant contribution to the growth and development of a spirit of catholicity in Islam, which itself is a tolerant faith. According to Rumi, who is pre-eminent among such contributors, not only are the prophets one in essence with God, but also with each other. Jesus was the soul of Moses and Moses the soul of Jesus (M.I, 325). David, Solomon and all the other prophets are one. If we disbelieve in any of them, our faith in any one prophet will not be perfect. As God says about the prophets in the Koran, 'We make no distinction between any of them' (Koran, ii,136).

But this does not mean that all prophets are equal. Rumi does not believe in the equality of prophets or saints. Though there is no established hierarchy of prophets, some prophets are above others. Thus, Moses was not given knowledge of the Mystery of the Divine decree, lest it should interfere with the performance of his prophetic mission to guide and instruct people. Khidr, the mystic sage and guide, was superior to him in esoteric knowledge. Rumi cites a couple of instances of his superiority from the Koran, where Moses was unable to understand Khidr's seemingly senseless behaviour. The first is when he staved a boat in, and the second, when he slew a youth. Explaining the significance, Khidr says that he thought of damaging the boat, as there was a king behind who was forcibly capturing all boats and would not have spared theirs; and he slew the youth as he was afraid that, by his rebellion and unbelief, he would oppress his parents who were believers (Koran, xviii,80–81).

Again, while the station of Moses was that of converse,

Muhammad's was that of seeing. The latter was the chiefest and divinest of the prophets, combining in himself all stages of Perfection, and all the attributes of the other prophets. What made Ahmad, that is, Muhammad, different from Ahad (One) was the inclusion of the letter 'M' (*mim*) in the spelling. The word *ahad* has no 'M'. Now every letter in the Arabic alphabet has a numerical value. The numerical value of *mim* is forty, which symbolises the forty grades of Divine emanation from Universal Reason to man. The first emanation becomes one with the last in the Perfect Man of whom Muhammad is the supreme type. The letter *mim* is 'otherness' added to Ahad who is Perfection, and the latter suffers a decrease by addition of any 'otherness'. Remove the *mim* and it becomes complete Perfection (*Discourses*, p.226).

The prophet's relation to God is like that of a true witness to a judge. The Prophet represents this relation at its best. When he ascended the seven heavens and was within two bow-lengths of the presence of God, he closed his eyes to the treasury of the Seven Heavens; houries and genies came arrayed to see him, but he had no eyes for them. In unity with God, there is no room for another, whether a prophet or the angels or the Spirit. Muhammad just kept beholding God, his gaze never swerving, never roving (Koran, liii,17; M.I, 3949–54). His eyes received collyrium from God, and the Divine Sun caused a light to dwell in his heart. He was able to behold the mysteries in their nakedness. He beheld the journey of the spirit of the true believer and the infidel. The faith and deeds of men are within his ken and he will give testimony about them at the Resurrection. Nothing is hidden from the Perfect Man and the Prophet was supremely Perfect. No self-interest, no love of created things, blinds or deafens him. His testimony is equal to that of the eye, as he has seen the reality of every event with a selfless eye. Consequently, God has named him the 'witness', the just 'witness' who is the eye of the Beloved. Other prophets and perfect men also are 'witnesses', but in lower degrees according to their spiritual stature (M.VI, 2861 etc.). God judges by their testimony. They bring His attribute of Justice into manifestation.

As stated earlier, the believers are mirrors of each other. Rumi gives the instance of the Prophet. Abu Jahl, his bitter enemy, referred to him as an ugly figure, while Abu Bakr, his first successor, said to him: 'O sun, you are neither of East, nor of West; shine majestically.' Muhammad told each that he was right. When asked how both could be right when they had said contrary things, Muhammad explained that he was a divinely polished mirror of Truth in which Turcoman and Indian beheld what each had in himself, white seeing white, black seeing black (M.I, 2365-70).

The prophet's mission is to connect the parts with the Whole. These parts are separate, except in the sense that all are connected with the Whole. We are separated by individualisation from the Absolute. If we slay selfhood or our sense of separateness, we are connected with the Whole. The prophet's task is to act as the unifying principle, harmonising appearance with reality, the particular with the universal. When he deviates from this mission, the deviation is disapproved by God — as in the story of Moses and the shepherd. In this story, when Moses rebuked the saintly shepherd for praying to God in terms that were 'blasphemous' and the shepherd, with penitent cries, vanished into the desert, God's revelation came to Moses that he had parted His servant from Him, and it reminded him that, as a prophet, his mission was to unite, not to separate. The most hateful thing to Him is divorce (M.II, 1750-2).

The prophet is not alien to this world. He reflects all the Divine attributes which constitute the world's reality. But he is independent of carnal men; in fact, he finds them as irritants, as disturbers of his communion with God. The Prophet himself said that since he had trained the carnal souls, he had received many kicks from those beasts. It is always an affliction to impart training to the ignorant (M.IV, 2007-9).

The prophet is like the moon that is disgraced by the company of stars, but is amongst them as a generous gesture (M.I, 3018). His mission to guide mankind, teach them the *tawhid*, bring them good tidings, warn them, etc., involves association with all and sundry, and such association involves, apart from kicks, a sacrifice on his part. The Prophet refers to this sacrifice when he says that he is faint and somewhat dark compared with the spiritual suns, because the common man cannot bear the full splendour of the Sun (M.I, 3661-2). If he were all spirituality, he would have been invisible to us. He had to be our congener, one like us, so that he could meet people and give them spiritual guidance as man to man.

Complete perfection of the prophet or any perfect man consists not in 'the flight of the alone to the Alone', with all relations with the created world severed, but in abiding with the One Eternal and, at the same time, descending to work for the Many, knowing that God is everywhere, ever revealing Himself anew, and that there is no real dualism of *Nirvana*[8] and *Samsar* (world), as there is nothing but God. It is only when he has combined the One and the Many that he can be said to have reached the highest perfection.

In other words, as Rumi explains, the Perfect Man has two figures, one in this world, and the other in heaven. His one mouth is discoursing with people on religious matters, while the other mouth is discoursing with God. His outer ear is apprehending what he hears here, while his spiritual ear is taking in the mysteries of the creative command 'Be'. This is true of all members of him. His bodily part is within Time's framework and endures till his bodily death, while the spiritual part is timeless and knows no death (M.V, 3601-7).

In Buddhism, the *Boddhisattva* (corresponding to our Perfect Man) renounces the state of *Nirvana* and stays back to help mankind to salvation. For 'How can there be bliss, when all that lives must suffer? Shalt thou be saved and hear the whole world cry?' (Blavatsky, *The Seven Portals*).

The masses were quite content to receive the revealed Law as the guide and the divines (*ulama*), as the inheritors of the Prophet and preservers and exponents of the Law. But the Shiites, Partisans of the fourth Caliph Ali, chose as their guide the unerring *Imam*, who was descended from the Prophet and the Royal House of Sasan in Persia. The Sufis also had their guides, but they were not traditionists like the *ulama* of the orthodox, nor genealogically descended from the Prophet like the Shi-ite *Imam*. They were spiritual children of the Prophet and they received mystical knowledge from God or through a chain of holy men spiritually descended from the Prophet. These holy men are the saints, who, after the prophets, are the elect of God, canonised by the people during their lifetime, unlike the Christian saints, who are canonised by the church long after their death.

Saintship is an essential part of Sufism. To quote Hujwiri, 'The principle and foundation of Sufism and knowledge of God rests on saintship' (*Kashf*, 210).

Rumi calls thousands of blessings on the spirit of Muhammad and on the cycle of his Caliph-born sons born of the substance of his soul and heart. They may belong to Baghdad or Herat or Rayy, but they are his progeny, with no admixture of earth and water; they are one with his light. No matter where the rose-bough blossoms, the rose is the same; no matter where the wine-jar bubbles, it is the same wine. (M.VI, 175–8).

In every age after Muhammad, a saint arises, descended from Umar or Ali — not necessarily from Ali, as with the Shi-ites. He is the *Mahdi* (Guided One) and the *Hadi* (Guide); he is the living *Imam*, not one of the twelve Shi-ite *Imams* of whom the last disappeared in mysterious circumstances, and, it is believed, will reappear at the end of the world. He is the supreme saint, the *Qutb*, and Universal Reason is his Gabriel. Just as Muhammad, the first emanation of the Divine Essence, had to leave Gabriel behind and proceed alone towards the Presence of God, the *Qutb* also leaves Universal Reason behind, when nearing His Presence.

The *Qutb* is the head of the Sufi hierarchy and has dominion over the visible as well as the invisible world. The saint that is lesser than he is his lamp, and one still lesser is the lamp niche which receives light from the lamp (M.II, 815–20; Koran, xxiv,35). The Apostle said that: There shall always be in my people forty who have the nature of Abraham (*Kashf*, p.161).

The saints at the time of *alast* saw their Lord and became drunk in spirit, utterly unconscious. They acquired knowledge and vision in pre-existence and can recognise the signs of His fair attributes in the heart of phenomena. They know the scent of the wine, because they have drunk it before (M.II, 1666–8).

Seeing by the all-seeing Light of God, the saint is above the temporal process and knows the beginning and the end of every created thing, as the perfect *pir* also does. Rumi compares him to the divine gardener who knows one tree from another and rears them according to their specific needs. Though they look alike in appearance at present, he knows they will bear different fruit. His eye is conscious of the end. He can distinguish the rose from the thorn in the orchard of existence, the righteous from the wicked, the blessed from the damned (M.II, 1563–6).

Distinguishing the essence of the saint from his form, Rumi says that his essence is beyond the reach of thought and is its ruler, and that thought is the ruler of men. It is only to bring himself within our reach for our benefit that he comes down from his lofty zenith, yielding himself to thought. When this world disgusts him, he soars aloft bird-like with outspread pinions. In any case, it is not he, but his shadow, his form that sits beside us; he himself is winging his flight in the highest heaven (M.II, 3555–63).

The saints generally remain hidden; they have no visible marks by which they can be recognised, except that the mystic knows them when he sees them. As Rumi says, they may be seated in the front, but the animal soul cannot see them. 'Below' and 'above', 'before' and 'after' are attributes of the body, but the radiant spirit of the saints is above all spatial relations and is hidden from the eye of flesh. In order to see the saints, one has to open his inward eye with the Light of God (M.I, 2006–9). Spirit life can be seen only by the eye of spirit. The ordinary eye is only blinded by that Pure Light.

According to Hujwiri, there are four thousand among the saints who are not only concealed from us and from each other, but are also unaware of their own saintship.

The saints also are unequal like the prophets, and their grades are clearly defined and institutionalised. To use the symbolism of light, the Light of God has seven hundred (or seventy thousand) veils.[9] Behind each veil, there is a rank of saints. The seven hundred veils ascend right up to the *Imam*, that is, the *Qutb* or *Ghawth*. Each rank of saint receives illumination from the next higher, and as the saint tears a veil at each ascent, he drops one earthly attribute which is represented by the outer dark side of the veil. He is where he is because he cannot bear the light in the higher veils; his vision is feeble (M.II, 821–4).

Rumi also speaks of saints like the *nuqba* and the *abdal*, who form a part of the invisible hierarchy of saints which is believed to govern the universe. They are among the officers of the Divine Court, who, as classified by Hujwiri, consist of three hundred *akhyar* (Good), forty *abdal* (Substitutes), seven *abrar* (Pious or Holy), four *awtad* (Pegs or Supports), three *nuqba* (Overseers or Leaders), with the *Qutb* (Axis) or *Ghawth* at the top (*Kashf*, p.214). But neither this hierarchical order nor the number under each head is fixed. Thus, Rumi seems to classify the *nuqba* among three hundred saints of an inferior order, taking the place of the *akhyar* (M.I, 2773, heading), and assigns a higher rank to the *abdal* (M.I, 1434). The accursed Satan before his 'fall' was of the rank of *abdal* and was the prince of believers (M.I, 3296). Considering his proximity to God, the *abdal* would seem to rank next to the *Qutb*.

According to a Tradition which Rumi cites, God has friends who move about wholly hidden and are unknown on earth; even the *abdal* do not hear their names. They possess spiritual dominion and are celebrated in heaven, and they and their miracles are in the sanctuary of God (M.III, 3104–6).

For us on earth, the *Qutb* is the supreme saint. He is the governor not only of the earth, but also of the spiritual world.

He is the axis on which the entire existence, including the celestial spheres, revolves. His soul is the mirror of the Divine Essence. Speaking of Husamu'd-Din as the *Qutb*, Rumi says that he belongs to God and God belongs to him (M.IV, 7). As Universal Reason, the *Qutb* controls the body of the world, attending to God's creatures either as an apostle or as a spiritual director. As Rumi says, he is like the reason and the people are like the members of the body, and the body's management depends on the reason (M.V, 2343, 2345).

It may be mentioned in passing that it is not only the prophets and saints who are unequal, but every angel also has a particular rank in respect of the light and radiance received by him from the Spiritual Sun and, according to his rank, has three or four luminous wings, representing his portion of the radiance and his spiritual worth. They are just like the wings of the human intellects which also vary in quality. Every human being is believed to be associated with an angel whose quality or rank corresponds to his rank.

Rumi believes in the doctrine of pre-election. According to him, saintship is not acquired by self-discipline; it is determined essentially by pre-election. God elects in eternity those who will inherit the Scripture, read it and establish worship (Koran, xxxv,29). In other words, God first elects the righteous and then causes them to inherit the knowledge and love of God (M.I, 747). And the saints have knowledge of their pre-election as saints and, also, of their ultimate salvation. When one is purged of evil and has realised that he is a grain of sugar, he knows that he belongs to the house of sugar. He does not have to make trial of himself. For when God has created him to be a spiritual king, he will surely not place him in a lowly porch, but assign a high seat to him. Even among us, no intelligent person throws a pearl into the midst of filth, or despatches wheat to a straw barn (M.IV, 369–73). And God is All-knowing.

It is said that God scattered of His Light over all spirits, but only the lucky ones gained that Light, while others, the loveless ones, lost their share by eternal foreordainment. The illumined hearts of the saints suffer no obscuration, for they are between the two fingers of the Light of God, His Beauty and Perfection (M.I, 759–62). The saints, says God, are His children in exile, but He is always aware of what befalls them, and, secretly, He is their friend and intimate (M.III, 79, 81–2).

TYPES OF SAINTS

A distinction is generally made between saints who believe in the efficacy of prayer (*ahl-i-du'a*) and those who are perfect quietists (*ahl-i-rida u taslim*) and consider prayer ineffective, even unlawful and against what is ordained.

The *ahl-i-du'a* can pray to God for favours; they can bless or curse people. Their blessings are believed to bring good luck and their curses bad luck.

Of the perfect quietists, Rumi mentions more than one class. In some cases, the difference between the two main groups — the *ahl-i-du'a* and the.*ahl-i-rida* — is only relative.

There is one class of quietists that is wholly content with destiny and does not seek to avert it in any circumstances. Rumi refers to this class in the story of the saint Daquqi. When, by his prayer, Daquqi saved a sinking ship and its passengers, seven saints of this order of quietists who had manifested themselves to him earlier and lined up for prayer behind him, regarded his invocation of God on behalf of the sinking voyagers as an unwarranted interference with God. Taking offence at his acting like one of the *ahl-i-du'a*, they just vanished, leaving no footprint or dust behind (M.III, 2281, heading; 2289–91). They belonged to the category of *ahl-i-rida*.

Daquqi had not really acted as one of the *ahl-i-du'a*. Rumi says that it was not conscious invocation from him. As Daquqi had lost consciousness of his individual self, both the invocation and the answer were from God (M.III, 2219–20). But he did pray, though unconsciously, for a special favour on behalf of the sinking passengers. The distinction between the *ahl-i-du'a* and the *ahl-i-rida* is thus not rigid.

In Rumi's story of the Blind Man and his reading the Koran,

we encounter another class of quietists. The blind man, who believed in the goodness and mercy of God, prayed to Him to give his sight back to him, whenever he intended to read the Koran. God granted his prayer. Saints and Sufis of this class believe that the merciful God sends compensation for whatever He takes away — grapes, if He burns your vineyard, festivity amid mourning, a hand to the handless paralytic, intoxicating joy to a grief-stricken heart, sight for the Koran to the blind. They are wholly quiescent. What cause for lament? they say. If God extinguishes your fire, He gives you heat; or if He puts out your lamp, He gives you light (M.III, 1872-7).

There is another superior class of quietists. The saint who belongs to this class makes the predestination of the Lord his pleasure and becomes a willing slave to His decree not as a matter of religious obligation, but because of his goodly nature. He does not seek to live for his own sake, for riches and sensual pleasure, but lives and dies for the sake of the Lord. He does not hold faith for the sake of Paradise, or shun infidelity from fear of Hell-fire, but acts wholly in obedience to God's Will. If the slave has a nature like this, which is not acquired by personal exertion, but is an original gift from God, the world may be said to run according to his will and command, which are merged in God's Will and Command and have no separate existence (see pp.223-4 *infra*). Why should he, then, pray to God to avert destiny or seek His help or favour out of pity and mercy for himself? He seeks His help only when he inwardly feels that the Lord has commanded him to do so. As God says: Pray unto Me and I shall hear your prayer (Koran, xl,60). In the absence of any such feeling, he remains resigned and silent, and even if he dies, death is sweet to him for the sake of the Lord, and his children's death agony is to him like honey cakes to a penniless old man. He prays only when he sees in the prayer the Will and decree of God. He is the absolute slave of God (M.III, 1905-19).

Speaking of another class of perfect quietists, Rumi says that saints of this class object to nothing in this world. They do not seek to avert destiny. Their mouths are closed to invocation. They say that God has already made a decree concerning them, and so are prepared to receive whatever comes from Him. They have no consciousness of themselves or their interests. To quote Ibnu'l-'Arabi, 'Amongst them are some who know that God's knowledge of them in all their conditions is identical with [His knowledge of them in] their state of potential existence.... Thus they know the source of God's knowledge concerning them [i.e. the connection of the Eternal Will and Power with their coming into existence]. No class of the people of God is more sublime and illuminated than this class, for they are acquainted with the mystery of Determination (*sirru'l-qadar*)' (M.III, 1873; Ibnu'l-'Arabi, *Fusus*, 32,22, etc. — quoted in Nicholson's *Commentary*, M.III, ibid).

The saint is a touchstone for good and evil. He indicates and also removes sensuous and spiritual veils. He is a blessing to the righteous whom he guides to salvation, but a bane to the wicked, who, spiritually blind and deaf, deem him an impostor, scoff at him, hurt him, thus making a war on God Himself. Their action recoils on their own heads and takes its full toll.

Rumi says that the saint is the shadow of God, dead to this world, and living through God. When that saint becomes a man's nurse, he delivers him from the forms and phantoms which he so fondly pursues and which only lay waste his life. They are passing and unreal, and the wise man, like the prophet Abraham, says concerning them: 'I love not them that set' (M.I, 421–6).

Rumi describes the saints as alchemists, the spiritual makers of the philosopher's stone, whose heavenly influence transmutes our copper into gold, that is, purifies us of the taint of worldliness we have gathered (M.IV, 3074).

Speaking of the Sabaeans, and this applies to the saints also, Rumi says that they are spiritual physicians of deeds and words who, unlike the natural physicians of food and fruit, do not have to feel the pulse to know the condition of the heart. Seeing by the Divine Light, these 'spies of the hearts' know, without any intermediary like the pulse, what our hearts are like, and which word and action would be beneficial to us and which injurious. They seek no fee. Their reward is with God; it is the Vision Beatific (M.II, 576; M.III, 2700–8).

Nor is it only spiritual food, knowledge and faith, that the saint provides for us, contingent beings. Having freed himself from 'howness' and attained to the full life of 'howlessness', he, in his absoluteness, dispenses both 'howness' and 'howlessness', that is, material goods as well as spiritual food, according to our capacities, and, like dogs, we hover round his table for crumbs. Without him, God does not bestow bounty directly on anyone. The saint is the essential medium through whom all sustenance comes from the Lord (M.VI, 1192–3; M.V, 877).

The saint in ecstasy is often taken for a madman by the public, as his actions may be odd, wholly unorthodox, or at least seem as such. Rumi cites the instance of the Egyptian mystic Dhu'l-Nun who was put in a prison, as the people could not bear his unorthodoxy. The reason for this public hostility to the saint's non-conformity is that the multitude is spiritually blind, and the spiritual kings carry no external signs of sovereignty — no purple mantles or gilt sceptres — and their illumined hearts, their infinite spirit, is hidden. Hence, when a profligate rules, a Dhu'l-Nun is in prison; when a traitor rules, a Mansur (Hallaj) is on a gibbet; and when the foolish are in power, the prophets are killed (M.II, 1386 etc.).

Rumi places the saints above criticism, as they act according to the Divine command and inspiration and are not motivated by hope or fear or by personal desire or intention. Their actions may appear wrong to our limited understanding. The piety of the ordinary man is sin in the elect. He that is veiled from the Essence sees the Divine Action proceeding from His attributes, not from His Essence. But how can the saints look upon His attributes as the cause of His action? Union or oneness with His attributes, which is the farthest limit of one who is not fully perfect, is to the saint separation from God (M.II, 2812–13, 2816).

115

HOW THE SAINTS AND THE PROPHETS DIFFER

The word 'saint' has a wide application among the Moslems. Its usage, as Dr Nicholson says, 'extends from the greatest theosophists like Jalalu'd-Din Rumi and Ibnu'l-'Arabi, down to ... victims of epilepsy and hysteria, half-witted idiots and harmless lunatics' (*The Mystics of Islam*, p.125). Here, of course, our concern is with the Perfect Man.

The saints and prophets have visited the other world and surveyed it in depth, and have come back and summoned mankind, saying: "Come to that original world! For this world is a ruin and a perishing abode, and we have discovered a delightful place' (*Discourses*, p.177).

With Rumi, except for the apostolic mission of the prophet, there is hardly any difference between the prophet and the saint. Saintship is the inward aspect of prophecy, so that every prophet is a saint. Every saint, however, is not a prophet. Also, while prophecy is finite, ending with Nuhammad, saintship, derived from the Logos, is super-temporal. There is also the Tradition that the prophets were benevolently envious of the saints.

While considering his exoteric or law-giving mission the prophet is superior to the saint, the prophet as saint is superior to the prophet as prophet. Thus, Khidr, representing esoteric knowledge, the inner light of saintship, is more perfect than the apostolic Moses who was not given knowledge of the mystery of the Divine decree, lest it should interfere with the discharge of his apostolic mission. Moses, therefore, said that he would make Khidr a means to the achievement of his high purpose, of higher esoteric knowledge, as, otherwise, left to himself, he would be flying with wings and pinions for thousands of years in quest of his goal (M.III, 1969-70).

In the story of the Merchant and the Parrot in which the parrot flies away from him, Rumi appears to place the spiritual intoxication (*sukr*) of the saint above the sobriety (*sahw*) of the prophet, whose mission is to be with people and call them to God. The merchant, representing in this context the enraptured lover — Rumi himself moaning for his beloved

116

Shams — says that if the prophet Solomon possessed a 'bird' like his, he would not have bothered about other 'birds', about other souls or people, and in his drunkenness, cries: Alas for my melodious bird, my bosom companion and intimate; alas for the wine of my spirit, my garden and sweet basil, whose like even Solomon did not possess (M.I, 1695–7). But this cry is wrung from the separated lover by his uncontrollable longing for union with the beloved, and not because *sukr* is superior to *sahw*. The prophet has to bother about other 'birds', other people, and has to be like them, not all spirituality; sober, not drunk. Elsewhere, Rumi unequivocally ranks *sahw* above *sukr* — though in the end, when *sukr* merges in *sahw*, they cease to be distinct.

It is commonly believed that when the cycle of prophecy closed, the sending down of revelation also ceased, meaning that knowledge by revelation (*wahi*) comes only to the prophets, and not to the saints or to anyone else. But this sign of the prophet's superiority, according to Rumi, is only nominal. The fact is that revelation, which is a speech hidden from sense-perception, is sent down after Muhammad also, but it is called *ilham* (inspiration), not *wahi*. Citing the Prophet's saying, 'The believer sees by the Light of God', Rumi explains that this means that as nothing is hidden from that Light, the believer sees everything, regardless of time and place, and this, in its true sense, is revelation, though it may not be called by that name. As his human attributes are in abeyance, this is the only light by which he can see, hear or know.

Another distinction generally made between the prophet and the saint relates to the concept of 'ascension' (*mi'raj*), the prophet's being in the body, that is, in person, and the saint's, only in the spirit.

Here also, Rumi's view is, in a sense, different. He does say that 'through love, the earthly body soared to the skies' (M.I, 25), the reference being to prophets like Idris (Enoch) and Jesus, and, particularly, to Muhammad whose ascension carried him to within two bow-lengths of God's Presence. But,

in principle, the same can be said of the saints. For like those of
the prophets, their bodies, speech, soul and form are pure as
absolute spirit, with no external trace (M.I, 2000–1), and, in
each case, whether it is a prophet or a saint, the ascension is in
the illumined body. In any event, what is of basic relevance is
that ascension does not involve any bodily movement; it is
essentially an interior or spiritual ascension. Cf. Plotinus: '...
all of Soul that is in body is asleep and the true getting up is not
bodily, but from the body — from corporeal things' (*Enneads*,
III,vi,6).

Elsewhere, Rumi says that the Prophet himself did not
consider his ascension above in Heaven — the zenith of the
heart's Heaven — superior to that of Jonah, son of Matthew,
whose ascension was in the body of the whale. For God is
beyond the spatial concepts of 'far' and 'near', 'above' and
'below', 'front' and 'rear', and His Self-manifestation is the
same, whether above or below or in the body of the whale
(*Discourses*, pp.114–15). In other words, nothing ascends or
descends through space, all actions and movements being
aspects of His timeless epiphanies. The only difference, and it
is vital, is in the degree of proximity to God that one is able to
attain in the spirit. This, of course, depends on one's degree of
perfection, the Prophet's ascension being the closest to God.

With Rumi, it is not only the prophets and saints, but also
other Perfect Men not classed as saints who can scale the
ramparts of the stars and see 'God's light shining in God's own
Town'. As the ascension is in the spirit and the spirit is infinite,
the Sufi has to cross countless stations, and die to self countless
times.

Again, a difference is made between the evidentiary
miracles (*mu'jizat*) of the prophets and the secret miracles
(*karamat*) of the saints. The former are an open breach of the
customary order, and if they immediately affect the soul of the
beholder, it is because through a hidden link the soul of the
beholder is brought into connection with the spirit of the
producer of the miracles. That, in fact, is their main purpose;
the effects produced on the inanimate objects are only

accessory and are really for the sake of the invisible spirit, so that by means of such objects the inmost heart may be affected (M.VI, 1304-6). The saints' miracles are direct and secret.

According to some Sufis, the saints and their miracles are the means by which the proof of the Prophet continues to be manifested, their miracles being derived from him.

It is held by some eminent Sufis that the prophets perform miracles while sober, and the saints only when they are in a state of ecstasy. Other equally eminent Sufis hold that the saints must also be sober before they can perform miracles. According to Rumi, the saints can perform miracles both when sober and when in a state of ecstasy, depending on the particular saint, and, in proof of this view, two instances may be cited from him.

The first is that of Bayazid Bastami, who declared in a state of intoxication before his disciples that he was God. When the ecstasy ended, his disciples told him what blasphemy he had uttered. He said to them that if they found him repeating such impiety, they should stab him to death. When ecstasy overwhelmed his reason again, he spoke even more strongly than before, saying that within his mantle there was naught but God. His disciples struck him with knives, but each stroke was reversed and wounded the striker, his own act thus recoiling on him. Rumi concludes the story with the mystical truth that the selfless one who has passed away in God has become a mirror, so that if you spit at it, you spit at yourself; if you see an ugly face or Jesus and Mary, it is your own image, fair or foul. This miracle was performed by Bayazid while he was mystically intoxicated, and he was not even aware of it (M.IV, 2102 etc.).

The second instance is that of Ibrahim bin Adham.[10] In this story, an Amir (a prince; grandee), who was previously his servant, saw him by the sea, stitching his Sufi mantle, and was wondering why the Shaykh had given up his kingdom, if it meant that he had to ply the needle on his dervish cloak. Reading his thought — no thought in the world is hidden from the saint — Ibrahim quickly threw his needle into the sea, and loudly called for it. Myriads of divine fishes, each with a gold needle in its lips, lifted their heads from God's sea and said: Take these God's needles, O Shaykh (M.II, 3210 etc.). Here, the saint performs a miracle while sober; he performs it at his will and is fully conscious of it.

It is worthy of note that, in early Sufism, miracles were hardly given any importance. Bayazid, for example, says that when he paid no attention to miracles, God gave him the means of attaining to knowledge of Him. According to Junayd, reliance on miracles is a veil which obstructs the way to the truth. The Prophet also regarded himself as a man, with nothing supernatural about him. But neither the Prophet nor the saints could suppress the appetite of the public for the unnatural. They demanded miracles, as, to them, a saint without them was no saint. Their demand had to be met if they were not to be alienated from the influence of the saint. Hence, a saint would perform or pretend to perform miracles. In the latter case, the pretensions would be given currency as actualities. Sometimes, a saint would present plain magical feats, which are always based on natural laws, and let them pass off as miracles. A rich legend of miracles thus grew, certainly exciting because of their unnaturalness, but not of real spiritual value, except that the acceptance of the unintelligible on the evidence of miracles may lead us to overcome our incredulity in matters beyond our perception and set us on the religious Path. That may be said to lend justification to miracles, and, according to Rumi, even make them necessary (M.I, 2143–4). It is, of course, understood, he adds elsewhere, that, without Divine Grace and inward illumination, evidentiary miracles can effect no real conversion.

Nor do miracles affect all alike. Rumi tells the story of an ascetic whom a group of pilgrims saw standing on the burning sand, enraptured in the ritual prayer. When he returned to consciousness, an enlightened pilgrim saw his garment wet with traces of ablution. When asked whence the water had come in that waterless desert, he said: 'from Heaven'. 'Reveal to us one of your mysteries', he prayed to him. The ascetic lifted his eyes to Heaven and prayed to God for an answer to their prayer. In the midst of his orison, a cloud appeared and there was a heavy downpour of rain. This miracle turned one group of unbelievers among the pilgrims into believers, increased the faith of another group, and left unaffected a third group that was entirely unreceptive and doomed to eternal imperfection (M.II, 3788 etc.).

Like the prophets, the saints are endowed in pre-existence with the cosmic consciousness, and coming into this world with knowledge of what is beyond this world of five senses and six directions, they know and remember every stage the soul has traversed in its journey to plurality; they know not only its way down from the source, but also to its heavenly destination, as the way up is the same as the way down. Hence, both prophets and saints are fully competent to shepherd mankind.

INSTITUTIONALISATION OF SUFISM

What lends special importance to the saints in Sufism is not only the belief that they are the Prophet's spiritual heirs, but the growth of the practice of saint-veneration in the later stages of Sufi development.

Initially, Sufism involved a simple master-disciple relationship, with Sufis wandering from place to place in search of a master, and also as a part of their way of life. They were free to live and worship as they liked, subject to no group discipline or method as such.

Gradually, with time, Sufism became institutionalised. *Khanaqahs* (rest-houses) and *ribats* (hostels) came to be founded for the wandering dervishes. These followed no standard pattern, but, broadly speaking, they were training centres, with a collection of aspirants under a *Shaykh* or director, except for some *khanaqas* which provided Sufis with opportunities of common living and companionship, but no training facilities. The real training centres were the *zawiyas* (cells), which had a spiritual instructor, with his own collection of disciples. During this stage, which may be called the *khanaqah* stage, the individual aspirant enjoyed ample liberty both in his way of living and in pursuit of Sufi practices of his own choosing. Conformity was at the minimum.

In the next stage, an eminent director, with his own *tariqa* (way, doctrine, method), would set up a centre which would run as a Sufi school or training centre, designed to pass down the founder's name and *tariqa* through a chain of successors, hereditary or chosen by election, who, it was believed, inherited the spiritual power of the founder. The growth of *tariqas* took away the liberty of the individual aspirant to pursue Sufi methods and practices of his own choice. He had to adhere to the doctrines and rules of conduct of the particular *tariqa*.

The next stage was that of the rise of *ta'ifas* or Sufi Orders, each with its own *tariqa*. The individual follower of the Order had not only to adhere to a particular *tariqa* or way, but had also to swear allegiance to the founder of the Order and to his present successor. He was now doubly bound — bound to a particular way, and also to a man, the chief of the Order.

Then followed the association of the saint cult and also the tomb cult with Sufi Orders. *Khanaqahs* and tombs of saints came to be built together. Rumi's own *zawiya* was built around his tomb. Saint veneration was a new development in Sufism.[11]

The saint cult, involving virtually the worship of a saint and of his relics, visits to his tomb, making offerings to his spirit, seeking blessings or favours from it, in brief, self-dedication to the spirit of the departed saint, has been described by some as a mark of Sufi degeneracy. Thus, Dr Nicholson says: 'It may be dangerous to worship God by one's own inner light, but it is far more deadly to seek Him by the inner light of another. Vicarious holiness has no compensations' (*The Mystics of Islam*, 146).

But a caveat must be entered here. Nothing is without the 'soul of goodness' in it. The saint-and-tomb cult has, at least, awakened interest in Sufism among the masses, which is not without value in these busy materialistic times, when people have little leisure or inclination for religious or spiritual things. On occasions, the layman visits the shrine of a dead saint and makes offerings or gives grateful thanks for favours believed to have been received from him or prays to him for some favour, and the visit gives him some inward satisfaction, some sense of holiness, some light of hope, even if temporary, which is all to the good. Interestingly, not only the Moslems, but members of some other faiths also undertake such visits, guided not by their particular religion as such, but by living faith in the holiness and supernatural powers of the departed saint. The Sufi, of course, comes with a higher aspiration. He comes to receive spiritual communion and inspiration which, he believes, will carry him forward in his spiritual quest.

In Rumi, the saint cult finds its basic justification in the Logos doctrine which identifies the saint with the Logos. The voice of the saint, of the Perfect Man like Rumi's spiritual director Shams or of his disciple and alter ego Husamu'd-Din, is the Voice of God. As he explains, whether the Voice of God is heard from God Himself or through the larynx of a saint or from his ever-living spirit after him, it is the same voice. It is like the light which is the same, whether one receives it from the last candle in a row of ten candles or from the candelabrum (M.I, 1947–9).

Rumi firmly believes in the tomb cult and he told his disciples always to be with him after his death, so that he might show himself to them and shed in them the light of heavenly inspiration (see p.135 *infra*).

WOMAN THE RAY OF GOD

Celibacy is not an essential condition for a Sufi, though many Sufis have been celibates. Rumi himself was married and had children. The Prophet said: 'Marry that ye may multiply.' He also said: 'Satan is with the solitary', for he can tempt them more easily than the married.

What is more relevant to our purpose is that in Sufism itself woman has a place. Her sex is no handicap. Like her male counterpart, she has only to be spiritual enough to be accepted as a Sufi. There were regular convents for women generally called *ribats*, just as there were convents for men. One of the early Sufis was a woman, the eminent Rabi'a of Basra (died AD 801).

According to Aflaki, Rumi himself had a female disciple, a saint named Nizama Khatun, a friend of his wife's (Redhouse, *The Acts of the Adepts*, p.97).

Like man, who has both devil and angel in him, woman also has two facets, evil and divine. In both cases, evil is relative, as it always is, existing only in relation to us, not in relation to God. Let us take her evil side first.

Rumi likens woman to the appetitive soul. Satan preferred her as an effective means of temptation to other attractive means shown to him by God. It was Eve, a woman, who made Adam eat of the 'forbidden' tree and caused his expulsion from Paradise. Again, it was his mother's lust that caused man's fall in the prison of the body. Thus, both his falls were caused by women.[12] Understandably, any Perfect Man — Joseph, for example — seeks delivery from the wiles of women (M.VI, 2795-9; Koran, xii,33).

Again, the first murder committed in this world was for the sake of a woman; it was the murder of Abel by his brother Cain, both Adam's sons. Whenever Noah tried to inspire infidels with faith, his wife Wahila would interfere and nullify his missionary efforts. Stories of women's wiles abound in Rumi, some of them seasoned with ribaldry, but always carrying a moral. The guile of woman is infinite (M.VI, 4471-5).

The Prophet believed in consultation with intellect, as it helped to avoid repentance in the end. When asked what should be done if a woman lacking in judgement and understanding came along, he said: 'Consult her, but do the contrary; he who does not disobey her, will be ruined. Know that one's fleshly soul is woman and worse, for woman is part of evil, while the fleshly soul is wholly evil' (M.I, 2956; M.II, 2269-72).

But that is one side of the picture. An equally vicious picture can also be painted of man.

Woman is not perfect, nor is man. The Lord has made her attractive to man. He created her in order that he might take comfort in her. This is a divine arrangement which he cannot escape. How can Adam be separated from Eve? (M.I, 2425-6).

Often, woman is the dominating partner. Rumi says that, outwardly, a man may be dominating his wife, but, inwardly, he is dominated by her, and seeks her love (M.I, 2431). This, however, is only true of the wise and intelligent man, not of one who is ignorant of love and tenderness and is ruled by lust and anger, by animality. Rumi cites a Tradition in this context: 'Woman prevails over the wise, and the ignorant man prevails over them [women]' (M.I, 2433-6), for, apart from being physically stronger, such a man lacks the human qualities of softness, kindness and affection.

Like man, woman is nobly planned. She is the highest type of earthly beauty and is man's natural beloved. But the object of love is not the form, whether it be love of things of this world or of the next. For if we loved a woman for her form, why abandon it when she is dead? Her form still is intact. But as the spirit has departed, we love her no more, we do not love her form (M.II, 703-5; also, see p.46 *supra*).

Beauty in humankind is like gilding, withering, passing, not permanent. It is like borrowed gold on our copper. It is not this gilding that inspires love, but the spirit whose beauty is lasting (M.II, 712-16). Just as God has poured out a draught of His Beauty on gold, rubies and pearls, He has poured out a draught on the curls and faces of the beauteous ones. It is this draught of Divine Beauty mingled with dust that we love and kiss with a hundred hearts. How wonderful must be the pure wine (M.V, 374, 380-1). The real inspirer of love is a woman's spiritual and divine qualities, not the clay in her tulip lips or anemone cheeks.

Rumi sees the eternal Beauty in woman. It is through her that the Divine Beauty reveals itself, and performs the creative function. In Rumi's words, she is a ray of God, and not the earthly beloved; she is, so to speak, creative, not created (M.I, 2437).

As both love and spirit, which are different aspects of Divine Being, are veiled like a bride, Rumi calls God 'the Bride' (M.I, 1992), and says that while the Bride unveils before all Sufis, that is, manifests her Beauty, none is with her in the bridal chamber, except the bridegroom — the Perfect Man, who alone enjoys the rapture of mystical union with God, his Spouse (M.I, 1437). Incidentally, the Arabic for spirit (*ruh*) is feminine.

Elsewhere, Rumi refers to the Koran as a bride (*Discourses*, p.236). He also narrates that the Prophet would say to his wife Humayra (Ayesha): 'Speak to me, O Humayra, speak and cause me to be ensorcelled by your beauty and drawn closer to you, so that the radiance of pure love may enter and transfigure my bodily nature.' Ayesha to him symbolised the Divine Spirit — the Heavenly Aphrodite or the soul at its divinest (M.I, 1972–3). Communion with her was communion with spirit.

Rumi says that it is no fault to address God as feminine. God has no share of male or female. He is above male and female, just as He is above 'up' and 'down' and 'before' and 'behind'. All these are bodily attributes and do not apply to the essence of the luminous Spirit. The fault is with us who see nothing but fault; the Pure Spirit of the Invisible sees no fault (M.I, 1995, 2007–8).

MAN THE ASTROLABE

To conclude, man is the astrolabe of God. For just as the astronomer knows the condition of the heavens through the metal astrolabe, a man with knowledge of self has knowledge of God, and, through the astrolabe of his own being, sees the perpetual manifestation of His ineffable Beauty.

It is argued that the heliocentric theory of Copernicus (AD 1473–1543) dethroned the earth from its geographical pre-eminence, and, with its dethronement, took away from — an the cosmic significance he had arrogated to himself, reducing him to quintessential dust, which he is at his lowest. But Copernicus had made no new discovery. Confucius and his school taught the sphericity of the earth and the heliocentric system around 600 BC (Blavatsky, *The Secret Doctrine*, Vol.I, 441). This theory was also known to the priests of Egypt from immemorial ages. 'Pythagoras took [it] from the Egyptians, who had it from the Brahmans of India' (Jablonski, *Pantheon Aegypti*, II, Proleg.10, quoted in *Isis Unveiled*, Vol.I, 532).

Today, the position is that science and ancient wisdom are not so much in conflict in certain fields as in the past. According to both, time, space and motion are relative. 'Modern science will tell us that the Copernican or heliocentric description is simpler rather than truer. Simpler for certain purposes no doubt, not so, for certain others.'[13] Not so in the ancient philosophical or in the Sufi context. To the Sufi, man and earth are virtually where they were before Copernicus or at any time in history or prehistory, and except for occasional attacks on his pre-eminence since his evolution as Man, he, the Perfect Man, continues to be the crown and pattern of the eternal Plan.

5

The Sufi Path I

The Path refers to the progress of the Sufi's spiritual life; it refers to his progressive interiorisation. As no two individuals undergo an identical experience, the paths are countless, being 'in number as the souls of men'. But in spite of the infinite variety of mystical experience, they have a common hard core.

Rumi speaks of classes of persons and says that each class has a different ladder. The reference to the ladder means that the interior ascent is gradual, rung by rung, not in one leap. The ladder is hidden as it is a spiritual ladder and the spirit is hidden. Each ladder leads to a different heaven, to a distinctive spiritual experience. Plurality continues as it must in this world of manifestation, till the ultimate unity is reached, when all differences will vanish. In the meantime, each spiritual wayfarer is aware of his own path, but, because of their hidden nature, he is unaware of other men's paths. This one wonders why that one on the other ladder is happy, and that one wonders why this one is amazed (M.V, 2556–9). But should anyone think that his path is the only right path, he is off the path from the start.

The Sufi treading the Path progresses by self-mortification, which means self-purification, through a series of spiritual 'stations' to contemplation of God, and ultimately to mystic union with Him. It is rising from light to light. On the Way, the Sufi experiences a succession of spiritual 'states'. Stations and states are the essential aspects of the Path.

STATIONS AND STATES

A station (*maqam*) is acquired by personal striving, and it

128

denotes the earned rank and standing of the Sufi before God. A mystical state (*hal*), on the other hand, has no direct connection with his efforts; it is not an acquisition like a station. It is a sudden flash of knowledge or spiritual feeling that comes as a free gift from God; it simply descends on the Sufi. He who is favoured with a state is in actual vision of an attribute or attributes of God and is dead to self.

But states as gifts and stations as acquisitions are really not unconnected. The former is the psychical and the latter the ethical aspect of the journey. Without self-mortification, there is no revelation; without toil, no illumination. Action and vision must go together or must alternate, with the disciple assimilating every new knowledge gained, retaining it, acting on it, thus preparing for the next flash.

The number of stations and states is not fixed, nor is their sequence or grading. God Himself is said to have sent over one hundred and forty four thousand apostles to explain the way, and they came with as many stations (*Kashf*, 371). When one station is attained, another lies ahead. There is no end to stations.

Distinguishing between the higher and the lower stages of mystical experience, Rumi says that *hal* is like the unveiling of a beauteous bride symbolising the manifestation of Divine Beauty, and *maqam* is like being alone with her. (The reference to God as feminine is only a figure of speech, with a hint of His attribute of beauty.) All Sufis may see the unveiling, but when she is alone in the boudoir, none is with her, except the king, the perfect Sufi. He alone tastes the rapture of union with her (see p.126 *supra*). There are many among the Sufis who experience *hal* — here, considered in its passing aspect — but those who attain the station of Perfection are rare (M.I, 1435–8). In any case, when perfection is attained, no distinction remains between stations and states.

Rumi speaks of two grades of Sufis, one termed 'the son of the time' (*ibnu'l-waqt*), and the other, 'the father of the time' (*abu'l-waqt*).

The term 'time' is a technical term in Sufism which denotes

the predominant spiritual state and rank of the Sufi at the moment; it also means the preservation of one's spiritual state (*Kashf*, p.13, footnote).

Rumi calls 'time' a cutting sword, as it cuts the roots of the past and the future, making the Sufi oblivious of both. He is kept absorbed in contemplation of God with whom 'is neither morn nor eve', neither past nor future, neither time without beginning nor time without end — no divisibility of any kind. In the spiritual world, it is 'indivisible continuity'; 'an eternal Now in which all things co-exist' (M.VI, 2714, heading).

'The son of the time' is an imperfect Sufi who seeks purity. He swings between states of elation and depression, joyance and grief, and because of his changing states is technically said to be in the state of *talwin* (change). He waits for the 'moment', for *hal*, and when it comes, he clings to it as if it were his father which it is in the sense that it keeps him from the necessity of looking to the morrow. He loves the eternal Light of the Beloved which shines in the mystical states (M.I, 1323; M.III, 1425–6).

The other type of Sufi is the Perfect Man, sunk in the Light of the Lord's Majesty. The Sufi has become the *safi* (pure one). He is not the 'son' any more; he is free from 'times' and 'states'. He is the lord of states of feeling; they depend on his decision and judgement. He can vivify any state by his Messiah-like breath. If he so wishes, death becomes sweet, and thorns and stings become narcissi and roses (M.III, 1420–7).

According to Rumi, everyone has a specific station wherein he finally abides. Abraham's spiritual station was that of casting himself in the fire of asceticism and mortification. His personal being was of no consequence in his sight. Moses was in the station of converse, whereas Muhammad was in the station of seeing. Another Sufi, seeing from another point of view, may assign other stations to them. Thus, the station of Moses is also said to be that of contrition, and of Muhammad that of praise (*dhikr*). Similarly, while from one point of view Adam was the Logos, from another his station was that of repentance.

REPENTANCE

The Way of *Mujahada*, or the Way of Purgation, as Christian mystics call it, begins with repentance (*tawba*), which marks the soul's awakening from heedlessness of God and its determination to 'return', which is the etymological meaning of *tawba* (*Kashf*, 294), from what God has forbidden to what God has commanded. It is the stage of conversion (*inabat*); according to some, repentance leads to the stage of conversion which is a separate stage.

With repentance, the aspirant is ready to start the journey. But there are hurdles to overcome, which arise mostly from the weakness of the flesh, from the imperious desire for sensual enjoyment. Even health and wealth can be hurdles. For though good in themselves, they often make us heedless of God and tempt us to evil. Often, it is when some illness or calamity befalls us that our conscience wakes up and we are shaken out of this heedlessness and become humble and penitent, and beg the Lord's forgiveness for our wrong-doing, which is shown to us by the Lord while we are penitent, and we vow that henceforth our choice of action shall always be in obedience to Him. The greater our pain and anguish, the fuller our awakening and the greater our pining and love for God, though we may revert to heedlessness when our calamity or anguish is over (M.I, 623–7).

But failure is no cause for despair. The Lord loves a contrite heart. As we are told, on his expulsion from Paradise, Adam went and stood penitently in the shoe-place (M.I, 1633–5). A similar self-humbling practice prevails among the Sufis. In the secluded company of Sufis, the erring Sufi stands in the shoe-place, his head down, and lays shoes on his head as a mark of penitence. If we also in sincere repentance let our eyes weep tears, and our heart burns with grief, the all-forgiving Lord may look down kindly on us and, in His Mercy, grant us pardon. He may even turn our evil deeds into good, if we are truly penitent. If we mean business, we should follow the Koran, and, as a measure of self-purification, 'repent, believe, and do a righteous deed' (Koran, xix,60). A rocky heart can

131

never take the plough.

Rumi knows the busy world of men. A penitent sinner, he says, is better equipped than one who is ignorant of the ways of sin. He is like a clever thief who has become a policeman. The ways and habits of thieves are known to him, as he himself has practised the trickeries of thieving. If such a man becomes a *Shaykh*, his previous trickeries will become a power for beneficence and justice, and he will naturally be superior to all other policemen who never were thieves (*Discourses*, p.143).

The door of repentance, says Rumi, is open to men till the Resurrection, and, like alms-giving and prayer, repentance is one of the doors of Paradise, and it is always open, while others are sometimes open and sometimes shut (M.IV, 2504-7). But the time for repentance is now. God will not forgive an evil-doer who repents at the time of his death. Ours is a probationary existence and we shall be judged after death and paid for every atom of good and evil we do in life. Death-bed repentance cannot save us from that judgement and its consequences. We should also know that, as the years grow on us, our weaknesses will strengthen their grip upon us, while our strength and will to resist them will grow increasingly feeble (M.II, 1235-6). Why, then, defer bleeding till blood ceases to be of any use? Why not bleed now, when our blood will not be rejected? (M.I, 3822).

But the initiative for repentance is not a matter of personal effort alone. The savour of repentance is not the portion of every wrong-doer (M.II, 1643). Pride and infidelity bar its way. Repentance is from God to man and is one of His countless gifts.

A question that is often debated in Sufi circles is whether repentance consists in remembering one's wrong-doing or in forgetting it. The answer depends on whether one has the novice in mind or an adept. The novice is taught to remember and regret the wrong-doing, so that he may not repeat it. But the case of the adept is different. Rumi says that it is only a self-conscious person who keeps remembering and forgetting his past sin. If an adept repents of a state that is past, his repentance is worse than his sin, and he should repent of such repentance. For the greatest sin is the sin of self-consciousness (M.I, 2205–6). The adept must be dead to self.

Here, Rumi is following Junayd, according to whom repentance consists in forgetting the sin. In fact, as both remembrance and forgetfulness are connected with one's self, both are sins. With the adept in mind, Rumi says that 'being is a sin' (M.I, 517), a thought more strongly expressed in the following hemistich quoted by Junayd: 'Thy existence is a sin with which no other sin can be compared.'

THE *PIR*

The aspirant who has been 'converted' by repentance is now ready for the journey. But he needs a *pir*, a spiritual guide. For he is ignorant of the Way. The knowledge he seeks is not head-learning, not knowledge by description, but the wordless knowledge which is universal and abides in his heart, as in every other heart, and can be gained by treading the inward Path. He must, therefore, be initiated and guided by a *pir* who possesses such knowledge, and, having trodden the Path, is well acquainted with its twistings and turnings and how they can be overcome, and is eminently fitted to guide the aspirant.

The novice is understandably nervous at this stage. He knows practically nothing about the journey, except that it will demand his all. He is afraid he might prove inadequate or backslide and succumb to the lure of the flesh. He needs mental assurance, and it is the *pir* who can provide this need. In Rumi's story of the Caliph Umar and the Ambassador of Rum, representing the *pir* and the *murid* (disciple) respectively, the former's 'Fear ye not' (Koran, xli,30) reassures the disciple and soothes his fear (M.I, 1429).

Speaking of fear, both fear (*khawf*) and hope (*raja*) haunt the aspirant in the beginning. As he progresses, hope grows and fear declines, and, later, they are succeeded by what in Sufism are called *bast* (expansion with spiritual illumination) and *qabd* (contraction with spiritual occultation). In his prose work, the *Fihi ma fihi* (Dr Arberry's *Discourses*), Rumi likens *bast* to spring and *qabd* to autumn. But all dualities disappear when the unitive state is attained.

It is said that the real Teacher is within us, not without. Can he not guide us on the Path? Why is an external *pir* necessary?

It is true that the Teacher is within us. But the clang and clatter of the world of sense and desire has deafened us to the voice of the inner teacher. The novice needs an embodied teacher, a *pir*, who can transmit the inner teacher's message in a form which the external ear can hear. The teacher has to be of his own kind, as it is from one's own kind that one can receive and absorb instruction.

The *pir* is the external teacher *par excellence*. For, as Rumi says, the disciple's thought is the outward form, while the *pir*'s thought is the soul. The latter is the Universal Soul. The disciple should listen to the impersonal voice of the embodied *pir* and seek himself in him (M.II, 1986–7). He can act without instrument and give lessons to his disciples without speech.

But the *pir* cannot plant anything new in the substance of his disciples. He is only an instructor. But when he delivers the inner teacher's message, the disciple should exercise his personal free will to hear and obey. The choice is his. There can be no compulsion on the Path. The disciple, even if he be king, should be lowly before him.

There is another reason why a *pir* is necessary. The light that the aspirant seeks is too strong for him. He needs a filtering medium, an intermediary, to soften it for him. The teacher is that filtering medium. He receives the first full brunt of light, and, knowing the inward state of his disciple, he transmits that light duly proportioned in intensity to the disciple's receptive capacity.

According to Rumi, the *pir* does not have to be present in person or even be living to guide disciples. He may be remote in space and time. His light and spirituality can guide lone aspirants without any formal initiation. Thus, Abu'l-Hasan Kharraqani, a well-known Sufi, received lessons every morning from the tomb, that is, from the spirit, of Bayazid who lived 165 years before him and is said to have predicted Hasan's birth and discipleship (M.IV, 1925–34). The spiritual descendants of Uways al-Qarni, a contemporary of the Prophet, also belonged to the same category and received instructions from no living *pir*. He lived in seclusion and never met the Prophet, though the wondrous scent of God coming from him in Qaran intoxicated and enraptured the Prophet. Dead to self, that earthly Uways had become heavenly (M.IV, 1828–30). Rumi is said to have told his disciples shortly before his death that, as after 150 years the light of Hallaj revealed itself to Shaykh Faridu'd-Din Attar (see Introduction, p.9), and became his spiritual guide, they should always be with him after his death, so that he might manifest himself to them and infuse into them the light of heavenly inspiration (Redhouse, *The Acts of the Adepts*, pp.91,92; also, see p.123 *supra*). But if the absent *pir* can accomplish so much, the present *pir* can accomplish more and is undoubtedly better (M.I, 2976).

Understandably, the aspirant looks for a living *pir* whom he can see face to face. But a living *pir* is not easy to find. Rumi warns us that, as many Adam-faced devils exist, we must not give the hand of discipleship to every hand (M.I, 316). The genuine *pir* is not mere beard and frock, not one who uses golden words stolen from a genuine dervish, or indulges in miracles that are plain magical feats. All his performance is calculated to spellbind and deceive simple people for his own selfish ends (M.I, 319). He is a hypocrite by any standard, and we must not fall into his trap. This warning is particularly relevant today, when we are literally invaded by a whole host of such men — 'the wretched quack-squadron' of Carlyle — who find easy victims among the growing number of those who are weary of the rat race or feel frustrated in life or whom pleasure has ceased to please, and who are prepared to clutch at any straw and trust it to carry them past the Slough of Despond to the uplands of hope and happiness. But it is a vain hope. Disillusionment comes to them early or late, and back in their original state of misery, sadder and, perhaps, wiser, they are apt to find their life wasted, the road far off, and the day late (M.II, 751). The danger is real.

Not that true *pirs* do not exist. At this very moment, Rumi says, there are many 'Companions of the Cave', many saintly men, beside and before us, who are lost in contemplation of God. But how can we perceive them? Their reality is hidden from the common gaze of men. Our inward eye which alone can see them and our inward ear which alone can hear them are sealed. We are spiritually inadequate (M.I, 405–6).

Rumi's advice to the seeker of a *pir* is that he should sit with many Sufis, look long on every face, watch it attentively, and do service to the Sufis. This way, God willing, he may be able to know the face of a true saint (M.I, 315), or of a true *pir*. Only his quest has to be genuine, and his guide his conscience, the spirit, not the flesh; that is, he has to be ready for discipleship.

Fortunately for the aspirant, as is natural, the teacher also is in search of promising disciples. The two are correlates. There can be no teacher without a disciple and no disciple without a teacher. The teachers are as much on the look-out for disciples as the disciples are for teachers. Just as God manifested His attributes by creating this creation, the *pir* must manifest his secret knowledge by transmitting it to true seekers. In this respect, he is like the Buddha who is said to scan the world every morning to see if there was one anywhere who would benefit by his teaching. The sad fact is that spiritually adequate disciples are rare. But where there is one, he finds the master, or rather, 'When the disciple is ready, the Master appears.'

The *pir* sows the good seed in the good soil. When he has found the right disciple, he puts him through a rigorous course of ascetic discipline generally for a period of three years of which the first is devoted to service of the people, not as their equal, but as their servant; the second year is devoted to service of God, not for any personal gain, but wholly for His sake; and the third to keeping a watch on his heart, lest any heedlessness of Him should creep in at any time. On satisfactory completion of his probation, the *pir* invests him with the *muraqqa* (patched frock), and the disciple takes a vow of allegiance (*bai'at*) to the *pir* in terms of the formula given to him by the *pir*, and his initiation is complete.

In the story of the Caliph Umar and the Ambassador of Rum, after reassuring the disciple (the Ambassador), the *pir* (the Caliph) seeks to encourage him to embark on the spiritual journey by speaking to him of the holy attributes of God, of His beneficence, and of His kindnesses to the *abdal* (saints). He explains to him the meaning of spiritual 'stations' and 'states', and of free will and compulsion. Going into greater subtleties which, in actual practice, are taught at a later stage, the Caliph tells him of the stages or stations the soul has traversed in its downward journey; of the Time that is void of time, that is, eternity; of the pre-existent atmosphere where the transcendental Spirit has seen boundless flights, each greater than the horizons themselves. In reply to the question as to how the spirit descended to the earth and got encased in matter, the Caliph explained that God recited spells and incantations over the non-existences and they joyously danced into existence. His creative command 'Be' was uttered, and it was (M.I, 1427 etc.; also, see p.29 *supra*). God needs no cause. His Will is supreme.

The *Shaykhs* have no time for kings or worldly dominion. Rumi narrates the story of a king who said to a Shaykh: 'Ask me to confer some bounty on you.' 'Are you not ashamed to say such a thing to me?' retorted the *Shaykh*. 'I have two vile slaves and they are rulers over you. One is anger and the other is lust' (M.II, 1465-8).

Speaking of how the disciple should behave towards the *pir*, Rumi says that, having found the *pir*, the disciple should place himself in his hands 'like a corpse in the hands of the washer', remembering that God has declared that the *pir*'s hand is as His own. In the words of the Koran, 'The Hand of God is above their hands' (Koran, xlviii,10); M.I, 2972). He must efface himself and obey the master's instructions implicitly, even when he does not understand them, submitting to him as Moses submitted to the authority of Khidr (Koran, xviii,67

137

etc.). Whether the *pir* speaks to him 'hot' or 'cold', that is, roughly or gently, he should listen to him joyously, for his 'hot and 'cold' is life, a new spring-tide; it is the source of faith and sincerity and service; it is the way of escape from the 'hot' and 'cold' of Nature as well as from Hell-fire (M.I, 2055–7). Unless the disciple is wholly obedient to the *pir*, he cannot be receptive to the teaching, as doubts or self-regarding acts will keep hindering its assimilation. As the great Hafiz says:

> Dye your prayer-rug in wine, if the Magian chief tells you so,
> For the spiritual wayfarer is not unaware of the ways and rules
> of the stages.

The disciple should regard his master as a model, and even in externals, his effort should be to become like him by imitating his ways and actions. He must listen to him in silence. For the *pir* is the tongue and the disciple only an ear. When a suckling child is born, it is, at first, quiet and all ear. If it be not ear, but keeps babbling, he is going to be the creation's dumbest being. One born deaf remains dumb. In order to be able to speak, one must hear; it is via hearing that one comes to speech. As God says: 'Enter the houses by their doors and seek the ends in their means.' It is only by constantly listening to the *pir*, which is the proper means of knowledge and speech, that the disciple imbibes spiritual knowledge and can meaningfully open his mouth and speak (M.I, 1621–9).

Rumi warns the disciple against certain actions in his relations with the *pir*, if he is serious in his spiritual quest. Firstly, having found the right *pir*, he should never think of testing him. The *pir* has already passed all tests, and, according to Rumi, is aware of his pre-election and sainthood, though, according to some Sufis, the saint possesses no such knowledge. In any case, for a novice to make trial of him is an act of ignorance and effrontery, for he is applying his scales of judgement and intellect which cannot contain the *pir*. The *pir* has cosmic judgement, and, consequently, shatters these scales. How should a mote weigh a mountain in its scales? (M.IV, 374–80).

Nor must the disciple harbour thoughts of disloyalty or rivalry against the *pir*, thinking that his thoughts are hidden from him. This warning is relevant, especially as it is not uncommon to mistake one's little achievement for perfection. The disciple must know that there is a window between heart and heart, and, having passed away from all human attributes, the *pir* sees by the all-seeing Light of the Lord; the occult and the manifest are no different to him. The imagined veil over the hearts of the disciples is no better than a hundred-holed blanket through which the *pir* can see their thoughts clear as daylight. Their hearts give testimony to him about their thinking. The *pir*'s heart, they should not forget, is the factory of their fortune. They receive mental and spiritual sustenance from him. Why seek to destroy the factory? They will only harm themselves, not the *pir* (M.II, 1578, etc.).

There may be occasions when the disciple is aware of something of which the *pir* may appear to be unaware. The disciple must not attribute the *pir*'s unawareness to his ignorance, and imagine himself to be superior in knowledge. The *pir*'s unawareness is only the result of his preoccupation with something else at the time. Nothing is hidden from him. The World of the Unseen is an open book to him. If he appears unaware of anything here, it is generally because, in moments of ecstasy (*fana, istighraq*), though ignorant of nothing, he is only conscious of God as One (M.III, 2063). Rumi describes a miracle in which an eagle snatched the Prophet's boot, and, flying up with it, turned it upside down, when a black snake dropped from it. When it brought the boot back, the Prophet thanked the eagle and said that though God had shown him every unseen thing, his heart was occupied with his own affairs at the time he was about to wear the boot. The eagle said that it never could dream that the presence of the snake was beyond his knowledge; the truth was that it was the reflection of the Prophet's own light (*nur-i-Muhammadi*) that enabled it to see the hidden snake. Rumi tells the disciple to take a lesson from this anecdote and not be of less understanding than the eagle (M.III, 3238 etc.).

139

The disciple should never relax his watch over his heart. For if he goes astray and indulges in sensuality, pride or conceit, becoming or re-becoming the 'clay-eater', the *pir* may not bother to check him and bring him back on the Path, and may even let him think that his back-sliding had not been observed by him. Also, if the disciple becomes inattentive to the *pir's* teaching, the *pir's* inspiration which comes from the Logos will not come to his lips, and he will let it return to its original source rather than be wasted (M.I, 3087–90). In either case, the disciple is not ready for discipleship.

The *pir* demands complete obedience from the disciple not to boost his own ego, but because, without it, he cannot effectively impart instruction to the disciple and transmute his copper into gold. The disciple, on his part, should be like the hunter who follows the footprints of a musk deer in the beginning, and then takes his musk-gland for a guide. He should follow the footmarks of the *pir*, that is, his spiritual instructions in the Sufi Way, up to a certain stage, and then take his navel, symbolising the essential knowledge of the *pir*, for his guide. To travel one stage guided by the scent of his navel is better than travelling a hundred stages following the *pir's* footprints, just rambling or racing in neutral (M.II, 160–4).

THE BODY IS NOT TO BE DISHONOURED

Rumi does not hold the body in dishonour. It was not in a moment of aberration, but in His infinite Wisdom that God bound the pure spirit in the earthly body. If pure spirituality were enough for His Self-manifestation or for manifestation of any created thing, the creation of this external world would have been purposeless. Form is necessary to manifest the invisible, and so the body is a purposeful part of the creation. It is an outward manifestation of the spirit in this world, and without it, the body cannot live. Bodily acts reveal our hidden intentions and thoughts in this world of externality, thus manifesting our real selves. If lovers exchange gifts which have form, it is because they are outward tokens of their inward feelings of mutual love which are hidden (M.I, 2624–8). The body is thus a valuable frontispiece, a reflector of our interior.

There is another useful purpose that the body serves. Without bodily development and sensual appetite, there would be no question of self-conquest without which no spiritual growth or perfection is possible.

When the Prophet called the 'deficient' man accursed, he was referring to his deficiency of mind, which can be remedied if properly tackled, not to bodily deficiency, the cure of which is beyond our power and which is, therefore, fittingly the object of Divine Mercy. God says in the Koran: 'It is no crime in the blind or the lame or the sick' (Koran, xlviii,17; M.II, 1536–41).

Quoting from the Koran, Rumi says that when a blind man comes seeking the Truth, do not hurt him by turning him away, and he cites the instance of a righteous blind man who approached the Prophet, while the latter was occupied with urgent religious talks with certain influential lords and chieftains. The Prophet excused himself from seeing him because of this important preoccupation. But this excuse was not good enough in the eyes of the Lord, and he said to Muhammad: 'O Ahmad, before God, this one blind man is better than a hundred Kaisers and a hundred viziers.' One single mine of hidden ruby and cornelian is better than countless mines of copper, and, as goes the adage, 'men are mines'. In the sight of God, riches have no use; what is wanted is a breast brimming with love, pain and sighs. The blind man of enlightened heart has come. Give him counsel, for counsel is his right, said God (M.II, 2068 etc.; Koran, lxxx,1–10).

The body is at once dark and light. It is dark as a part of the world of appearance; it is light, as the knowledge of reality first descends into the soul through sense perception. The senses as faculties of the soul can receive illumination, and when they do, it is 'light upon light'.

Elsewhere, speaking of the connection between the heart and the body, Rumi says that it is by means of the heart that the body functions, speaking and seeking when the heart speaks and seeks (M.II, 837). If the heart wills, the feet begin to dance and the hand begins to write. The hidden hand within, 'mystic, wonderful', has set up the body outside as its instrument of action.

THE CARNAL SOUL AND ITS MORTIFICATION

In Sufism, there is an evil element in man whose seat is *nafs*, the carnal soul or the flesh (not the body), which drugs us with every evil anodyne. Its mortification is an utter necessity on the Path; for such mortification is an indirect means of contemplation (*mushahada*). According to the Sahli Order of Sufis (one of the twelve Sufi orders mentioned by Hujwiri) it is the direct cause of contemplation. But the conquest of the inward enemy is far more difficult than that of the outward enemy, the infidels. Hence, the Prophet referred to the holy war against the infidels as 'the lesser war' (*jihad-i-asghar*), and that against the inward enemy, against oneself, as 'the greater war' (*jihad-i-akbar*) (M.I, 1373, heading).

Explaining the Tradition, Rumi says that the idol of the carnal self is the mother of all idols, that is, of all that is not God. The idol without is only a snake, but that within is a veritable dragon. The carnal soul is like iron and stone which, when struck together, bring forth fire; the idol without is as sparks from the fire. The sparks can be quenched by the water of faith, by observing the religious obligations and prohibitions. But how should these external, religious ordinances quench stone and fire within? How should they quench the flame of sensuality? (M.I, 772–4).

Rumi also compares the outer carved idol to black water in a pitcher, and the carnal self to the feeding fountain for the black water. A piece of stone can break a hundred pitchers, a hundred idols, but the water from the fountain keeps gushing out uninterruptedly; the fleshly soul lives and grows, churning out new evils (M.I, 775–7).

The carnal soul is also invested with a form. To some, it has appeared in the form of a young fox, a yellow dog, a mouse, a snake — forms bodied forth by the minds of Sufis. Rumi describes it as the seven-gated Hell mentioned in the Koran (Koran, xv,44; M.I, 779), and he calls Hell the seven-headed dragon (M.VI, 4657). These seven limbs of Hell are the seven vices that lead to Hell.

Our base self is truly a part of Hell, and, like all parts, it has the nature of the whole (M.I, 1382). It has praise of God on its lips, the Koran in its right hand, but dagger and sword in its sleeve (M.III, 2554). Every instant, a deceitful action outrushes from the fleshly self, and, in every deceit, a hundred Pharaohs and their hosts are drowned; a single deceit catches and destroys the mightiest of men (M.I, 780).

Not only is the carnal soul Hell, which is a dragon and such a dragon that its flame not even the waters of the Seven Seas can quench, but it makes a morsel of a whole world and devours it, and, still unsated, its belly cries out: 'Is there any more?' (M.I, 1375–80; Koran, *l*,30). Hell and destruction are never full.

Commenting on the verse in the Koran, 'And raise the battle cry against them with thy horsemen and men on foot' (Koran, xvii,64), Rumi explains how difficult it is even to get started on the Path. We resolve to do so, but the devil, our carnal nature, raises his voice and says that if we followed the way of religion, we would become prisoners of distress and poverty, and be cut off from relatives and friends, and would only repent our action. We defer the journey, saying that there is enough time to make a start.

But on seeing death and other woes of life around, Buddha's First Noble Truth — the Truth of Suffering, we, out of deadly fear, resolve afresh to be religious, and manage to re-start on the Path and advance a few steps. Again, the devil cries out at us that we should be fearful and turn away from the sword of poverty. Fear overcomes us again. We waver. Even if many a ray of Divine faith and love had shot forth from noble works, that devilish soul, taking advantage of our weakness, lays its finger on them, extinguishing them one by one, so that success eludes us again and we re-become darkly earthy (M.III, 4326, heading, etc.; M.I, 384–6). 'To be weak is the true misery'.

To uproot a mighty mountain with a needle is unimaginably difficult, but still more difficult is it to mortify the lower self. It is only God's foot that can kill it by stamping on it. Rumi, therefore, seeks strength and help from God to uproot by painful mortification this Hell-born fleshly self. The act of man must be blessed by God, if it is to succeed (M.I, 1388).

The real trouble is that, within us, a constant conflict is waging between the reason and the flesh (*nafs*). The reason pulls us forward and the flesh backwards. In the words of St Paul, 'The flesh lusteth against the spirit, and the spirit against the flesh: and these are contrary one to the other' (Galatians, ch.5, 17).

Rumi cites the analogy of Majnun, the lover, and his she-camel, symbolising the flesh (*nafs*). While Majnun's desire is to speed to his beloved Layla, the wish of his she-camel is to run back after her foal. Whenever Majnun forgot himself or became heedless, and the ever-alert she-camel saw her toggle slack, she would go back towards her foal. Eventually, realising that, because of this constant battle between his desire and that of his she-camel, he would never attain to his beloved Layla, he flung himself down from the camel so violently that his body cracked and his leg broke. He tied his leg and said that he would become a ball and go rolling along in the curve of the Lord's bat (M.IV, 1533 etc.). He had subdued the flesh and the devil.

Rumi quotes a verse from Attar the first hemistich of which reads: 'You are a sensualist, O heedless one, drink blood amid the dust.' The meaning is that the craving for sensual enjoyment, the pride and ignorance of a Nimrod and other evils, are present in the children of the flesh. We must go through the fire of self-mortification and purge ourselves from self's pollution. We must kill selfhood while still in this body of clay (M.I, 1603, heading). We must remember that even bread does not give strength until it is broken, nor grapes yield wine till they are crushed (M.I, 2932).

Rumi refers to the curse uttered by Sana'i on the rider who does not dismount from the body. That spirit is lost which does not so dismount and turn to God.

One cannot, however, go the whole way by one's own effort, symbolised in the story of Majnun and his journey on the she-camel. After the conquest of the flesh symbolised by the act of dismounting from the she-camel, further progress is possible only by the pull of God, the pull of the flesh having ceased (M.IV, 1559).

We may remind ourselves that the Light of God sustains the entire creation, and is 'the master light of all our seeing' on all levels of being. Even the gross senses and the outward world of sense-objects are illuminated by that light (M.II, 1292–3).

All kinds of thoughts, not only good, but also bad arise in the heart of the aspirant, as in every other heart. This duality in the kind of thoughts is inevitable, as duality is the basis of manifestation. Man is seated on the threshold between the Upper World of unity and peace and the lower world of diversity and strife. From Above comes the call of Duty, stern daughter of heaven, the call of conscience which symbolises the Voice of God, and from below comes the siren call of desire. Man is free to decide which voice to heed, the unifying and harmonious voice or the separative and discordant voice.

Referring to what the Prophet calls 'the greater struggle', Rumi says that we must draw up armies of good thoughts, in order that they may throw bad thoughts out of the kingdom of the body.

If this object is to be achieved, no thought must be rejected as too trivial. For, as Rumi says, every thought is a message from God, indicating His Wrath or Mercy, and it calls for deep meditation; it must be investigated in depth, as Solomon investigated each new plant that grew in the Farther Mosque (*masjid-i-aqsa*). Just as study of the plants in the earth tells us about the secret nature of the soil, the thoughts, when meditated upon, tell us about the secrets of the heart (M.IV, 1314–18). As each thought is the objectification of the archetype in the spiritual world, through such meditation real knowledge begins to grow in the mystic's heart.

Obviously, mere study of the thoughts is not enough. We

must learn to appraise them and classify them into those good and those bad, and follow the good and discard the bad. To this end, we must concentrate wholly on good thoughts. As it is not possible to concentrate wholly on two different things simultaneously, bad thoughts will then automatically disappear (M.II, 1505).

Such self-introspection and appraisal and follow-up action is the way to self-knowledge. But the process must be continuous, so that, gradually, the appraisal and response may become more and more accurate. Here, the *pir's* guidance can be invaluable. He can help the disciple to ensure continuity of self-introspection and correct appraisal of each thought, followed by appropriate action in each case, till, ultimately, the disciple is able to rise from ignorance to knowledge of the real or true self.

As man reflects all the attributes of God, self-knowledge is Universal Knowledge; it is knowledge of God. As the Prophet said: 'Whoso knoweth himself knoweth God' (M.V, 2114). Hence the inscription on the Delphic temple: Know thyself. When this stage is reached, the *pir's* task is done; he is needed no more — not as a *pir*. A new Jerusalem has been born. The disciple, with all his limitations transcended, now himself becomes the *pir*, fully equipped to shepherd others to safety.

But that wondrous knowledge is yet a far-off thing. We must return to the point of quest where we were. The Path is long and toilsome, and we can only progress step by step. As is said in *The Secret of the Golden Flower*, 'One must not wish to leave out the steps between.'

In the formal teaching of the Way of *Mujahada* (Purgation), certain methods, some external, others internal, are prescribed. There is no uniformity in this regard among the different Sufi schools, except that their ultimate aim is the same. Some of the major methods are dealt with below.

OUTWARD AND INWARD METHODS
Religious rituals and obligations

Like any good Moslem, the aspirant must observe the rituals

and obligations prescribed in the Koran, even if he does not understand their inner meaning.

The worldling is spiritually sick. He would only become sicklier if he did not abstain from what is forbidden and do what is commanded. In this respect, he is no different from one who is sick in body, who also would become sicklier if he were to eat any of the forbidden things.

The aspirant's compliance with the religious injunctions may only be formal at this stage, but that does not render them valueless. They will restrain him, as they would any good Moslem, from grosser forms of evil, and promote a sense of unity and brotherhood with others in the community. The unity may be loose, and may disintegrate later, but the act of compliance constitutes a useful step on the Path.

Good behaviour (husn al-adab)

Good behaviour is, in brief, good manners and feelings, self-control and discipline.

Nothing is of greater merit in this world of trial and tribulation than a good disposition, says Rumi. For it is from a good disposition that good manners arise. Good manners, he says, are forbearance with the ill-mannerly (M.IV, 771).

The Apostle said that good manners are a part of faith.

Rumi exhorts us to implore God to help us to self-control, as, without it, one is deprived of His Grace. He cites the instance of the people of Moses who were receiving bountiful trays of food from heaven, when some of them, blinded by greed, insolently cried: 'Where is bread and lentils?' It was, on their part, an act of ingratitude and irreverence to the Lord. Punishment was inevitable. The bountiful supplies were cut off not only from these impudent wretches, but from the rest also (M.I, 78 etc.).

Whatever of gloom and grief comes upon us is the result of our insolence, that is, of flouting religious injunctions; it is the result of our indiscipline (M.I, 89). It is through discipline, Rumi says, that heaven is filled with light, and the angels become sinless and holy (M.I, 91). Why not take a lesson from them and exercise self-discipline and observe priorities relevant to each place and occasion?[1]

Further, good behaviour is valuable not only because it creates a friendly feeling and makes for social harmony, but especially because it breaks down selfhood in some measure and makes for outward calm which creates favourable conditions for inward peace and spiritual progress.

Abstinence (taqwa)

Abstinence is the result of piety. It involves abstaining from what the Lord has forbidden and, in this sense, it forms a part of the religious prohibitions. It involves abstaining from what is lustful. In the later stages of the Path, it involves abstaining from everything except God. Full abstinence cannot be achieved so long as desire is not renounced.

There is another method which is associated with dervishes and Sufis and which an average Moslem does not practise. That method is asceticism. What is its value in Sufism?

Asceticism (zuhd)

In the early days of Islam, overwhelmed by fear of sin, of after-death Judgement and Hell, the religious Moslem would tend to seek salvation in jungles and deserts, away from the haunts of men. There was also the belief that everything was unalterably fixed, and even with good works, man's salvation depended on the inscrutable Will of God, and this promoted practices that made for passivity — for acquiescence, renunciation of exertion and blind trust in Providence. The stress was on God's Wrath and Vengeance. But this was a temporary phase. In due time, God's Mercy and Lovingkindness and the positive side of man's purpose in life began to receive attention. Man was not a mere automaton, but was born with a Divine purpose, and with free will, and he must strive after purity and perfection in order to fit himself for return to his Divine source. In consequence, asceticism came to lose its pre-eminence, and was relegated to the early stages of the Path.

Exertion is necessary in our daily life as well as on the spiritual Path. As Rumi says, gnosis is the fruit of past asceticism. Asceticism is the toil of sowing, while gnosis is the growth of the seed and the reaping of the harvest (M.VI, 2090-1). An ascetic's is only one day's journey in a month, and a day is of great value to him. But a day cannot be equal to 50,000 years which is the length of every day of our reckoning in the life of the adept, the reference being to the Lord's timeless Self-revelations. Every moment, the mystic has an ascension peculiar to himself, to the very throne of God (M.I, 1580).

According to Rumi, the externals of asceticism like nightly orisons and vigils, retreats, abstinence and fasting divorced from their inner meaning, are of little avail on the Path. To perform any religious obligation or any good act for the sake of ostentation or for the sake of Paradise, or to attribute any action or thought to one's personal will, instead of to God, is polytheism in Sufism. It is the attitude that lends value to the act.

Outward methods of mortification belong to the lower reaches of the Path, and are a journey in the body. Inward methods, which are more difficult, belong to its higher reaches and are a journey in the spirit. Outward methods commonly receive greater attention, not only because they are easier to understand and practise, but also because of the not uncommon belief among the masses that mind and body are separate and independent, and that it is the body that is the source of evil, and not the mind which is something noble and divine. The truth is that not only the noblest, but also the vilest pleasures are mental, and the senses only act according to the dictates of the mind; and that the mind, the world of thought by itself, that is, unregulated by the unifying spirit, is personal and separative, and is the creator of the illusion of independent selfhood, which is the root-cause of evil in the world. 'The mind is the great Slayer of the Real,' says Blavatsky, 'Let the disciple slay the Slayer' (*The Voice of the Silence*).

Inward methods involve the killing of all ignoble attributes, which are like so many idols in the human heart. Envy is the worst of all evils, according to Rumi (M.II, 805). Many a worthy becomes unworthy through envy (M.II, 809). Pride and envy led Satan to disobey the Lord's command to bow to Adam, and the result of this disobedience was his expulsion from Paradise. Self-conceit and self-approbation made Adam look contemptuously on Iblis and laugh at his sorry plight. God pulled him up and Adam expressed repentance for his prideful look (M.I, 3893–8). These two attributes — pride and envy — must be overcome, if spiritual harm and retrogression is to be avoided.

Again, anger is king over kings (M.I, 3799). Apart from upsetting the other party, anger disturbs one's own peace of mind, and, consequently, one's power to concentrate on God. We must remember that the wrath of God is terrible, and as Jesus said, the only way to save ourselves from that wrath is to master our own wrath (*Discourses*, 239).

Another common vice is greed and covetousness. They are a sign of discontentment with our lot; a sign of ungratefulness for what God has given us or enabled us to earn; a sign of lack of faith in Him. Not that man should not strive to earn his daily livelihood; he cannot survive without it. Greed comes in when the limit of propriety is exceeded. The mouth of greed is never full. It leads us on and on, without our ever reaching the fountain where we can slake our thirst and find satisfaction.

Rumi mentions another stumbling block on the Way, and that is man's craving for worldly fame, for wealth, power and position, for self-assertion and expansion, stemming from the false conviction that he is separate from all beings and lives only for himself.

In Buddhism, the Second of the Four Noble Truths is Craving, the thirst and lust of things, which is the cause of the First Noble Truth of life's Suffering. Iron fetters which are visible can be mechanically broken, though with difficulty. But the fetter of public reputation which is deep-rooted in the heart and is invisible to the outward eye is far more difficult to break. But unless it is broken, the aspirant will remain self-regarding and cannot progress on the Path (M.I, 1546).

So strong is the craving for public fame that Rumi tells us to look ill and miserable, so that we may be freed from the snare of reputation (M.I, 1545).

Be munificent, says Rumi. Munificence, in Rumi, means the giving up of lusts and pleasures; it is a branch of the cypress of Paradise. If clutched, it will carry one aloft to Heaven and show him the delights of the spiritual realm. Woe to him who lets go this branch. He will only sink in the mire of lust and never rise again (M.II, 1272–5). We must not wait till the day is late, but sow while the sowing can be fruitful.

The disciple has to learn under the guidance of a *pir* that all bad qualities, of which the outward evil acts are the fruit, spring from the lower, finite self. So long as selfhood prevails, the aspirant will regard himself as a 'windowless monad', independent of others, and his actions will be self-regarding. He will cease to be selfish and overcome his base qualities only when, through ascetic practices and devotional acts, and by withdrawal of the light of consciousness from the world of sense-objects, he begins to realise that the individual 'monads' are not 'windowless', separate and independent, but are harmoniously interlinked, and the same One Life runs in us all. 'To see a world in a grain of sand, and a Heaven in a flower' is not a mere poetic flourish, but a profound truth of life.

Poverty and renunciation

As there can be no poverty in Sufism without renunciation, the two may be dealt with together.

Poverty is the absence of desire for worldly possessions as well as for other-worldly blessings. Contentment is its accompaniment. 'Poverty is my pride', said the Prophet. A Sufi is said to be 'poor' when his heart is empty of phenomena, of everything other than God. One must not possess poverty either, for poverty is as much a possession as wealth. One must renounce regard for renunciation of words, deeds, wealth and reputation, and do so not out of fear of God's

Wrath which is His Justice, nor from hope of Paradise, but out of sheer love of Him.

When God asked Bayazid what he desired, he answered: 'I desire not to desire' (*Discourses*, p.138). Even the desire for union with God separates one from God, and has to be killed.

But desire is not easy to renounce, not by sheer will power, which will only subdue it temporarily, not kill it. We must conquer the senses, which are its wings and pinions. Detaching the light of consciousness from the sense-world, we should seek to identify ourselves with the light itself, so that it does not stream out, but ingathers, and the mind begins to realise that within lies what it was seeking without. For the sense-objects outside are only a manifestation of their inner archetypes which the inner senses can sense, and, without which, there would be no world of sense-perception. The realisation that all is within, possessed, of course, in common with other souls, is the natural death of desire.

According to the Koran and the Sunna, poverty is superior to wealth, which is so often the root of evil. By acting as a cover for his sins, wealth makes its owner believe that he can do no wrong or evil, and that he is a superior individual altogether. But when one claims no property as his own, knowing that all goods belong to God, and has renounced all desire, wealth cannot corrupt, nor poverty bring greed or covetousness. One should be content with whatever state, whether of wealth or poverty, is his portion.

Knowing that the worldling tends to look down on the poor as inferior beings, Rumi warns them not to jeer at the poverty of the Sufi and despise him merely because he is materially poor. For it is not outward wealth, but the inward eye that is the true measure of man, the eye that can reach God Himself. The rest of man is but skin and bones (M.I, 1406). The Sufi's inward eye is open and can span horizons, while the worldling is spiritually blind.

Beggary

Beggary, though associated with poverty in the common mind

and apparently an outward method, has a special significance in Sufism.

In Islam, alms-giving is an ordinance of faith, as the poor are always with us. If there were no beggars, none to receive alms, this religious obligation would remain unfulfilled and the defaulters would be punished at the Resurrection. The beggar is, therefore, necessary, and is even ranked above the giver, as he enables the giver to fulfil his religious obligation.

The goodly beggar does not beg of men with importunity (Koran, ii,273). He does not make a pest of himself — a test by which an average person can roughly judge whether the beggar who approaches him for charity is genuine or not. Also, the Koran tells him who can afford to give: 'Do not drive away the beggar' (Koran, xciii,10), unless good reasons exist. Charity is one of the noblest virtues, and, in a wider sense, with its basis in love, it is the noblest.

Beggary is a practice that belongs to all stages of the Path. While the novice is required to practise beggary as a part of his probation, some of the *Shaykhs* also who have attained perfection find the practice useful, even necessary at times. Rumi tells the story of Shaykh Muhammad Sar-razi whose spiritual experience was higher than the throne of God and who came to Ghazna from a desert after many years, and, in obedience to the Divine command, turned a beggar and started carrying his basket around from door to door. Whatever he collected he distributed among the poor. He would purposely use vile expressions while begging, so that he would hear vile abuses from high and low. The Shaykh sought the humiliation of begging and these abuses not for the sake of his gullet, but because God had commanded him to be a beggar. There was an Amir (chieftain; grandee) whom he would visit and pester with his begging basket four times a day. The Shaykh explained to the Amir, who was disgusted with his importunity which, in a novice, would be inexcusable, that during his seven years in the wilderness, he ate nothing but vine leaves, and that if he had found in himself any craving for bread, he would have ripped his bread-craving belly (M.V, 2686 etc.). His importunity was justified. The Koranic text, 'Do not drive away the beggar', is relevant in a case like this.

Not only the Sufis, even the prophets would beg in the name of the Lord, crying: 'Lend to God, lend to God.' As the Koran says, 'If you help God, He will help you and make your foothold firm' (Koran, xlvii,7); 'Lend unto God a goodly loan and you will find a richer recompense with God' (Koran, lxxiii,20; M.V, 2700–1).

Speaking of the Sufi doctrine of poverty in relation to the beggar and the giver, Rumi says that just as the beggar seeks and loves the bountiful giver, the bounty of the bountiful giver also seeks and loves the genuine beggar. He speaks of two types of such beggars and two types of bountiful givers. If the giver has more patience, the beggar will come to him and beg; but if the beggar has more patience, the giver will come to his door and give him bountifully. Patience in the beggar in the second case, indicating his abstention from self-activity, is a virtue, while in the giver in the first case is a blemish.

Genuine beggars, says Rumi, are the mirror of the Lord's bounty. The first type of beggar just mentioned is a seeker of God. The giver's bounty, and all bounty is the Lord's, causes the beggar to beg and mirror His bounty. The other type has negated himself and is always with God; he is united with the Absolute bounty. To refrain from begging and every kind of self-regarding act is his perfection. In this case, the giver himself comes to his door and lavishes on him more than his need, wholly unasked (M.I, 2744, heading, etc.).

Any third kind of beggar is like a dead man; he is like a lifeless picture on a screen; he is the land-fish (*bi-ruzi*) that is scrupulously avoiding the Sea of Divine Essence; he wants a morsel of food; he does not want God (M.I, 2751–4).

While detachment and renunciation are vital on the Path, and the *pir* often enjoins his disciple to wander from place to place in order that he may learn not to get used to persons, places or things, and some *pirs* may even appear heedless of the well-being of men and the world, it must not be thought that they hold the creation or any part of it in low esteem. The saint Daquqi is a case in point. In Rumi's story of him, Daquqi would not spend even two days in a village or in a house, lest he should get attached to it, and his heart should get defiled. He would tell his soul to migrate and travel to independence, that is, to non-attachment. Not that he was ill-natured or he isolated himself from men and women, regarding them as wholly other than God. On the contrary, as a Perfect Man, as a created form of Universal Spirit, his spirit was the whole of which their spirits were parts, and it is natural for the whole to love its parts. A part severed from the whole is useless till it is rejoined to it. We may recall in this context the Prophet's words: 'Ye all are parts of me.' To continue Daquqi's story, he was kind to the good and the bad alike, better than a mother, dearer than a father. He would intercede for people and his prayers on their behalf were granted. But inasmuch as he contemplated nothing but the Divine Unity, he was isolated from the people. The human terms 'separation' and 'union' do not really apply in such cases (M.III, 1926 etc.).

True dervishhood is not escapism; its object is not to forget one's responsibilities to fellow-brethren or to avoid worldly entanglement. Absolute poverty is absolute detachment from all 'otherness', from all except God, because nothing exists but God (M.II, 3497). There is nothing to escape from. True dervishhood cannot be attained if one is concerned with its theory or is aware of possessing it.

Rumi treats poverty as synonymous with self-abnegation (*fana*) and non-existence (*adam*), as when he says: Poverty is your Mahmud (M.VI, 1400), the Mahmud of non-existence (M.VI, 1446).

Poverty is not easy to learn. Book and tongue cannot teach it. It is learnt by companionship with a *pir* or saint. Soul receives knowledge of poverty from soul (M.V, 1063–4).

Speech and silence

It is common knowledge that the tongue conceals the man. It is a curtain over the soul's gate; and it is only when it is rolled up that his interior is revealed (M.II, 845–6). Speech is the curtain-raiser and silence a veil. Some Sufis rank silence above speech, others speech above silence. Both are right, each in his own way. Whether one should keep silence or speak depends on the object one has in view; it depends on the spiritual station of the wayfarer.

God has commanded the believers to speak well and give Him thanks and praise, and He has promised to answer the prayers of His invokers. The believer has also to make the declaration of faith with his tongue.

Further, even when one is seeing the Beloved, and His cup is at his mouth, his ear may ask for its portion. As a poet has said: Give me wine to drink and tell me it is wine (M.IV, 2078–9).

Placing silence above speech, Rumi says that the gnostic who drinks of the mysteries of God is like a lily — hundred-tongued and mutely eloquent. Silence is basic to contemplation, while speech, an expression of selfhood, is as dust that covers the heart, incapacitating it for the reception of light (M.I, 577). 'Speech is of time; silence is of eternity.' It is not in speech that Truth abides, but in the silence of the inmost centre in us 'where silence is more than all tunes'. Rumi says that he thought of rhymed couplets for communication with God, but He says that he wants him to think of nothing but vision of Him, and that 'I [God] will throw word, sound and speech into confusion, so that without these three, I may converse with you' (M.I, 1727–30).

Rumi tells the story of the Caliph Uthman, who mounted the pulpit, but instead of preaching as the congregation expected, kept looking at the people in silence. His steady look, his silence, imparted instruction and revealed secrets to the congregation, and accomplished more than a hundred sermons could have done. An ecstasy descended on them. The entire mosque was filled with the Light of God, and those with vision saw that Light. At the end, the Caliph remarked: 'The preacher who exhorts by deeds is better than one who exhorts by speech.' A working *Imam* is better than a speaking *Imam*, for true work is that of the soul, and external, visible works, like prayer and alms-giving, are its forms (M.IV, 496–9; *Discourses*, pp.139–40).

In the same congregation, there was a blind man, typifying the novice, who imagined from the heat he felt from the Light of Eternity that a sun had arisen, and said that he had gained sight and could now see. But it was not an experience of real vision (*iyan*), but only of a fleeting state of ecstasy (*hal*). The novice must not equate himself with the adept. The meaningful silence of Uthman affected the novice and the adept differently (M.IV, 498–504).

The gnostics who have drunk of the cup of God and have been taught the mysteries of His action are understandably silent; their lips are sealed and closed (M.V, 2238–40). As Junayd said: 'He who knows God is dumb.' For in actual vision, speech or exposition is a veil, a thorn hedge that bars access into the vineyard of Reality (M.I, 1729). God knows our inmost thought. Our words explain nothing to Him. It is only others they can inform, not the All-knowing God. In Sufism, silence is 'bewilderment'; it is self-abnegation.

Trust in God (tawakkul)

Trust in Providence is an important station on the Path. Some equate it with renunciation of all exertion, with utter impassivity. This, however, reduces this beautiful, mysterious creation to a cosmic folly, and our life to nothing better than a walking shadow — a view to which Rumi does not subscribe.

According to Rumi, trust in Providence belongs to the inner man, while efforts and means belong to the outer. God is Omnipotent and can render any cause or means ineffective. But that does not mean that man should not use his God-given means and faculties and allow them to rust in idleness. Like the Prophet, he must exert his best, but for the flower and fruit of his exertion, he must wholly rely on God. This is the correct spiritual attitude — a principle already discussed at length in chapter 3.

According to the extreme order of Compulsionists, to rely on anything other than God is contrary to the *tawhid*; it is hidden associationism (*shirk-i-khafi*). Even to take medicine in grievous sickness is a denial of trust in God, though, as stated earlier, the Prophet himself took medicine when ill, and advised his companions to do likewise. When a camel-owner asked if he should leave his camel to God's care, the Prophet told him: 'Along with trust in God, bind the knee of the camel.' The earner is said to be beloved of God, and to earn one must work. In indolence alone is there perpetual despair (M.I, 912–14).

Even hunger is not without relevance or devoid of value. It is the prince of aperitifs. Rumi calls it the king of medicines. It lends savour to unsavoury things, adding to our enjoyment of food, whilst its lack robs even savoury things of their savour, or is a consequence of indigestion which is the mother of so many afflictions (M.V, 2829–33).

For the disciple, hunger has another significance also. He is urged to get used to hunger as an exercise in self-denial, as a part of the process of self-mortification, as a means of strengthening his trust in God. Hunger is the food of such trust; it is a means to that end.

The elect do not tremble for fear of hunger. In trust in God, they live full-fed. Trust is the daily bread of their souls. Rumi tells us to provide them with their daily needs, so that they may concentrate on devotional practices, and on provision of spiritual instruction to mankind, exempt from any thought of food or other physical needs. Such a gesture would also bring us inward satisfaction. In any case, the Lord will always look after them. If the lilies of the field neither sow nor spin, and yet they grow, arrayed in peerless beauty, would the Lord neglect His elect? Ascetics live in jungles and deserts and they do not starve. John the Baptist lived contentedly on locusts and wild honey, and Sar-razi on vine leaves.

Recollection (dhikr)

There is no standard ritual of the *dhikr*. As described in

various order manuals, it is complex and varied. It can be individual or congregational, spoken or silent. Rumi's concern is not so much with rites and ceremonies as with their inner meaning.

Remembrance of God, involving repetition of God's name or some recognised formula, and full concentration on its meaning, is the essence of *dhikr*. It is generally practised with the aid of a rosary (*tasbih*), and with eyes closed. In Sufism, it is a withdrawal from the *la* of negation, this phenomenal world, and return to the day of *alast*, before we were separated from God. The true *dhikr* is the loss of consciousness in the *dhikr* (*fana fi'l-dhikr*). According to the well-known Sufi Shibli, it 'is that you forget *dhikr* and get absorbed in the Sea of Divine Unity'.

Rumi says that remembrance of God strengthens the spirit and acts as its wings and feathers in its heavenward flight. Even if the spirit does not reach heaven, every moment it achieves a loftier height. We may not attain to the Essence of God, but remembrance of Him, whether it be with the tongue (*dhikr-i-jali*) or in the heart (*dhikr-i-khafi*), will leave its mark upon us.

Like every other act, our remembrance of God does not result from our initiative. As God says in the Koran, 'It is We who have sent down the Remembrance, and We watch over it' (Koran, xv,9). While this Remembrance may well refer to the Koran, it can also mean: 'We have placed in you a substance, a seeking, a yearning' (*Discourses*, p.125), so that this remembrance is from God to man. It belongs to all stages of the Path.

Meditation (muraqaba)

The disciple has by now scoured the windows of his soul. Having renounced desire and emptied himself of self, he is now in a position to meditate on the symbol of the Supreme and gradually fill his being with the Light of God.

While practising meditation, the Sufi usually rests his head on his knees. Rumi says that 'the knee is the Sufi's school' (M.III, 1173). The ingathered limbs help the ingathering of the light and prevent its streaming out and getting wasted. As is stated in *The Secret of the Golden Flower*, the meaning of the Golden Flower, of the Light, of the Elixir of Life, depends entirely on 'the backward-flowing movement', that is, on progressive interiorisation. Meditation is the inner door to the Way of Contemplation, which is the second stage of the Path in Christian mysticism.

Rumi tells the story of a Sufi who, in the course of his wanderings, reaches a Sufi monastery, and is taken in as a guest. He sits on the dais with other Sufis, and they all engage themselves in meditation. The presence of another Sufi is not a source of disturbance. On the contrary, it is a help. A Sufi is like a book, not composed of ink and letters, but a snow-white heart whence shoot forth beams of Divine Light, unfolding the Reality. There are different grades of Sufis in the group. The juniors can follow the footmarks of senior Sufis, and those more advanced can go after the 'musk-gland', that is, the Divine Knowledge reflected from the hearts of the *pirs*. The *pirs* meet as friends, as one in essence, only bodily separate. When such friends meet, it is a wonderful experience for them, with each seeing himself in each. In Rumi's story, the congregational meditation ends in ecstasy. Thereafter, the guest is served with food (M.II, 156 etc.).

In Rumi's story of the saint Daquqi, the latter was participating in meditation in company with seven saints of a lower order, and he became unconscious of his individual self and lost all sense of time. As change arises from time, he became free from change (*talwin*) also, and with this liberation from time and change, he became acquainted with timelessness and familiar with the incomparable Lord (M.III, 2072–5).

It is understood that a saint can experience 'timelessness', whether alone or in company. There is a time and place for both kinds of meditation, individual and congregational.

As for the disciple, his sense of values changes as he advances on the Path. The weaning from the world and its pleasures and vanities seemed to him in the beginning like giving up the light and casting himself in fire. But, gradually, he begins to recognise that what seemed fire to him was in essence the light, while the fire of carnality which falsely seemed light was only a burner. At the end of the Way, the light will illumine the heart of the wayfarer who is inwardly present with God, not even thinking that he is meditating, for the thought itself is enough to inhibit meditation. The man of God is filled with radiance, like the 'tree of Moses', and is the light, not fire (M.III, 4369-76). But that stage is not yet.

In any event, we shall do well to bear Rumi's counsel in mind. We must not be content, he says, with any spiritual station, howsoever lofty, or with any mystical state, howsoever intense or intoxicating, but keep on advancing. We should be like a dropsy patient who is never sated with water. The Lord's Court is the Infinite Plane. It has no boundary. We must leave behind what we consider the seat of honour. The true seat of honour is the journey, the journey which never ends 'the journey in God' (M.III, 1960-1).

The Sufi Path II

In the last chapter, which was concerned with the Way of Purification (*mujahada*), it was stated that progress on the Path was not possible without a growing realisation that we all are one in essence, hiddenly interlinked, and not 'windowless monads', separate and independent. It was also stated that the aspirant treading the Path experiences spiritual states (*hal*) and stations (*maqam*). It is understood that if he is earnest, he will assimilate the new consciousness or illumination experienced in a particular spiritual state and discipline himself for the next state and the next station. The light, of course, is the same, but it appears in increasing splendour to the Sufi as he progresses on the Path.

Sufism has many grades, but often, for the sake of convenience, it speaks of two grades, the lower and the higher, like 'the son of the time' and 'the father of the time' mentioned in the previous chapter. Adding the worldling, Rumi speaks of three grades of men, technically called the 'fish' (*mahi*), the 'non-fish' (*juz mahi*), and the 'land-fish' or the 'breadless ones' (*bi-ruzi*) (M.I, 17; M.III, 3071).

The 'fish' is a perfect Sufi gnostic, the illumined one who is sunk in the Sea of Gnosis, which is also the Sea of Love. He is a lover of God and is never sated with love, as the object of his love is infinite. To him worldliness, this dry and dusty existence, is death — spiritual death.

The 'non-fish' is an average Sufi gnostic who is sated with a little water from the fountain of Divine Knowledge. His capacity to love God is limited, and he is generally content with the observance of the religious Law (*shari'at*), with its

162

prohibitions and injunctions, and its promise of reward in Heaven.

The fish concept, as we may know, is not new. It is believed to have originated with Lord Vishnu of Hinduism, who was half-fish and half-man. The ancient Babylonian Dagon, the man-fish, was an instructor or interpreter to the people. In the Talmud, the Messiah is often called 'Dag' or the 'Fish' (*Isis Unveiled*, Vol.II, pp.256–7).

The 'breadless ones' neither love God, nor are they interested in knowledge of Him. Sense-bewitched, disinherited of soul, their life ends in the grave, unillumined by faith or hope in the future.

Elsewhere, we referred to two kinds of journey. One is the 'land' or exterior journey which is our speech and action. The waves of earth are our imagination, thought and understanding. It is a journey in the body, not in the spirit. The other is the interior journey, a journey not in the body, but in the spirit, not on 'dry land', but in the Sea of Unity. The waves of water are self-effacement (*mahw*), intoxication (*sukr*) and the death of self (*fana*) (M.I, 570–5). That journey is endless.

Referring to the water journey, Rumi speaks of the man 'absorbed' and the 'swimmer', both of whom are in the water. The former, his personal will in abeyance, is borne along by the water; every movement proceeds not from him, but from the water — from the Sea of the Divine Essence which is the source of all action. The swimmer, on the other hand, moves by his own effort and at his own free will (*Discourses*, p.84). He has not surrendered his will to the Divine Will. He is guided by the injunctions of exoteric religion. They who still are on dry land, lost amid the trifles of life, are the breadless ones. The Sea of Gnosis does not let them in, as it does not let the 'fish' out (M.III, 3071).

The work of religion is nothing but 'bewilderment', not such bewilderment that one turns away from the Beloved back to his personal self, lost in error and astray from the Path, but bewilderment which is a ruin wherein the Divine Treasure is buried; it is that entrancing bewilderment in which one is sunk in the Friend and drunk with Him (M.I,312–14, 2474–5). His dazzlement arises not out of error, but from reason's incompetence to comprehend the infinite diversity of forms of the Lord's manifestation, and from proximity to the Divine Light which is dark with excess of splendour.

In Attar's *Mantiqu't-Tair* ('Conference of the Birds'), Bewilderment is the Sixth of the Seven Valleys which the Sufi has to cross before attaining to Reality. It is a story of the quest of thirty birds (*si murgh*), typifying the Sufi pilgrims, for the fabulous 'Bird' Simurgh (also meaning thirty birds when broken into *si* and *murgh*). This fabulous 'Bird' symbolises the transcendental Spirit (see p.101 *supra*) or God 'the Truth'. As this allegory is a simple and excellent account of the Sufi Path, which it divides into Seven Valleys, that is, seven mystical stages, a brief summary of it is given below.

The first is the Valley of Quest (*talab*) where the aspirant has to undergo a hundred trials and hardships every instant. He has to renounce all worldly possessions as of no worth, and detach himself from all that exists. His purified heart will then glimpse the pure Divine Light, and, filled with longing, he will abandon himself completely to the quest.

The second is the Valley of Love (*ishq*), which is fire and where the entrant himself must become a flaming fire. Reason is of no avail here. For where reason enters, love flees. Here, the lover burns in the fire of love, yearning for the Beloved, with no thought for the morrow or the end, and no awareness of religion or disbelief, doubt or certainty, good or evil.

The third is the Valley of Gnosis (*ma'rifat*). It has no head or foot, no beginning or end. The Sun of Gnosis shines, and the entrant becomes a seer of mysteries according to his merit. There are degrees of gnosis. Each one's proximity to God is in measure with his spiritual state.

The fourth is the Valley of Independence and Detachment (*istighna*). Here, the entrant desires nothing. Nothing has any worth. The seven heavens are just a corpse, and seven hells are congealed like ice. If the skies and the stars were scattered into fragments, it would mean less than the fall of a tree leaf. If the parts and the whole were wholly destroyed, it would be like the loss of a blade of straw from the world.

The fifth is the Valley of Unity (*tawhid*). Here, all who lift their faces lift them from a single collar. Whether you see a few or many, in reality, there is but one, and the many complete its unity. Nor is that which seems as unity different from that which seems as number. The Supreme Being is beyond unity and number.

The sixth is the Valley of Bewilderment (*hayrat*) to which we referred earlier. Here, the entrant is subject to pain, sighs and burning. Whoever, bewildered and lost, has the Unity of Being imprinted on his soul, forgets all, himself included. If you ask him whether he is dead or living, hidden or manifest, mortal or immortal, his answer is this:

> He says: I know not a thing at all,
> I know not that, nor this I know,
> I am a lover, but whose I know not.
> I am not a Moslem, nor an infidel; what then am I?
> Of love I have no awareness,
> I have a heart at once full and empty of love.

The Seventh Valley is the Valley of Poverty (*faqr*) and self-abnegation (*fana*). Its essence is forgetfulness, dumbness, deafness and unconsciousness. Here the aspirant is lost to self and sunk in the fathomless Ocean. He is existent and yet non-existent.

Beyond this Valley is the abode of the Simurgh.

Of the thousands of birds that set forth on the painful and hazardous journey, all perish, except thirty birds (*si murgh*) who arrive at the goal, all broken by fatigue and half-dead. Regressing into their inmost depths, utterly purified of all, they see the Divine Light shining within, 'the Light that shines beyond the broken lamps', and they see themselves through that Light. In the bird symbolism, they find the Simurgh and in finding it, they find themselves; it is self finding Self. They see that they are the *si murgh* and yet are doubtless the Simurgh, and the Simurgh that doubtless is there is nothing but the *si murgh*, and when both are looked at together, both are the Simurgh. This one was that, and that one this. It is a state not of unity or duality, but of identity-in-difference and difference-in-identity.

THE LIGHT SYMBOLISM

The spiritual journey is also described in terms of light-veils numbering 70,000 which separate the soul from God and which it has to go through in its descent into matter. The way up is the same as the way down. The exterior of each veil is of darkness and its interior is of light. In its descent, it sheds one veil of light and puts on one veil of darkness, and, in its ascent, it sheds one veil of darkness and gains one veil of light. The veils of light are symbols of the Divine attributes, and the veils of darkness, of earthly qualities. The soul has to perform seven series of purgations, rending 10,000 veils each time before it can attain to the One Reality.

Rumi also uses the light symbolism. According to him, the Light of God has seven hundred veils going up in tiers. Behind each veil is a rank of saint corresponding to the intensity of the light-veil. But his rank is not fixed for all time. If he strives to climb higher, the weakness of his eyes will gradually diminish, and he may attain, if that be his portion, the top rank of the living *Imam*, the *Qutb* or *Ghawth* (M.II, 821–6). Although Rumi is speaking of saints here, the light symbol is also applicable to the progression of Sufis not ranked as saints.

SPIRITS AND SOULS

Although the interior Path is concerned with the soul's progress towards God, we cannot ascertain the description and quality of the soul (*nafs*) (M.VI, 1624). Of the spirit (*ruh*) also, the Koran tells us that it is by command of the Lord, that is, it is created in time, but of its knowledge we have been vouchsafed but little (Koran, xvii,85). And yet, references to soul and spirit abound in religious literature. It is the light of faith that alone can give us some idea of their nature, and also of what is involved in the soul's pilgrimage to God.

While Rumi, like other Sufis and the Moslems in general, regards the soul in its lowest phase as synonymous with the flesh and the devil, the animal spirit as the seat of animal passions is hardly any different though Sufism always uses the term *nafs*, not *ruh*, when referring to the evil element in man. The difference between them is really a matter of usage and tradition.

Rumi says that both soul and spirit come from pre-existence. In the story of the Bedouin and his Wife, the latter, symbolising the appetitive soul, is thinking of the pre-existent state, when she says to her husband who symbolises the rational soul or spirit: Remember the time when I was lovely as the idol and you were my worshipper. The soul, then, was pure, untainted by sensuality (M.I, 2407), and it was the beloved spouse of the spirit, that is, they were in union like husband and wife, not apart; they were one.[1]

In the spiritual world, which is the vast region of the soul, the latter journeys without hand or foot; eats sugar without lip or tooth; sees a whole world without eyes; gathers roses and basils without a hand. It is drunk with the anemone field. It has no limbs or organs (M.I, 2090-5).

Both soul and spirit come into this world, bearing marks of damnation or salvation, all predestined. The recompense they receive in the other world is as much the result of what they do in this world as what they do here is the result of the recompense already fixed for them there. The effect of the cause is from another angle the cause of the effect. It is correlation, rather than causation.

Rumi also says that the spirit comes from God, from the world of souls and intelligences, but has deserted its origins (M.VI, 450). It is created like the soul to reflect God's attributes as good and evil.

Again, the divine soul is immortal. It is only the animal soul that dies. In proof, Rumi cites from the Koran: 'All of them shall be brought into Our Presence' (Koran, xxxvi,32), and explains that this means that they are not non-existent; only their human attributes are steeped in the Divine attributes.

This is certain proof of the immortality of the soul, for, without it, they would not be existent (M.IV, 442–5).

The spirit also is everlasting like the soul, and is like the resplendent Sun, which is free from change, being neither of East nor of West, but without direction (M.IV, 3788–9).

The soul is celestial and is in exile from light in this world. It longs for Life and the Living One, remembering its origin in the Infinite Soul, which is a mode of the Absolute Being. Its desire is for knowledge, for ascent and exaltation to its original Home. The soul loves God and God loves the soul. His love for the people precedes their love for Him. In fact, the soul's love for God originates in God's love for the soul. As Hafiz says: 'Love is born first in the heart of the beloved' — not in the heart of the lover.

The spirit, which, as stated earlier, is from the world of the souls and intelligences and has deserted its origins, is constantly receiving admonition from the pure, celestial souls and intelligences that it has forgotten its old heavenly companions and attached itself to new friends on earth who are mean and temporary (M.VI, 450–2). Here, the souls on high are speaking to the spirit on the earthly plane. Cf. Hafiz:

> They are whistling to you from the battlements of Heaven,
> I know not what has befallen you in this dust-pit.

In another place, Rumi says that the spirit has a Spirit that is calling it. As the spirit is one, the reference here is to its two aspects, namely, the Holy Spirit (*ruhu'l-quds*) which is spirit in relation to God and is the eternal Divine Spirit, and the created spirit which is the same spirit viewed in relation to man, and is constituted by the Divine Spirit, as the individual soul is constituted by the Infinite Soul. It is the Divine Spirit which is calling the created spirit back into itself (M.III, 1274).

We spoke earlier of the form of the soul — the appetitive soul (see p.143 *supra*). Has the spirit also some form?

According to Rumi, the spirit has a subtle, immaterial body (*jism-i-latif*), and this visible external body is its garment. This physical hand is the sleeve of the spirit's hand. There is thus a spiritual body, with a spiritual hand and foot.[2] The body, hand and foot which the dreamer sees in a dream are real to him, not imaginary, and yet distinct from the physical body, hand and foot. Why should, then, anyone be afraid of the exit of the soul or spirit from the body? (M.III, 1610, heading, etc.). The body is only the field for the operation of the spirit.

We often speak of the entry of the spirit into the body and its exit from it. This should not be taken to mean that the spirit is incarnated in the body. As no bodily limb can function without the presence of the spirit, the spirit may be deemed to be present in every part of the body, and, therefore, to possess its shape and form. Or we may say that the spirit's gaze covers and animates every part of the body, and, like light, may be said to assume the shape of the object on which it shines. But considered by itself, that is, not in relation to the finite body, it is infinite. No object, not even the entire physical universe, contains it. According to the ancient Neo-Platonists, the spirit never descended into man, but broods over and illuminates the physical body as well as 'the astral soul', which was believed to be the perishable, inner fluid body, quite distinct from the immortal, incorruptible Augoeides, or 'portion' of the Divine Spirit.

What happens to the spirit when the body disintegrates after death, which may be said to be the effect of the withdrawal of the spirit's gaze from the deceased?

Rumi's answer is that God puts together the spiritual faculties and fashions for them another body or vehicle, appropriate to the nature of the spirit. St Paul also speaks of 'the spiritual body' as distinct from the 'natural' or terrestrial body (M.III, 1613, 1759-60; p.232 *infra*).

Not only is the soul everlasting, but, according to Rumi, it neither grew, nor came to birth (M.I, 1927), that is, it knows no beginning, growth or end. An objection may be raised that this would make the soul co-eternal with God. The answer is that, here, Rumi is not thinking of the soul in relation to man which is created, but of the Heavenly Aphrodite of Plotinus, 'the soul at its divinest, unmingled as the immediate emanation of the Unmingled'; he is thinking of the *ruhu'l-quds* (the Holy Spirit), which is the Self of God, of His Essence in which His attributes inhere and whence they cannot be detached. He had yet to begin his descent into manifestation, and gradually make known the 'hidden treasure'. There is thus no birth of the soul as such, nor of the spirit, nor of any other being in the creation, but only a manifestation of the attributes of God (see p.30–31 *supra*).

It is a cardinal Sufi doctrine that the spirit or the soul bears the imprint of all knowledge from pre-existence, and, therefore, there is nothing for it to know that it does not already know. If the kingdom of God is within us, all knowledge is within us. But the drug of sensuality, the taint of worldliness, has made the spirit forgetful of its pre-existent knowledge. Purge it, and that knowledge will come back. Hence, it is said that knowledge is but recollection. The pure heart of the Perfect Man, illumined by the Divine Light, is able to see the existent things as ideas in the Nous, the Divine Mind, and as every soul existed as an idea, it had foreknowledge of the entire creation, of all that is or will be. Time does not exist for the Perfect Man. It is the eternal Now, with no past or future (M.II, 168–77; also, see p.103 *supra*).

Rumi says that the soul's inmost nature and essence is consciousness. The soul is conscious of good and evil. Kindness makes it rejoice, and injury makes it weep. Awareness is the spirit's effect. The more aware is one, the more spiritual is one. One who is super-abundantly aware is a man of God (M.VI, 148–50).

Broadly speaking, there are consciousnesses that relate to our bodily nature and consciousnesses that are beyond them in the spiritual world. The former belong to the sensual soul which belongs to this world of scent and colour, and the latter is the Soul of the soul which is the mirror of the Divine Essence (M.VI, 151–2).

Elsewhere, Rumi speaks of three grades of soul. First, there is the kind of understanding (*fahm*) and soul (*jan*) that is in the ox and the ass; second, there is the kind that is in man; and the third, the kind that is in the Perfect Man, saint or prophet. In his *Commentary*, Dr Nicholson explains that 'The three souls or faculties mentioned here are the animal spirit (*al-ruhu'l-haywani*), the intelligential spirit (*al-ruhu'l-'aqli*), and the transcendental prophetic spirit (*al-ruhu'l-qudsi al-nabawi*)' (M.IV, 409–10).

The animal soul or spirit grows by eating, and is variable. It is vital; without it, the body is a carcase. Animal sensation and perception depend on the light of this soul.

The intelligential soul or spirit is different. Not bread and roast meat, but the light of intelligence is the food of this soul. The bread that man consumes becomes nourishing from the reflection of that light; the animal soul transmutes it by 'the water of Salsabil' (a river in Paradise), that is, by power of spiritual absorption, and the inanimate bread becomes the glad spirit (*ruh-i-shad*) of life. The animal soul itself becomes soul from the overflowing of the rational soul (M.IV, 1954–8; M.I, 1474–5).

The First or Infinite Soul is the mirror of the Divine Essence or an aspect of the Absolute. It determines the character of the particular souls, which are its emanations or individualisations (M.III, 3080).

In grading the spirits, Rumi adds another level between the human and the Divine. It is the shore of the Sea of Gabriel's Spirit Gabriel, the First Intelligence, the trusted custodian of the treasure of gnosis. But the Perfect Man is above him. And Muhammad was supremely Perfect. Gabriel guided him towards the Presence of God, but on reaching his limit, he crept back, saying that if he took one more step forward, he would be instantly consumed. Muhammad then went ahead alone and attained to within two bow-lengths of the Presence of God (M.IV, 1888–90). The Perfect Man is above Gabriel, as he is dead to self and steeped in the Divine Essence, whereas Gabriel is the spiritual guide to the adepts on their celestial ascent, a role he cannot perform if he is consumed.

Referring to Adam in whom the soul or spirit of Muhammad took earthly form, and to the subsequent spiritual heirs of Muhammad, Rumi says that they all are superior to Gabriel. For they all sought to get consumed moth-like in the fire of Divine Love, while Gabriel, the highest spiritual Intelligence, is 'neither the candle nor the moth'. He cannot be either, as one dead-burnt cannot function as a guide (M.IV, 3807–8).

Spirit is knowledge and reason, and is beyond spatial relations. It has nothing to do with Arabic or Turkish. Human speech is helpless before it. It is simply bewildering (M.II, 56).

The spirit is the life of man. It is independent of the body, but becomes its fellow-traveller in order to free it from bodily ills and give it spiritual guidance. It is like the moon, which is disgraced by the company of faintly twinkling stars, but, as a gesture of goodwill, it is with them to give them light (M.I, 3018).

The appetitive soul is not beyond redemption; if it were, there would be no interior journey, no inward ascent. If the self is subdued and killed, the higher consciousness is awakened and its light completely overshadows the lower phases of the soul, and the latter, now illumined, assumes the nature of the spirit. In the case of saintly men, who are dead to this world and are steeped in the Divine attributes, even their body is illumined and is essentially pure as spirit; their soul and form and speech — all is absolute spirit, with no trace of externality. Their state may be likened to a star that loses all traces of itself in the radiance of the sun (M.I, 2000–1; M.IV, 442–3).

Here we are speaking of the Perfect Man whose image is ever looming before the aspirant as the ultimate ideal, howsoever distant. The soul of the Perfect Man comprehends all; nothing is external to it. All phenomena are but reflections of its Divine attributes. Though hidden, the soul is the only real actor. The figures the Perfect Man meets in his bodily existence and that appear as others are like the figures seen in a dream. This vast universe is but a dream-grotto, wherein the dreamer only goes from the presence of himself into the presence of himself. No 'otherness' is involved. The Perfect

172

Man himself is subject and object, beholder and beheld (M.I, 1715–18; M.III, 1300–2). He comprehends both this world and the next, not in his bodily self which is so puny, but in his essence which is infinite, divine and all-embracing.

THE SOUL'S ASCENT

To return to the training of the soul, the spirit's essential nature which God gave it in pre-existence is not impaired by association with the body or by training the soul and unifying it with itself. Nor does the soul bemoan the loss of its separate individuality. The phenomenal self, the soul, is like a jar; the more it is shattered, the more perfect it becomes, with every piece of it lost in dance and ecstasy (M.I, 2865–8). When it has reached Perfection, it becomes the transcendental soul, merged back in 'the pleroma of eternal light' of the gnostics.

The soul is one, but is fragmented and becomes many in relation to the bodies. It is like the light of the sun which is one, but becomes a hundred lights when it breaks into a hundred courtyards. Remove the separating walls of the courtyards, and the lights are one. Similarly, when we pass away from our individual selves and merge in the Universal Self and all sense of separateness goes, we all become one soul (M.IV, 408, 415–18).

In the story of the Bedouin and his Wife, Rumi gives an allegorical description of the ascent of the soul. The Bedouin represents the rational soul and his wife the appetitive soul, the flesh (*nafs-i-ammara*) (Koran, xii,53). Complaining of poverty in touching terms, she says to her husband: 'We are miserable because of our poverty. We have no bread; anguish and envy are our only condiment; our tears our only drink; and moonbeams our only coverlet at night. If I beg some lentils from someone, I am told: "Shut up, you death and plague." If a guest were to come to us, I am sure I would go for his tattered cloak, when he was asleep' (M.I, 2252–63).

The Bedouin's wife is a worldling, seeking household requisites, some riches and reputation, adopting humility or domination, as may be necessary, in order to gain her ends.

173

Her husband, on the other hand, is unaware of her guiles and devices, and regards poverty as his pride, and worldly possessions, these gauds and baubles, as trifling and temporary. He believes in contentment, and has nothing in his mind, except love of God.

The wife reviles her husband, saying that pride is ugly, and, in beggars like him, it is still uglier. He is not contented, as he pretends. He is just a fraud, full of deceit.

The reason does not give in to the arguments of the flesh. The husband tells her that the business of poverty is beyond her comprehension and she must not look down upon it. The rich are plunged in vice, but they have money and their money covers their vice. Through contentment, the whole world was within his heart. The dervish is above wealth and poverty. How should God in His Justice behave cruelly with the poor? He gives them abundant spiritual riches. Poverty hides a thousand glories. He ends by asking her to make trial of poverty and see the Light of the Lord in it, and by warning her that if she will not give up quarrelling, she should leave or he would leave her (M.I, 2315 etc.).

When the wife finds her husband so determined and stubborn and threatening her with desertion, she gives up her dominating attitude and becomes humble and 'self-reproaching' (*nafs-i-lawwama*). She turns from infidelity to faith and is like the spirit that turns penitently to God. Shedding copious tears, and amid sobs, she says to her husband: 'I am thy dust.... Body and soul, I am thine, though unworthy of thy companionship. I would gladly die for thee. I renounce all thought of gold and silver. I am thy slave, eager to obey thee. I was ignorant of thy kingly nature. I repent. Have mercy. Your hidden conscience always pleads on my behalf; O thou whose nature is better than honey' (M.I, 2394 etc.).

The husband is moved by his wife's tearful humility and penitence and yields to her request to seek a living, and views her dispute with him as a sign from God. He says to her: 'I will become non-existent in your existence, as I am your lover' (M.I, 2645).

But with suspicion still lingering in her mind, she says to him: 'I wonder if you are really my friend, or are making trial of me?'

He swears to her by God that his words were inspired by love, sincerity and humility.

She feels reassured, and the two work as one. She indicates the way to earn a living, and he accepts her suggestion.

The story as told by Rumi is a parable of our own flesh and reason. The man and wife, representing the reason and the flesh, are always in conflict, displaying God's attributes of Mercy and Wrath. Here, the wife, purified by love and reason, suggests to him to go to the Court of the Caliph, symbolising God. When feeling his inadequacy, he asks on what pretext could he go thither, she, speaking like a 'tranquil soul' (*nafs-i-mutma'inna*) (Koran, lxxxix,27,28) says: 'When God manifests Himself, the essence of every lack of means, that is, poverty, becomes the means. One needs truth as a witness to his poverty, and when one is entirely purified of self-existence, that is truth. Palaver and show are of no avail in the Court of the Lord. Take to him this jug of water, this body, stop its five spouts, the five senses, and keep it filled with water from the Sea of Reality to which it has a secret passage. As God says: "Close your eyes to vain desire." The best provision for the journey to God is knowledge of poverty.'

The Arab takes the jug to the Caliph, and is simply dazzled by the richness and splendour of his court. The all-sufficient Caliph, though lacking nothing, is pleased to accept the jug, rewards him most handsomely, as his bounty rewards all others, and delivers him from penury. The Arab is intoxicated by his regal munificence (M.I, 2684 etc.).

Apart from the soul's three stages of purification, there is an additional one mentioned in the Koran, that of 'the inspired soul' (*nafs-i-mulhama*) which precedes the third. For convenience of reference, a brief description of the four stages of the soul's ascent is given below:

In the first stage, 'the reprobate soul' (*nafs-i-ammara*), having got enmeshed in matter and acquired evil qualities, commands evil (Koran, xii,53).

By striving against itself, the soul rises to the second stage and becomes 'the reproachful soul' (*nafs-i-lawwama*), when it accuses itself of blameworthy qualities (Koran,lxxv,2). These can be overcome by persistent struggle for purification, and by recollection of God.

When the base qualities are overcome, the soul reaches the third stage and is now 'the inspired soul' (*nafs-i-mulhama*); it is inspired with consciousness of what is right for it and what is wrong (Koran, xci,7,8). By intensifying the struggle for purification and by increased devotion to God, it can attain to the fourth stage.

In this, the fourth stage, the soul becomes 'tranquil' (*nafs-i-mutma'inna*) and is at peace, free from all vacillation, steadfast in all conditions, and, given the necessary aspiration, it can return unto the Lord, content in His good pleasure 'well-pleased, well-pleasing' (Koran, lxxxix,27,28).[3]

In Rumi's story of Moses and the Shepherd, the latter prays: May the Divine nature (*lahut*) be the companion of my human nature (*nasut*). These two — *nasut* and *lahut* — form two of the four stages of cosmic evolution or worlds of existence which find mention in Sufi order-manuals and which the gnostic must span in order to attain to Reality. The process, of course, is spiritual. These are:

   i)   *'alam-i-nasut*: the phenomenal world; the world of humankind;

  ii)   *'alam-i-malkut*: the world of the Divine attributes;

 iii)   *'alam-i-jabrut*: the world of the Divine Essence; and

 iv)   *'alam-i-lahut*: the Divine Nature.

Only in respect of the first world is there agreement that it refers to the phenomenal world or the world of mankind. In respect of the other three, there is no standard description. Thus the second world is also described as the world of angels or of spirits or souls; the third, as the world of the Divine attributes or of Power or Universal Reason; and the fourth, as the quiescent world of the Godhead, or as the world of the Divine Essence.[4]

According to Rumi, at no stage of the ascent does man lose his outward, phenomenal self. On the contrary, the highest perfection consists in combining the eternal aspect of the One Reality with its outward, phenomenal aspect. It is for such perfection that the shepherd in Rumi's story prays (M.II, 1790).

The various descriptions of the Path are doubtless instructive and interesting. But there is no substitute for personal experience. Hearing is not seeing, and seeing is not attainment. Words can tell us what form of prayer to perform, what ascetic or devotional practices to follow. They may throw light on the Path. But grey is all theory. We have to tread the Path. None else can tread it for us. It is 'a regress into the hiddenness'. As Browning says:

> There is an inmost centre in us all
> Where Truth abides in fullness, and to know
> Rather consists in opening out a Way
> Whence the imprisoned splendour may escape,
> Than in effecting entry for a light
> Supposed to be without
>
> (*Paracelsus*)

7

Knowledge and Ecstasy

Some philosophers deny the very existence of real or essential knowledge, so that the question of knowing the reality of things does not arise. Rumi rejects this view. He believes both in the existence of knowledge and in the possibility of its attainment. 'Seek knowledge in China', that is, wherever it can be found, said the Prophet.

Rumi distinguishes between the knowledge of the religious law (shari'at), that is, the exoteric revelation, and the knowledge of the Truth (haqiqat), that is, of God's Essence, attributes and actions, and says that the shari'at is knowledge; the tariqat (Path) is action; and the haqiqat is attainment to God, the Truth. This brings to mind what the Prophet is reported to have said in reference to himself: 'The shari'a is my words (aqwali), the tariqa my actions (a'mali), and the haqiqat my interior states (ahwali).'

Rumi gives the following three examples for clarification of the difference between these three concepts:

a) The Law is like a candle showing the way; one's personal wayfaring is the Path; and his arrival at the destination is the Truth. If the Truth were manifest, the Law would be purposeless.

b) The Law is like learning the theory of alchemy; the Path is like using chemicals and rubbing the copper upon the philosopher's stone; and the Truth is like the transmutation of copper into gold. When the transmutation occurs, we become gold and are delivered from the theory and practice of alchemy.

c) The Law is like learning the science of medicine; the Path is like using its teachings in sickness and in health; and the Truth is like gaining permanent good health and becoming independent of the knowledge of medicine as well as the observance of the rules of health (M.V, Preface).

The Law, as these examples indicate, serves as a means to the end of Truth; it is not an end in itself.

With Rumi, as with the orthodox, the Koran and the Traditions of the Prophet are the ultimate standard of the Truth. Of the Traditions, some are said to have been invented by Sufis themselves and attributed to the Prophet, in order to gain support for their views, and, at times, to escape persecution. The Koran contains the Laws of God. But in its interpretation, differences arise between the orthodox and the Sufis. The gap varies with different Sufis, becoming unbridgeable in certain cases. Rumi's teachings, though not always strictly orthodox, generally fall within Islam's framework.

Let us turn to his reference to the Koran, for which, without doubt, he has the highest reverence.

THE KORAN

According to Rumi, the Koran possesses two aspects, the exoteric and the esoteric. It is a double-sided brocade. Some enjoy the outer side, some the inner. This is in keeping with God's desire that both types of men should benefit from His Word (*Discourses*, p.173).

The inner side is not a single layer. Rumi cites the Tradition of the Prophet that the words of the Koran have an exterior meaning, and, under it, an interior meaning, and under that interior meaning another interior meaning, and so on to seven interior meanings (M.III, 4244, heading). Even the first interior meaning is exceedingly overwhelming, and in the third meaning all intellects get lost. The fourth sense none has perceived at all, except the Peerless Lord (M.III, 4244–6). Rumi is silent about the other interior meanings. Even what he says about the three interior meanings only hints at the great depths involved. These seven meanings are related to seven ascending spiritual states and are beyond the reach of speech.

Rumi tells us not to regard only the exterior meaning of the Koran, lest we should miss the deeper meaning. When the devil looks at Adam's exterior, he sees nothing but clay. The Koran's exterior is like someone whose features are in view, but whose spirit is hidden (M.III, 4247-8). We should, therefore, seek out the inner meaning of the Koran, according to our measure. There is food for all in the Koran.

Rumi does not admit the competence of any external authority, any Moslem jurist or divine, to act as the ultimate interpreter of the Koran, or to decide which act or view is in order and which heretical. Nor does he believe in any rationalistic or personal interpretation (*ta'wil*) of the Koran. Such an interpretation is narrow-visioned and opinion-based and only degrades the sublime meaning of the Holy Word.

According to Rumi, the prophets and saints are taught the essence of the Koran in pre-existence, and they can recognise its signs in their hearts. The Sufi who is not a saint learns its meaning directly from God; it descends into his heart. One can also learn the inner meaning from a man of God. As Rumi says, seek the meaning from God Himself, or from the Koran or from one who has sacrificed himself to the Koran, so that the Koran has become the essence of his spirit (M.V, 3128-9; M.VI, 2292).

The Koran is the Word of God, the Logos that feeds the elect spirits; it is the pure Sunlight that illumines them without becoming separate from the Sun; it is the Fountain of the Water of Life that gives them eternal life by uniting them with itself as the Logos (M.III, 4287-9). Whoever feeds on the Light of God becomes the Koran, that is, one with the Logos (M.V, 2478), or, as already stated, the Koran becomes the essence of his spirit.

The Koran is acknowledgedly the Word of God, but in the external form in which it is made available to us, it is not the whole Word. It is said in the Koran itself: 'Say, if the sea became ink for the words of my Lord, the sea would be spent before the words of my Lord were exhausted' (Koran, xviii,110).

This relates to the outward form of the Koran as distinct from its meaning. Fifty drams of ink, says Rumi, would suffice for the transcription of the whole of the Koran. The Koran is a symbol of God's Knowledge. Since the world began, God has revealed the same faith to man through the prophets. 'In the time of Moses and Jesus', says Rumi, 'the Koran existed, God's speech existed, but it was not in Arabic' (*Discourses*, p.93). As is said in the Koran, 'And We have revealed to thee the Book with the Truth, verifying whatever Scripture was before it' (Koran, v,48). The Preserved Tablet (*lawh-i-mahfuz*) on which are inscribed all the events of the past, present and future, and which is regarded as the Koran's celestial archetype, predates its historical revelation, and has always existed, though not wholly manifested in any external form.

The Mu'tazilites reject the orthodox doctrine that the Koran is uncreate and eternal on the ground that it made the Koran co-eternal and co-existent with God. The answer to this argument is that the Koran is the Word of God, a symbol of His Knowledge. As St John's Gospel has it: 'In the beginning was the Word, and the Word was with God, and the Word was God.' There was no 'otherness', nothing that could be said to be co-eternal with Him (see p.246 *infra*, n.6.)

THE WAY TO DIVINE KNOWLEDGE

How can we attain to knowledge of God?

Certainly not by means of the physical senses, though 'some people expect to see God as they would see a cow' (Eckhart). If the animal sense could see and hear God, every ox and ass would hear and see Him. But they do not not in their animality. God has called the eye of the sense blind. It is an idolater and an enemy of intellect and religion. It sees the pen that writes, but not the writing Hand; it sees the arrow flying, but not the Bow and the Archer. It sees the foam, but not the sea; it sees the present, but not the future (M.II, 65, 1607-9). 'How paint to the sensual eye what passes in the

181

Holy-of-Holies of man's soul?'

Sense-perception cannot go beyond the world of the senses, the world of form and colour. The worldly sense is the ladder to this world. It has no knowledge of the world of Unity, no knowledge of God, who is without form and colour and is utterly unlike any creature. Hence Rumi's exhortation: Plug your outward ear with cotton wool, as this ear is the cotton wool of the ear of conscience, and the latter ear cannot hear, until the outward ear is plugged and becomes deaf. Become without sense, ear and thought, so that you may hear God's call to the soul: 'Return' (M.I, 303, 566–8; Koran, lxxxix,28).

Most people rely on opinion, generally, with some admixture of faith, for their conception and knowledge of God. But opinions vary and clash. They lack certainty and faith. At best, they are a search for certainty. If an opinion were infallible, it would not be opinion, but knowledge, which it is not. In the words of Rumi, knowledge has two wings, whereas opinion has only one wing. The one-winged bird is greatly restricted in its flight, and keeps falling and rising, instead of flying smoothly (M.III, 1510–12).

How about imagination with its fabulous flights?

No, sensuous imagination can be a deceiver, a deluder in the quest, giving to airy nothings a local habitation and a name. Rumi tells the story of a stupid school-teacher whose students worked out a plan to keep him away from school in order to free themselves from work and weariness. The plan was that when the teacher came to school the next morning, they all should tell him, one after the other, that he looked pale and not at all well, so that, hearing the same remark from so many, he might begin to believe them. The plan worked. When so many students told him that he looked ill, he began to imagine that he really was ill, and returned home to rest, cursing his wife, accusing her of being so intoxicated with her beauty as to be blind to his sickly complexion and anguished state, which even strangers — his pupils — noticed and bemoaned (M.III, 1522 etc.).

In the case of Pharaoh, it was because everyone addressed

him as lord and king that he became terribly conceited, and imagined himself to be God. There is no madness to which one cannot be driven by imagination and opinion (M.III, 1555–7).

Nor can fantasy be of much avail on the Path. Fantasy in this world of external existence records sense-data as mental images and runs the world. In the spirit, it is nothing (M.I, 70). How should it know of the world of non-existence which is the world of Formlessness and Unity? The proper home of fantasy is the world of similitudes where ideas exist in ideal forms, a world narrower than the world of non-existence, but more spacious than our phenomenal world.

Here, only the fantasies of the saints exist in such ideal forms. They are faithful pictures or scrolls of the Lord's attributes and are a class apart. They are fantasies of His Light which are reflected in their hearts. But the aspirant is not a saint, and sees no such fantasy or image (M.I, 72).

Our much-vaunted intellect is unable to lead us to knowledge of the essence of things, because it is subject to fantasies and can get lost in the mists of speculation. By itself, it is a stranger to the archetypal ideas which are the source of our knowledge. Intellectual knowledge is only the outward form of mystical knowledge. It is like bread whose outer form is visible, but whose savour is hidden. The intellect can do no more than receive and perfect up to a point the second-hand material supplied to it by the senses and imagination. It needs to be taught, and its teacher is a divinely inspired man who is an organ of the Universal Mind. For apprehension and enlightenment of the intellect is not its own, but is from the Universal Mind, from the Spirit (M.III, 2543, 3584; M.IV, 1295–7).

There is an increasing tendency among philosophers to rely on the logical method for the discovery of truth. This method is analytical. It selects a limited number of elements out of an unlimited number and seeks inferentially to reach the knowledge of the whole. But the coverage is inadequate. Partial reason can never comprehend Universal Reason. Nor is the method of observation always free from error. Even the same object can appear different to different people.

The analytical method is wholly unsuitable in our context. Rumi calls the syllogists wooden-legged, and a wooden leg, he says, is very infirm. Their method is opinion-based, untrustworthy, and breeds controversy because of the inadequacy of the data covered. We were given the arts of syllogism and demonstration to serve as the staff on the way to God; but as they have become a weapon of quarrel between us, Rumi tells us to break that staff to pieces and seek God under the guidance of a seer — a *pir* (M.I, 2128, 2135–9).

The Divine Knowledge is synthetic. It is the knowledge of things in their interconnectedness, and of the world of Divine Unity, not of things separate and mutually independent. It involves no mental postulates. It is knowledge of the whole arising out of spiritual experience or mystical illumination, needing no coil of premise and conclusion, no logical proof, no support of sense and intellect. It is above the duality of cause and effect. It is vision. It gives us knowledge of the parts also, as the whole is reflected in each part (M.I, 1506–8).

All the usual means of knowledge fail us in the spiritual quest. They can give us knowledge of the products as they appear to us, not of their origins. For no origin resembles its product. Jesus does not appear like the breath of Gabriel, nor Adam earth, nor the jinn fire. Even the bough or blossom does not resemble the seed (M.V, 3975–85). Spiritual reality is simply outside the field of operation of all branches of exoteric learning. This explains the reason for Rumi's exhortation: Sell intelligence and buy bewilderment. Intelligence is conjecture and bewilderment is vision. Sacrifice understanding and say: God is sufficient for me (M.IV, 1407–8).

Yet, typically, Rumi does not reject empirical knowledge, or ignore sight and hearing as sources of knowledge. They tell us of what we know of the world of externality, and are not irrelevant to spiritual wayfaring. True, they deal with the world of appearance, but there is no appearance which is divorced from reality, no subject without an object, no significant name without the named (M.I, 3454–6), no means which cannot lead from knowledge of the outward to the inward, from the lower to the higher.

Take the senses. They correspond to the faculties of the soul and emanate from the Universal Spirit. To each sense is allotted a portion of the spiritual sense. The latter is distributed among the five senses and is king over them all, and can lead the physical senses from the darkness of the carnal self towards the Sun of Divine Knowledge. Each sense is thus given the means of access to the Unseen. What is needed is the Light of God without which all means come to naught. But when His Light rides the sensuous eye, the soul pines for God; it is an ornament to the light of sense. 'The good eye, O King, defeats the evil eye ... or rather, from Your eye come alchemies which make the evil eye the good eye', and the worldly sense which is the ladder to this world is purified and transmuted into the religious sense, and becomes the ladder to heaven (M.I, 303; M.II, 1290-3; M.VI, 2806-7, 2813-15).

Elsewhere, Rumi says that the five spiritual senses, which are derived from the Universal Spirit, manifest the Divine attributes and are not separate, but involved in one another. When one has been delivered from the body, the ear is an eye to behold, and the eye an ear to hear. All the senses unite in one sense (M.II, 49, 3236-8; M.IV, 2400).

But while all external means of knowledge, the scriptures and the *pir*'s teaching included, serve as bridges of light to the other shore, they do not carry us there. It is we who have to do the crossing.

Unfortunately, we tend to regard the created things as things in themselves, separate from one another, forgetting that they are interlinked, each being illumined by the same light and reflecting the whole. If we forget the Cosmic Unity that governs them all, and become 'logic-choppers' and pursue the analytical method, we shall only succeed in stressing the illusory independence of the elements. If, on the other hand, we view them in the unitive way, our stress will be on their relatedness and harmony.

The unitive seeing itself is of two grades, the lower and the higher. The lower gives us relative knowledge of what is knowable, and its range covers the cosmic plane, which is the farthest limit of manifestation. The higher takes us 'beyond the known, beyond the unknown'. Speech and thought are unavailing there. Absolute knowledge is beyond the reach of man. As the *Kena Upanishad* has it: 'The man who claims he knows, knows nothing; but he who claims nothing knows.' The former's is, at the best, 'a learned ignorance'.

Rumi refers to a series of grades of knowledge and proceeds on the principle that each grade seeks the higher grade. Take opinion (*zann*), the self of which is the mind. Every opinion, as Rumi says, is thirsting after intuitive certainty. Its basis, however, is probability, which also has degrees. Opinion cannot fly to the garden of certainty; it is only the starting point. Faith (*iman*) takes over from opinion, and leads us to religious knowledge, which is knowledge grounded in faith and is superior to opinion, but inferior to certainty. Religious knowledge also is a seeker of certainty; it scents certainty, but, exoterically, is not certainty. In the third stage dawns the knowledge of certainty (*'ilmu'l-yaqin*), which is heard by the ear and which transforms attributes, but not essence. Certainty also is a seeker; it is a seeker of vision, as hearing is not seeing, the ear being only a mediator. This knowledge must penetrate the heart and be apprehended by the *oculus cordis*, by the third eye, by the eye of spiritual intuition; the ear must become the eye. It is of certainty that vision is born, so that the knowledge of certainty becomes the vision or intuition of certainty (*'aynu'-yaqin*), which transforms essence. But seeing is not attainment. The vision of certainty must be realised in immediate experience; it must become the truth of certainty (*haqqu'l-yaqin*).[1] The Sufi is not content with the certainty of fire. He sits in it and burns, deriding death. He gains the essence and the ultimate source of Gnosis (*ma'rifat*). Mystically self-effaced, 'the dew drop slips into the shining Sea' (M.II, 857–62; M.III, 4117–27).

Nor do the outer senses cease to be of value even to an advanced Sufi. With his inward eye open, he sees God in every object of perception; He sees 'His Beauty burning through the veil of outward things'. But it is his senses that perceive the object. It is through sense-perception that the knowledge of reality comes into the soul. Every object he perceives is identical with the image of God he has in his heart. In other words, it is from the outer senses which are the faculties of the soul that the heart receives the outward idea of God, and that idea cannot be separated from the inward idea.

Theoretical knowledge cannot be a substitute for experience on the Path. Rumi narrates a story to illustrate this truth, the story of the Police Inspector and the Drunkard. The latter was lying on the ground in a drunken state. When the former asked him what he had drunk, the drunkard said that he had drunk of what was in the jar. When asked what was in the jar, the reply was that it was some of what he had drunk, and instead of uttering 'Ah' in penitence, as he was told, he kept uttering 'Hu, Hu', which are exclamations of joyous drunkenness (Hu refers to God). When told to get up and accompany him to prison, the drunkard said that if he could walk he would have walked to his house and avoided this encounter, adding that if he possessed understanding and consciousness of self, he should be seated on the bench like the *Shaykhs*, instructing people instead of lying drunk on the ground (M.II, 2387–99).

The knowledge of the definition and conditions of drunkenness is not the same as the experience of drunkenness. As Thomas à Kempis says: 'I desire rather to know compunction than its definition.' The Sufi does not rely on books and erudition. He discards grammar (*nahw*) and jurisprudence (*fiqh*) and adopts mystical self-effacement (*mahw*). He relinquishes the form and husk of knowledge and relies on the inward eye of certainty. He abandons thought and gains light. Freed from scent and colour, his purified heart reflects all the Divine attributes (M.I, 3491–7).

Sufism speaks of the heart (*qalb*), the spirit (*ruh*) and the soul (*nafs*) as three distinct organs of spiritual communion though, as discussed in the last chapter, there is no rigid dualism of soul and spirit. According to Hujwiri, the Lord imprisoned the heart in the spirit and the spirit in the soul and the soul in the body. The soul attained to love, the spirit arrived at proximity to God and the heart found rest in union with God (*Kashf*, 309); or as Dr Nicholson explains, in Sufism, the heart knows God, the spirit loves Him, and the inmost ground of the soul contemplates Him (*The Mystics of Islam*, p.68). Words do not have a fixed meaning in Sufism. It is the context that indicates which meaning is implied.

Generally, the heart is said to be 'the psychic nerve-centre of Wisdom', the location of Divine Knowledge, a place for vision of God. It has no bound, and, being boundless, it reflects the form of the Infinite and Formless, which is not reflected in the earth, Heaven and the empyrean, because they are bounded and numbered (M.I, 3486–8).

Rumi says that God has dropped a pearl in the human heart which He did not give to the seas and heavens. The reference is to a black blood-clot in the heart (*suwayda-i-dil*), which, in Sufism, is the centre of Divine Knowledge (M.I, 1017). All the attributes of God shine in the heart in their dual aspect of plurality in Oneness and Absolute Unity (M.I, 3490).

The pearl, the 'white pearl' to which Rumi refers, may also be explained as the First Intelligence or the Logos (M.III, Preface), the original ruler and substance of all created things.

Not only the hearts of the elite, but every heart has a channel that leads to the Sea of Consciousness. All the different channels lead to the same Sea, and lose their individual identity in its limitless depths. The way to it must, therefore, be sought within. The light of the heart must be checked from flowing out into the world of externality, and assiduously ingathered, so that the heart's mirror may be illumined and, in its purity, reflect the entire Cosmos. That Way — the interior Way — alone can lead to that boundless Ocean of living Light, whence arise all life and manifestation on every level of being.

According to the Koran, 'Allah is the light of the heavens and the earth' (Koran, xxiv,35). And, as we have said elsewhere, gifts of illuminative flashes from God (*hal*)

alternate with acquisitions of stations (*maqam*) on the Way of *Mujahada*. But it must not be thought that the heart or any other organ can have vision of God. According to Rumi, that which gives light to the eye is the light of the heart, that is, the light of reason, and that which gives light to the heart is the Light of God. Just as the outward light is derived from the sun and the stars, the inward light, the colour of inward fantasy, is derived from the reflection of this Light of God. In other words, the ideal forms of knowledge are produced by the inner light of reason which is reflected from the Light of God (M.I, 1124–7) and 'is the fountain light of our day'. As Rumi says, "Tis the sun's self that lets the sun be seen' (*aftab amad dalil-i-aftab*), that is, the inner light is its own evidence (M.I, 116). The light of intuitive certainty which blesses the Sufi's heart with vision of God is a beam of God's own light which He has flashed into him. 'To spirit only is the spirit-life revealed, God alone can see God's glory, God alone can feel God's love' (Edmond Gore Alexander Holmes, *Nirvana*).

Rumi speaks of the gnostic's finding everything in his essence. 'This outer world is but the pictured scrolls of worlds within the soul.' A spiritual son of Adam, the gnostic reflects all the Divine names and attributes, and as these constitute the whole universe, the whole universe is found within the infinite spirit of man. By knowing himself, he knows God through His attributes reflected in him. We know ourselves through Him, and Him through ourselves. Ignorance of the way to knowledge of oneself is ignorance of the way to knowledge of God. To recall the words of Rumi, you are not this or that form as you may imagine, but you are the Unique One. You are your own bird, prey and snare; your own seat of honour, floor and roof. The whole progeny of Adam is in you (M.IV, 806–9; also see p.100–101 *supra*).

Gnosis, as stated earlier, is the fruit of past asceticism. It is by self-mortification, which is voluntary death (*mawt-i-ikhtiyari*), that the treasure of gnosis is obtained. The time for mortification is now, before the lease of the hired body ends, before we are seized by death (*mawt-i-iztirari*). After death, there is only recompense for what we have done during our earthly sojourn (M.IV, 2543-5).

God bestows the treasure of gnosis on saints, on holy men, who have caused their earthly nature to fall into ruin, and are empty of themselves. Just as no one writes on an already written paper, but seeks a blank sheet of paper, and no one plants a sapling on a plot already planted, but seeks an unknown plot, God seeks and inscribes the Wordless Knowledge or sows the seed of gnosis in the purified heart (M.V, 1960-4). It is only a burnished breast freed from greed, avarice and hate, a heart cleansed of all taint of corruption that can reflect the Divine Light.

In this context, Rumi tells the story of a dispute between the Greeks and the Chinese. The point in dispute was as to who were the better painters. The Sultan put them to the test. The Chinese used many tints and colours and turned out a beautiful picture. When the Sultan saw it, he was robbed of his wits by its beauty. A curtain divided this picture from what the Greeks had accomplished. All that they had done was to keep burnishing the walls, till every single stain was removed. When the curtain was removed, the Sultan saw the reflection of the Chinese painting striking upon the walls opposite, looking even more beautiful than what he had seen on the Chinese side, and 'it was snatching the eye from the socket' (M.I, 3467-82).

The Greeks in the story represent the Sufis with their pure hearts (M.I, 3483), and the Chinese the theologians, with their embroidered conventional ways.

The *Mundaka Upanishad* mentions two kinds of knowledge, a lower and a higher. The lower is the knowledge of the four Vedas and matters like pronunciation, ceremonies, grammar and etymology, and the higher, the knowledge of the One Eternal which having known, there is nothing more to know.

The Divine Knowledge cannot be directly communicated by any external teacher. No outward ear can hear it, no tongue can convey it. It descends into the heart as inspiration from

God; it is gained by direct perception (M.III, 1994–5). Some meditate on the light of consciousness and behold that it is in all forms and is their sustenance. Others discard all forms as Not-being and meditate on the isolated light. Some rely for their knowledge on the teachings of their *pir* or his spirit, or on the writings of saints and prophets; but in such cases there must be some mysterious voice in their heart which tells them that what they have heard is the truth. That voice is the Voice of Conscience, which is the Voice of God or is inspiration from God.

Citing the instance of Bayazid, Rumi says that his (Bayazid's) guide was the guarded tablet (*lawh-i-mahfuz*) which is guarded from error; it was Divine inspiration (*wahi-i-haqq*) which the Sufis call the inspiration of the heart (*wahi-i-dil*). In common parlance, the term *wahi* refers to revelation bestowed by God upon the prophets, and *ilham* to Divine Inspiration that comes to the saints. In Sufism, there is no difference between the two kinds of inspiration. With Rumi also, they are indistinguishable (M.IV, 1851–5; pp.116–117 *supra*). In any case, the heart is the location where God can be envisioned. There can be no mistake when the heart is aware of Him. The true believer, his heart empty of self-awareness and all 'otherness', sees by the Light of God. As nothing is hidden from that Light, nothing is hidden from him. All the mysteries of creation are inscribed on his heart's tablet by the Pen of God. This is the stage of contemplation (*shahadat*), with the whole, but finite, sphere laid bare within his infinite spirit.

As already stated, the physical and mental faculties, though useful on the Path, are not the immediate means to the attainment of Divine Knowledge. Means and faculties necessarily involve the existence of individual consciousness on the part of their user, and so are a veil between the seeker and the sought. The apprehension of the Real is not possible unless the means are discarded and selfhood effaced (M.I, 2696–7), unless subject and object become one. This is possible through union with Him. In the words of the great mystical

191

Arab poet Ibnu'l-Farid, 'And since I was seeking myself from myself, I directed myself to myself, and my soul showed the way to me by means of me.' There is no room for two at this stage.

When the gnostic attains to the state of contemplation, he can only view the attributes of God. That for Rumi is not the journey's end. The Sufi is not content till, having become the knower, he passes away in the Divine Essence, and knower, knowing and known are one.

ECSTASY

Ecstasy, another name in a sense for *fana* (self-abnegation), finds prominent mention in Sufism, as it is the way to union with God. As Rumi says, the oculist of ecstasy provides the collyrium of Unity to the Sufi's eye (M.V, 1701). Ecstasy involves the loss of individual consciousness, without which loss, Universal Consciousness or Self cannot be found. In itself, it is not the end.

Describing the state of the Sufi in ecstasy, Rumi says that such a Sufi has passed away from himself. His apprehensions are blunted. Not a vein of his is sensible (M.I, 128-30). He is like a star on which the sun shone and he has vanished in it. His senses and reason are effaced in the knowledge and wisdom of God (M.I, 3669-71).

Elsewhere, Rumi says that God is the Sun and reason is His shadow; when the sun appears, the shadow disappears. Similarly, when the saint becomes intoxicated by the wine of Divine Love his reason becomes distraught. Ecstasy sweeps away his personal consciousness (M.IV, 2109-11), and he is not aware of what he is saying or doing. This was the case with Bayazid who was in a state of ecstasy when he exclaimed: 'Glory to me! How very great is my estate'; 'Behold I am God'; 'There is no God but I, so worship me.' As we said before, when he returned to consciousness, he could not believe that he had uttered such blasphemy, and he told his disciples that if ever again he spoke like this, he should be put to death. To cut the story short, whenever Bayazid was overcome by Divine

intoxication, he would break into blasphemous speech (M.IV, 2102, heading, etc.; also see p.119 *supra*).

According to Rumi, a Sufi in a state of ecstasy or *fana* cannot be held responsible and punished for violating conventional speech. The fire of love is ever burning in the soul of God's lover, and it is such burning that the Lord seeks — not mere conformity with the externals of faith. Why order them to mend their garments who have rent them in spiritual ecstasy? They have lost their reason and are unaware of self. For the same reason, why seek guidance from those who are drunk with love of God? We should await their return to sobriety. The religion of love is different from all religions. For lovers, the sole religion and creed is God (M.II, 1762 etc.).

The rending and flinging away of garments has no basis in Sufism as such. But this practice is common among the Sufis. They rend them while in a state of rapture or ecstasy induced by music or otherwise, or do so at the behest of the *Shaykh*. The garment, after sewing if rent, is either returned to the owner or given to the singer in appreciation of his services, or to another dervish, or its pieces are distributed among the members of the party. Practice varies (*Kashf*, 417–18).

In Rumi, a certain Sufi in ecstasy rent his garment. As this brought him *faraj* (relief), that is, spiritual relief, he gave the name *faraji* (relief bringer) to the torn garment. To the common man, garment-rending is a mad act, but to the Sufi, it has a spiritual meaning (M.V, 354–6).

According to Rumi, the owner should not seek to take back the flung-away garment. To want it back means that he repents having given it; that his ecstasy was not worth his while; it was not worth the mantle; he was cheated. Such a Sufi is no lover of God. Dust be on his head! Love is worth a hundred such mantles (M.VI, 4415–19).

SAMA' (AUDITION)

The *sama'*, which literally means audition, but here includes music, singing and dancing, plays in Rumi's Sufism a very prominent part in the context of ecstasy, though apart from the chanting of the *adhan* (the call to prayer) and the Koran, music has no place in Islamic ritual. In fact, many Moslems, including Sufis, regard it as abominable and degrading, if not unlawful. In his chapter on 'Audition' in the *Kashf*, Hujwiri sets forth various views on the subject (*Kashf*, 393–420).

According to Rumi, music has a divine influence. He instituted *sama'* into the religious service. Because of the peculiar gyrations performed by his followers, the latter came to be known in the West as the Whirling Dervishes.

Rumi also introduced into the burial service for the dead the practice of joyous hymn-singing during the procession towards the burial place, meeting the criticism from canonists by saying: 'My singers ... testify that he [the deceased] was a Moslem, a believer and a lover of God', and that 'when the human spirit ... is at length set free, and wings its flight to the source whence it came, is this not an occasion for rejoicings, thanks and dancings?' (Redhouse, *Menaqib*, p.67).

Music induces mental collectedness and intensifies the flame of love. It is the food of lovers of God (M.IV, 742). The strains of the reed and the rebeck would entrance Rumi and exalt him to the plane of Universal Consciousness.

Philosophically, the Mevlevi *sama'* has been explained 'as a representation of the planets which love-desire impels to circle round the First Mover', but its origin is emotional, and it is this aspect, as found in Rumi, that will occupy us in the present context.

According to Rumi, what issues from the reed — here symbolising the human soul — is not an airy breath that is passing and endures not, but is the fire of love that burns up selfhood and carnality and all that is not God (M.I, 9), and urges the soul to speed onward and upward to the realm of Undifferentiated Unity, which is its Home and Origin. The very first line of the *Mathnawi* is an exhortation to the reader to listen to the tale of the reed-flute, the tale of the soul, the tale of the Perfect Man, of the Poet himself — a tale of the soul's painful severance from God and its passionate longing to return to Him.

The dance symbolises the ecstasy both of dying to self and of attaining to life everlasting, of *fana* and *baqa* — a doubly rapturous experience. Holy men clap when freed from self's dominion, and dance when freed from their own imperfection. They dance where they mortify themselves; they dance in their own blood (M.III, 95-7). 'Die before ye die', said the Prophet, echoing the words of Jesus. 'Slay me', said Hallaj, and he danced in his fetters, when he was being led to the gallows. He sought physical death, for when the lover is dead, God remains and naught besides Him.

Rumi likens the composition of the *Mathnawi* to *sama*, and says that its object was Husamu'd-Din, his disciple who inspired its composition and whose voice to him was the Voice of God (M.IV, 754, 759).

Explaining the inner significance of *sama'* in the *Diwan*, Rumi says that *sama'* is to hear the sound of *bala* ('yes') affirming the Lordship of God at the Primal Covenant; it is to sever oneself from oneself; it is to attain to union with Him. It is to be unconscious of individual existence and savour everlasting life (*baqa*) in absolute self-extinction (*fana-i-mutlaq*). It is to make the head like the ball before the stroke of His love, and run without head and foot.

Speaking of Ibrahim bin Adham, Rumi says that Ibrahim would listen to the sound of the rebeck, as it was to him an echo of the Voice of God and he desired to recall His Voice, proclaiming His Lordship at the Primal Covenant. That Voice is heard in the heart of the Sufi as trumpeting the spiritual resurrection, and it is like the blast of the Universal Trumpet that will be heard at the Resurrection (M.IV, 731-2). It is a call to retrieve our original state with Him, when He alone was and we had no individual existence and were not separate from Him.

Rumi also speaks of 'the music of the spheres', which is a Pythagorean concept. This music is interpreted esoterically as the Logos of the Greek philosophy, the Word of St John, the creative *kun* ('Be') of Islam, which makes the entire creation the speech of God, with all created things chiming like chords in a universal symphony. All rhythms and sounds are echoes or manifestations of 'the music of the spheres', of the Pythagorean Harmony, of the Voice of God. In the realm of spirit, as all human souls have known in pre-existence, all is melody and harmony. To quote Rumi,

> The songs of the spheres in their revolutions
> Is what men sing with lute and voice.
> As we all are members of Adam,
> We have heard these melodies in Paradise
> But while we are thus shrouded by gross earthly veils,
> How can the tones of the dancing spheres reach us?
> (E.H. Whinfield, abridged translation of the *Mathnawi*, p.182;
>
> M.IV, 733–8)

Cf. Byron:

> There's music in all things, if men had ears:
> Their earth is but an echo of the spheres.
> (*Don Juan*)

If we do not have ears and cannot hear the Voice of God or 'the music of the spheres', it is because the human soul has travelled through numerous levels of being, and the dust of the journey has clouded its perceptive faculty; it is because the soul has forgotten its heavenly lineage and divinity and has deserted to the dark realms of matter and sense. It is broken-winged and is powerless to soar back in memory to its pre-existent state and hear the voice of the Beloved. Why is the mirror of your soul dark and unreflecting? asks Rumi. It is so, he says, because it has gathered the rust of worldliness and sin, the rust of illusion — the illusion of selfhood and separateness, forgetting the unity and harmony of all elements in the universe.

There is an anecdote about Rumi and his rebeck-playing. It is said that once he was playing this instrument, completely lost in ecstasy, when a friend arrived and reminded him that people were already saying their afternoon prayer. Rumi retorted that his rebeck-playing also was a call to prayer. The formal prayer only called the external self to serve God, but his music called the inner self to love and knowledge of God, and was 'the prayer of lovers'.[2]

According to Rumi, the ears of men are ranked; they do not have equal hearing ability. They do not hear alike the words of the spirit or of the Koran or the Traditions (M.IV, 2020). Not everyone is able to hear aright; a fig is not the food for every little bird (M.I, 580, 2763).

The state of ecstasy has also been described as the state of intoxication (*sukr*) or self-effacement (*mahw*). Ecstasy or intoxication is not the ultimate aim of the aspirant. His ultimate aim is sobriety (*sahw*) to which intoxication or ecstasy is the prelude. Sufism speaks of 'the first sobriety' and 'the second sobriety'. The first sobriety involves a return of the naughted senses to normal consciousness, to the world of attributes, where the aspirant is veiled from God, and is again filled with a longing for union with Him. Intoxication and sobriety may alternate many times before the second sobriety is attained, which also involves a return, but not to normal consciousness as in the first case, but to higher, super-normal consciousness; it is a continuation of union and separation, with the essence revealing itself as attributes.

The Sufi tends to swing between intoxication and sobriety, between contemplation of plurality in Oneness and Absolute Unity, between His Immanence and Transcendence. Both are veils. Sometimes, the One veils the Many, and sometimes, the Many veil the One, that is, the outward world of phenomena veils its inward Reality. In either case, his vision of the Divine Essence is partial. The process of oscillation ceases and the veils are rent when the Sufi attains to the second sobriety, which is the unitive state at its highest. In this state, remaining full-rooted in the Divine Essence, he descends to this world of Divine attributes and mingles with people, affirming the One in the Many (M.II, 57, 58; M.VI, 637). Intoxication is lost in sobriety, which is no more its superior, nor even distinct from it. Both stand transcended, both harmonised in a single unity.

8

Sufism and Exoteric Religion

The Koran, as stated earlier, is a rich, double-sided brocade, the outer side of which represents the exoteric aspect, and the inner the esoteric, with seven interior meanings, so that there is food for all in the Koran.

The Koran lays down five basic duties to God: Faith, Prayer, Alms-giving, Fasting and Pilgrimage. Formally, they are not difficult to fulfil. It is their inner significance that is not always properly appreciated and is our main concern in this chapter.

FAITH (*IMAN*)

Formally, Faith is the verbal profession that 'There is no God except God', and 'Muhammad is the Apostle of God.'

The Apostle said: 'Faith is belief in God and His angels and His [revealed] books.'

According to some Sufis, apart from being a verbal profession, faith is both verification (*tasdiq*) and practice. Mere verification in the heart without right action is not enough; nor is anyone saved by his works alone, that is, by works without faith. Faith is religious knowledge, accompanied by performance of the Divine commands.

But faith, as commonly understood, is not real or mystic knowledge, for if it were, it would be knowledge, not belief or faith. Faith scents certainty, but is not certainty. It scents certainty, as it is a reflection in the lower empirical self of the true knowledge that abides at higher levels of being. It is not certainty, as the empirical self is not yet sufficiently detached from the outward sense-world and is not pure enough to rise to

198

union with the light that shines through the higher consciousness.

Speaking of the connection between faith and patience, Rumi says that patience in pain or distress is sweetened by spiritual thoughts, as in the case of Job, as such thoughts make grief and pain tolerable; and that relief comes from faith, 'the substance of things unseen'. Weakness of faith is despair and torture. It is patience, long-suffering patience, that nurtures and strengthens faith. He that has no patience can have no faith, no hope in the future. It is from patience that faith secures a crown. To practise patience is the soul of one's glorifications. In the words of the Prophet, God has not given faith to anyone in whose nature there is no patience. Patience, as the Arabic saying goes, is the key to relief and happiness; it is patience that through perseverance in self-purification burns the veils over our eyes and opens our breast to the Divine Light; it is like the bridge *Sirat*,[1] across which is Paradise (M.II, 71, 598–601, 3145–7).

Patience in Sufism often means abstinence — abstinence from greed, from desire, from wealth, rank and power, from everything other than God. God has created myriads of elixirs, says Rumi, but none has seen an elixir like patience (M.III, 1854).

According to Rumi, faith and unbelief are correlates. Faith cannot exist without unbelief, which is heedlessness or denial of God. For faith is the forsaking of unbelief and this is not possible unless there be unbelief to be forsaken. One cannot exist without the other. They are indivisible and their Creator is one. Hence both faith and unbelief may be said to be serving God's purpose and singing His praise; they are His lovers. Rumi quotes Sana'i:

> Both unbelief and faith are seeking Thee
> And shout Thy undivided Unity.
>
> (*Discourses*, p.215)

Faith is belief in the Unseen. Hope and fear are its pillars, each complementary to the other; for opposite manifests opposite. They both belong to the world of the Unseen. Faith is hidden in the heart, and both faith and the spiritual fruits that follow from it lie hidden in the mystery of God's eternal foreordainment. For faith that is seen is not faith, but knowledge.

Similarly, hope cannot be seen by the outward eye. For hope that is seen is not hope. What a man sees, why should he hope for? But if we hope for what we see not, we, with patience, wait for it (St Paul, Romans, viii, 24,25).

God wishes every prince and prisoner to be both hopeful and fearful (M.I, 3615). If we fear God in this, life and this fear will make us abstain from sin, we shall have no fear in the next life. If, however, we have no fear here, we shall have fear There; we shall not be safe. God does not put two fears in our heart, both here and There (M.III, 494–6).

Good and evil, which test the souls, have also been wisely kept in the world of the Unseen. If the veil separating the seen from the Unseen were lifted, opposites like hope and fear, good and evil, faith and unbelief, this earthly probation itself, would no more exist, and we would be as at the Resurrection, pure and sinless (M.II, 984–8; also, see p.88-89 *supra*).

Speaking of the Faith formula, *la ilaha illa 'llah*, Rumi says that we are only particles of *la*, that is negation. The phenomenal world is all *la* or Not-being. He therefore tells us to lift our heads from this phenomenal world, this 'otherness', and heed the call of God directly or through the larynx of a saint, and, dying to self, experience spiritual rebirth and attain the unitive state (M.I, 1925–6, 1933–6).

PRAYER (*MANAZ*)

Next to faith is prayer. Faith is superior to the prayer's form. Prayer can be dropped or postponed for a valid reason. In any event, prayer, without faith, is of no value. Faith, on the other hand, can never be dropped or postponed and, even without prayer, it is useful (*Discourses*, p.43).

Prayer can be for anything. It can be for the sensual pleasures of the world which are transient. On the religious level, it is for Paradise, which God has promised the believers who give their lives and possessions to Him. This promise is binding on God in the Torah and the Gospel and the Koran (Koran, ix,III).

Rumi distinguishes between the body of prayer and the soul of prayer. The outward form of prayer is the body of prayer, and it is time-bound, while the soul of prayer transcends time and is continual. Some of Rumi's prayers and supplications are about the finest in Persian literature.

Forms of prayer are far from God. The worshipper is carried close to Him only in proportion to the love and devotion with which he worships the forms. A mind 'rapt into still communion ... transcends the imperfect offices of prayer and praise'.

The Prophet, who introduced the formal prayer for his followers, said that the soul of prayer is complete absorption; it is a state of unconsciousness which has no room for any form, outward or inward, no room for thought or imagination. Even Gabriel, the highest spiritual intelligence, cannot enter therein. It may be likened to the 'dim' or 'dark' contemplation of St John of the Cross, or to Ruysbroeck's 'Prayer of Passive Union'.

No love relation can be unilateral; it must be mutual. There can be no lover without a beloved, and no beloved without a lover. They are two aspects of the single reality of love (M.I, 1740). If man seeks God in prayer, God also seeks His worshippers to glorify Him. But this does not mean that everyone can pray. God is the agent of action. The inspiration to pray comes from His inward presence. It is His gift for which we should be grateful.

If the initiative for prayer comes from God, the response to it also is from Him (M.IV, 3499). In this context, Rumi tells the story of a supplicant who was devotedly praying to God, when the Devil appeared and said to him: 'How long will you keep crying "Allah" when He has not responded to you even once?' Thinking himself rejected of God, the supplicant felt broken-hearted and stopped praying and fell asleep. Khidr appeared to him in a dream, and when told what had happened, he said that God says: 'Your crying "Allah" is My "Here I am".' Man's love for God has its birth in God's love for man (M.III, 189–95), and his selfless God-inspired prayer is accepted even before it is uttered.

As already stated, it is not everyone who is privileged to pray. A man of evil nature is not permitted to cry 'Allah'. What is needed is a sorrowing soul, a heart full of grief and pain, and a voice become pure and sad, crying 'O Allah', 'O You whose help is besought', 'O Helper' (M.III, 198–206).

But prayers which, if heard, would involve loss or destruction, He, in His infinite Kindness and Wisdom, does not hear. Thus, when a thief stole a snake-catcher's snake and was bitten by it and died, the owner of the snake was praying to God for its retrieval. God rejected his prayer and saved him from snake bite and death (M.II, 135–40).

A distinction is generally made between those who believe in the efficacy of prayer (*ahl-i-du'a*) and so ask for special favours, and those who are perfect quietists (*ahl-i-rida u taslim*) and consider prayer helpless against what is ordained, except that predestination itself may provide for the possibility of avoiding evil by means of prayer (see pp.112–13 *supra*).

Rumi says in the context of Daquqi's prayer that the ritual prayer is a reminder of the Primal Covenant, and signifies a return to the other world, as at the Resurrection. It also signifies the creative evolutionary process of man.

The ritual prayer consists of four postures: the standing up (*qiyam*), the bowing (*ruku*), the prostration (*sajud*), and the Confession of Faith (*tashahhud*), and repeated pronouncement of the words 'God is most great' (*takbir*). The Sufi is more concerned with the soul and spirit of prayer than with its outward form. Every external movement has an inner meaning. The former is the husk and the latter the kernel of the prayer.

To take the *takbir* first, the Law requires that the words 'God is most great' should be pronounced at the time of slaughter of an animal. It carries a similar significance in prayer. As Rumi explains, the essence of the *takbir* is self-mortification; it means that we should pronounce it in slaughtering the carnal soul, and, discarding greed and bestiality, become a sacrifice and pure offering before God (M.III, 2143-4).

The essence of 'standing' also is self-mortification. In this posture, one must throw behind his back all self-regarding interests, whether of this world or of the next. The bowing and prostration represent humility and self-abasement. God says: 'Prostrate thyself and draw near.'

The prostration is also a reminder that at the Resurrection the earth will be a witness to our actions on earth and must not therefore be lowly esteemed.

The Confession of Faith signifies contemplation of God; it is to recall the sound of *alast* which was heard in pre-existence. Thus, the ritual prayer, involving the sacrifice of self, draws us close to God, and takes us back in memory to the original Confession of Faith.

The ritual prayer in Rumi is also an enactment or prevision of the Resurrection scene. The worshipper should know that its real essence will be revealed at the Resurrection. The prayer contains such indications. In the standing posture, such words come from God as will come at the Resurrection. He asks the worshipper how he has lived, what he has accomplished on earth, how he has used his limbs, senses, intellect and the Divine Nature reflected in him. The inadequate worshipper is overwhelmed with shame, and all his strength to remain standing departs from him, and he bends double in the genuflexion, and, with bowed knees, recites a litany of praise. Asked by God to lift up his head from the genuflexion and answer his question, the shame-faced one lifts up his head at the Lord's command, but, under the burden of shame, falls flat on his face. When the Lord again asks him to relate his deeds and tells him of His determination to enquire about his performance on earth 'hair by hair', his soul is smitten by His overawing words, and, as he has no strength to stand up, he sits down and turns for intercession to the spirits of prophets and saints on the right, and, then, to his family and relatives on the left. But no help comes. He must bear his burden alone. Losing all hope, he uplifts his hand in supplication to the all-forgiving Lord and throws himself on His mercy (M.III, 2140–74).

Another allegorical interpretation of the four postures is that the standing up represents man, erect with pride and arrogance. The bowing posture of humility represents the animal stage, as all animals bend or stoop, none being erect like man. The anthropoid is the nearest to being erect, and, in the evolutionary scheme, is closest to man. The self-abasing posture of prostration represents the plant stage, as all plants 'bow themselves'. The Confession of Faith signifies the process of the soul's coming into this world, and, after self-abnegation, its return to the other world.

Certain preliminary conditions are prescribed for the performance of prayer — like outward purification from filth, cleanliness of the outer garment, freedom from contamination of the place where one purifies oneself, turning toward the *Qibla*, that is, towards the *Ka'ba*. These physical conditions certainly have their value. But more important than outward conformity is sincerity (*ikhlas*) of feeling in prayer. If the inside of the worshipper is not purified from lust, corruption and sin, of what avail is outside cleanliness, except as a measure of hygiene? Rumi speaks of an occasion when Ayesha, the Prophet's wife, said to him that he performed his prayers anywhere, even in places stinking with filth. The Prophet said that God makes impure things pure for the spiritual kings. To one in a state of contemplation, the entire universe is a sanctuary (M.II, 3424–8; *Kashf*, 327). The truth is, as St Paul said: 'There is nothing unclean of itself; but to him that esteemeth anything to be unclean, to him it is unclean' (Romans, xiv,14).

Prayer is not ordained, Rumi says, in order that we should be standing, bowing and prostrating throughout the day. That would be too tiring and impracticable. Hence, prayer at five times a day is laid down. But to the Sufi, this restriction is only nominal. His aim is that the spiritual state which possesses him visibly at prayer time should always be with him, and he should in all circumstances be in God's hand, continually at prayer.

Here, Rumi is referring to the prayer of the spirit and not to the formal prayer which, externally, is a prayer of the body and is limited to fixed hours.

The question is often asked whether the Sufi is exempt from the obligation to perform the ritual prayer. The answer depends on the spiritual state of the Sufi. In Rumi, although certain passages may give the impression that he favours exemption, others plainly make it incumbent on the Sufi to fulfil this ritual obligation, except when he is unconscious or in ecstasy.

In Sufism, spiritual states rank higher than mere bodily movements. The love of God cares nothing for external, religious forms. Love is love and ruby is ruby, even if they bear no seal in testimony (M.II, 1771). No time is fixed for remembrance of God. He is always in the Sufi's mind. What gain is it to him to subject himself to the formalities of five prayers of limited duration each day, when he is continually at prayer? The Prophet made the *Ka'ba* the place of turning in prayer for the sake of God. How much more is God Himself the place of turning? (*Discourses*, p.25). Why bother about the road, when the destination is already reached?

We have already narrated the anecdote in which Rumi was playing the rebeck when he was reminded by a visitor that it was prayer time. He said that his rebeck-playing also was a call to prayer and that while the formal prayer only called the external self to serve God, his music called the inner self to love and knowledge of God. God is jealous of anyone who, after seeing His face, prefers His scent or, having received the privilege of kissing His hand, prefers to kiss His foot (M.I, 1768–70).

The Sufi who has savoured ecstasy understandably finds his mission to mix with people and give them spiritual guidance and comfort an irritation, as it disturbs the continuity of his intimacy with God. Even the Prophet, who was, at first, wholly occupied with God, wept and lamented when God commanded him to 'call the people, counsel them and reform them'. Muhammad said to God: 'O Lord, what sin have I committed that I am being driven from Your presence?' It was only when God told him that, even when he was occupied with men or in any other matter, he would not be abandoned, but would always be in union with Him, that Muhammad felt reassured (*Discourses*, p.78).

Speaking of the obligatory aspect of the formal prayer, Rumi says that in the prayer of the spirit, the spirit also has its genuflexion and prostration, and they must be manifested in form. Meaning and form must go together if they are to be beneficial. For one is the root and the other the branch, and, without the branch, the root would remain unknown and even without a name (*Discourses*, pp.152–3).

God has made the Perfect Man the broker between Him and man. Having journeyed to the spiritual world of unity and gained knowledge of that world, he must return to this world of plurality and use the knowledge for the instruction of mankind and for their guidance to the original world.

None is exempt from social obligations. The higher the rank, worldly or spiritual, the greater are one's obligations to society. Although Rumi says that no obligation can be laid on those mystically intoxicated, the exemption is temporary. They cannot claim permanent exemption, without exposing themselves to the charge of 'spiritual selfishness' and dereliction of duty. Rumi calls the intoxicated one 'a false pretender' and tells him to open his eyes and see and rise from intoxication to sobriety, from this negation of self and the many, to affirmation of the One revealed in the Many, and bestow intoxication upon others, that is, inspire them with spirituality. Let your 'I see not' become 'I see' and your 'I know not' become 'I know' (M.VI, 627–30). The intoxicated are many, the sober are very few. Intoxication has no other aim and purpose than sobriety.

206

The Perfect Man knows his social duty. He must teach others to pray, not only for themselves and others whom they consider their own, but also for their enemies, who also are creatures of God, with the same life running in them as runs in all. To hate or ignore any creature is to hate or ignore the Creator, and betray ignorance of the unity of life. Aware of his obligation to those less fortunate than he, the Prophet David said: 'I am like the sun in the Light. I cannot distinguish myself from the Light. My going to prayer and into solitude is only to teach the way to the people.' In Buddhism also, the *Boddhisattva* renounces *Nirvana*, which, in a sense, is not the highest state of Perfection, as it involves spiritual selfishness, and, instead of undertaking the flight of the alone to the Alone — whence there is no return — he comes back to the world of men and stays for their salvation.

The prayer itself is a pleasure. The Prophet is reported to have said that he found in the ritual prayer the delight of his eye (M.II, 3235). Whenever he felt joyless and longed for proximity to God, he would say to his favourite Negro *muazzin* (the crier who calls the people to public prayer) Bilal: 'O Bilal, comfort me by the call to prayer.' While performing the prayer, he felt he was seeing God or was in His presence. As he said for general benefit: 'No prayer is complete without feeling His inward presence.' In his own case, every prayer was a spiritual ascension to God, an ineffable bliss, not a painful renunciation or sacrifice.

How important in prayer are the prescribed words and correct pronunciation?

It is generally believed that in prayer the prescribed words and their correct pronunciation are vital, and, in their absence, the prayer becomes null and void. But Rumi places sincerity of feeling above conventional speech. He narrates the story of a saintly shepherd and the prophet Moses. Moses heard him saying to God: 'Where are You, so that I can reach You and become Your servant and sew Your shoes, comb Your head and wash Your clothes, kill Your lice and bring You milk, kiss Your little hand, massage Your little feet and sweep

Your little room at bedtime? May all my goats be a sacrifice to You — to You in whose remembrance are all my cries and sighs' (M.II, 1720-4).

The shepherd was babbling in this manner, when Moses chided him, saying what blasphemy was this! The Lord was not like his paternal or maternal uncle; He had no body, and, therefore, no bodily wants. What he was saying would be irreverent even in respect of His servants of whom He has said: 'he is I and I am he' (M.II, 1735-40).

The shepherd heeded the chiding and said to Moses that he had burnt his soul with repentance. He rent his garment, as Sufis do in ecstasy, heaved a sigh and hastily turned towards the desert and went his way (M.II, 1748-9).

It is not uncommon for man to create God in his own image and invest Him with corporeality and with human attributes like grief and laughter (M.I, 1790). For to praise God, after all, is only to express one's subjective idea, necessarily inadequate, of the Divine Nature. And this is what the shepherd was doing in his own simple way. His sincerity was above question. Hence came God's revelation to Moses: 'You have separated My servant from Me. Did you come to unite or separate? The most abhorrent thing to Me is divorce. I have laid down a code of conduct and a form of expression for everyone. The Indian expression is praise for the Indians; the *Sindi* idiom is praise for the Sindis. I am free from all purity and impurity. I ordained worship, not in order to gain profit from My worshippers, but to do a kindness to them.' God desires of them no provision, nor does He desire that they should feed Him. He needs nothing from anyone. He is the all-provider. 'Whoever exerts himself does so for his own advantage; verily, God is independent of created beings' (M.II, 1750-8; Koran, li,57,58).

Continuing, God said: 'I do not look at the tongue and the speech. I look at the interior and the feeling. I look to see if the heart is lowly, even if the speech is not lowly. For the heart is the substance, and the speech the accident; the substance is the real object, the accident is secondary. What I want is not words, concepts and metaphors, but the burning fervour of love. Light up the fire of love in your heart, and wholly burn away thought and expression. O Moses, the knowers of the formalities of religion are of one kind and those with burning souls and spirits are of another kind. Lovers burn with the fire of love which consumes them at every moment. They are not liable to penalty for non-observance of religious forms; no tax or tithe exists on a ruined village. If they speak wrongly, do not call them wrong. If you are already inside the *Ka'ba* [the sanctuary at Mecca], you do not look for the *Qibla* [the direction of the *Ka'ba* towards which the Moslem turns for prayer]. If you are already in union with God, of what avail are conventional forms? The religion of love is separate from all religions. The lovers' only creed and religion is God (M.II, 1759-70).

Although, according to some Sufis, a word loses its magical meaning if mispronounced, Rumi ranks a sincere heart above a faultless tongue. He tells an anecdote about Bilal, the Negro *muazzin* mentioned earlier, at whose sweet voice the Prophet would feel wonderfully refreshed. Bilal would mispronounce *ḥayya* as *hayya* in the words 'ḥayy 'ala'l-falaḥ', which form part of the call to prayer and mean 'Hasten to welfare'. When people pointed out the mispronunciation to the Prophet and asked for another *muazzin* with a correct pronunciation, the Prophet flew into a rage and said: 'O wretches, to God, Bilal's *hayy* was better than a hundred *ha*'s and *kha*'s[2] or any words or speech' (M.III, 172-7).

ALMS-GIVING (*ZAKAT*)

Alms-giving to the poor and deserving is prescribed in all faiths. Islam, which is concerned with all facets of life, prescribes what proportion of one's income, profits, etc., is to be given for specified purposes. Alms-giving is not a state tax or levy, but a religious obligation in Islam. Also, it is thanksgiving for any benefit received, be it property or 'dignity'. As the Prophet said: 'Everything has its alms, and the alms of a house is the guest room' (*Kashf*, 314).

But alms must be given in the right spirit. A coin dropped reluctantly into the beggar's bowl just to satisfy the instinct for social conformity or for show is not real alms-giving. Alms-giving is giving something one loves and giving it gladly; it is self-giving; it is giving one's whole self for the sake of God. According to Rumi, riches spent in charity bring a hundred lives in the heart as recompense. When pure seeds are sown in God's earth, how should there be no income? (M.IV, 1758-9). The Caliph Abu Bakr gave away all his possessions, leaving for his family, as he said, God and His Apostle. The receiver is superior to the giver when he accepts charity not for himself, but for distribution to the deserving poor, and, in the process, enables the giver to perform his religious obligation, which, incidentally, breaks down the giver's sense of selfhood in some measure. (See p.153 *supra*.)

FASTING (*SAWM*)

God says: 'O believers, fasting is prescribed unto you' (Koran, ii,183). This prescribed fast is of one month's duration each year which the Moslems are required to observe in normal circumstances. Apart from this prescribed fast, Sufis often fast voluntarily for varying periods.

In Sufism, fasting is not just a formality, but an act of deliberate mortification which, in various forms, is a means to contemplation. Mere abstinence from food and drink is no fasting. 'Fasting is half of the Way' (Junayd). It includes the whole method of Sufism (*Kashf*, 321). All the five sense-organs must abstain from evil. 'Imprison thy tongue and thy senses', said the Prophet, which is complete mortification. The fast is broken, says Attar, with the attainment of contemplation.

PILGRIMAGE (*HAJJ*)

Like fasting, pilgrimage to the *Ka'ba* at Mecca also is an act of mortification, its object being to attain contemplation. It involves the performance of certain rites which, as in the case of other religious obligations, carry an inner meaning in Sufism.[3]

According to well-known Traditions, not only is there no monkery in Islam, but the congregation is deemed a mercy. The Prophet laboured for solidarity. Just as the mosques were created for the congregation of local people for public prayer, the *Ka'ba* was instituted in order that people from different parts of the world might congregate for the fulfilment of a religious obligation. Such assemblies, apart from the religious or spiritual benefits they may confer on individuals, tend to promote a sense of togetherness and brotherhood amongst them and, through them, in the world community at large (*Discourses*, pp.75-6).

As a part of the pilgrimage, one has to tread the valley of Mina (see p.253 *infra*, n.3, item viii). When Rumi says that this cannot be done unless one crosses the desert (M.III, 775), undergoing the terrible hardships of the journey, he has the mortification aspect of the pilgrimage in mind. Also, while the formal pilgrimage consists in visiting the House of the Lord, the true pilgrimage, according to Rumi, is to the Lord of the House. Compare Hafiz:

> Do not show off before me, O chief of the pilgrims, for you
> See the House, and I see the Lord of the House.

Bistami, in narrating the experience of the pilgrimage, says: 'On my first pilgrimage, I saw only the temple; the second time, I saw the temple and the Lord; and the third time, I saw the Lord alone.' That is, he was exclusively absorbed in contemplation of His Self-subsistence. 'Where mortification is', Hujwiri says, 'there is no sanctuary: the sanctuary is where contemplation is' (*Kashf*, p.327).

In Rumi, the *Ka'ba* means 'the heart of the prophets and saints, which is the locus of God's revelation'. The physical *Ka'ba* is only a branch of the other, the real *Ka'ba*. If it were not for the heart, what purpose would the *Ka'ba* serve? (*Discourses*, p.174).

Rumi tells the story of Bayazid, who once, on his journey to Mecca, was seeking, as was his wont, as Sufis do during

travels, someone who was the *Khidr* of his time. He met a holy
dervish who was a knower of God and also a family man.
Learning of Bayazid's intention to visit the *Ka'ba*, the dervish
asked him to lay before him whatever money he had and make
a circuit round him seven times and know that he had
performed the 'greater' and the 'lesser' pilgrimage, become
pure and gained everlasting life. In truth, he should consider
this circumambulation better than the circumambulation of
the other *Ka'ba*. For while the *Ka'ba* was the house of His
religious service, his own form was the house of His inmost
consciousness, and while God had never entered the *Ka'ba*,
none but the Living God had ever entered his house, and so, to
see him and serve him was to obey and serve God. God was
not separate from him (M.II, 2231–49).[4]

Sufism has no fixed attitude to religion. It depends on the
individual Sufi, on the mystic knowledge that God flashes into
his heart, on his personal experience of Reality. He is guided
not by the injunctions of exoteric faith, but by his inner
perception of what is right and true. His attitude to religion
may be one of general conformity or of positive rejection, or
of lip-service, as a shield against the wrath of the orthodox.
Take the Sufi gnostic (*arif*). His denial of all 'otherness' means
denial of any positive creed and morality. He sees the Light of
God not in this or that faith, but in all faiths alike; not in
temples and churches and mosques any more than in taverns.
Compare Hafiz:

> In the tavern of the Magians, the light of God I see,
> And behold this wonder what light from where I see.

The eminent Persian mystic Abu Sa'id ibn Abi'l-Khayr goes so
far as to say:

> Not until every mosque beneath the sun
> lies ruined, will our holy work be done;
> And never will true Musulman appear
> Till faith and infidelity are one.
> (Nicholson, *The Mystics of Islam*, p.90)

Though these verses sound like a denunciation of Islam, taken in a deeper sense they are a rejection of all duality, including faith and infidelity, and an affirmation of God as the sole Reality. If all is God (*hama ust*), what room is there for plurality and difference, except in form which is fleeting, not real and abiding?

Rumi's faith in Islam is above question. He repeatedly refers to the Koran as the Word of God, and Muhammad as His chiefest creature, as His Light, as the Logos, the final cause of creation. His great work, the *Mathnawi*, is known in Persia as a commentary on the Koran. But his interpretation is based on the truth that God has directly communicated into his heart, and, sometimes, it varies from the orthodox interpretation. There is no religion higher than Truth, and Truth's location is in the heart.

In his attitude to other religions, Rumi's catholicity is most exceptional. Certain stories in the *Mathnawi* — like that of the Jewish King and Christians — and his rejection of the Christian Trinity, and his questioning the ability of Jesus to save others when he could not even save himself from the Cross (M.II, 1401–2), may sound anti-Semitic and anti-Christian. But it was not hostility towards these faiths as such that prompted these denunciatory references. Where personalities are criticised, it is generally because they were bigoted and tyrannical. In the case of Jesus, Rumi speaks of him as the revivifying Messiah, as the Logos. It may be mentioned that, according to the Koran, Jesus was neither slain, nor crucified (Koran, iv,157). Not he, it is believed, but his phantom (or Titanus, the Jew) was hung on the cross.

As for Rumi's criticism of certain doctrines or dogmas of the Jews and Christians, it is generally directed more against their form than their substance. The forms in which they are represented arose in a different social environment, out of different traditions, and they are rejected as heresies in Islam as well as in Sufism, mostly because, according to them, they appear to compromise the Unity and Transcendence of God.

On the whole, however, taking the final purpose of all faiths, Rumi fully respects them all, and cites the following

Tradition, which, referring to what God said, supports not only his own liberalism, but is unmistakable proof of the tolerant nature of Islam: 'I God] am where My servant thinks of Me. Every servant has an image and an idea of Me. Whatever picture he forms of Me, there I am' (*Discourses*, p.61). One has only to be God's true servant and his views, whatever they be, are deserving of respect. The Lord's Mercy, Rumi says, is like sun and rain; it descends on all alike — whether believers or infidels, good people or bad (M.I, 2739).

Explaining how religious differences arise, Rumi narrates the well-known story of the elephant, with minor variations. In his version, there was an elephant in a dark place. People tried to feel it in order to know what it was like. But because of its colossal size, some could feel one part and some another part of it, each group thinking and describing the part it felt as the whole. Yet every person spoke the truth, since his description of the elephant and its shape was in proportion to the partial knowledge of the elephant he had acquired. But none of them, nor the entire lot, understood the real form of the elephant. If they had seen not with the eye of flesh, but with the eye of spirit, they would have beheld the whole of the elephant (M.III, 1259–70).

Rumi says that every prophet and saint may have his own path, but all paths lead to God and are really one (M.I, 3086). People may profess different faiths, but, to Rumi, the Jew, the polytheist, the Christian and the Magian are no different in essence. Their forms of worship differ only because of the infinite diversity of names and attributes in which He manifests Himself and the particular aspects of His nature which the different forms express. In any case, the forms of worship are only the means; once the end is attained, they become redundant. This will become evident at the Resurrection, when the preoccupation of one and all will be with God. Their objective having become one, they will then be 'one of eye and tongue and ear and understanding' (*Discourses*, p.40).

The kind of idol worship that Rumi disapproves of is one

that is bound to forms divorced from its inner meaning. In fact, such worship in any faith is only an exercise in sterility. Hence Rumi's exhortation: Abandon the form, and behold the meaning. For what matters is not the religious label one wears, but how pure his heart is. If you are a Mecca-bound pilgrim, seek a sincere fellow-pilgrim, whether a Hindu, Turk, or Arab. Do not look at his form or complexion, but at his intention, at the language of his feeling. If he is dark in colour, but has the same purpose as you and the language of his heart is the same as yours, call him white, for, inwardly, he is white (M.I, 2893–6). What counts is not the sameness of the spoken tongue, but spiritual homogeneity. Without speech, sign or scroll, myriads of interpreters arise from the heart (M.I, 1208).

Even unbelief which is forgetfulness of God is not without a purpose. As stated earlier, faith cannot exist without it. They are indivisible and spring from a single unity.

Rumi's catholicity stems from the simple truth that God is the Creator of the entire creation, and He created every creature in order that it would worship Him, and for every one He has laid down the form of worship. All things and thoughts reflect His attributes which are nothing but His Essence viewed from different aspects. He is thus the essence of every object, including any thought or belief one may hold about Him. There is no thought that is not from Him, not even disbelief in His existence; there is no thought that is not about Him. 'The fool saith in his heart that there is no God.' Little does he know that thought is created by God. The whole creation is the thought and speech of God.

In the words of Rumi, quoted in an earlier chapter, 'The religion of love is apart from all religions. For lovers, the only religion and creed is God' (M.II, 1770).

9

The Unitive Life

The unitive life is the summit of the spiritual ascent. It involves a positive as well as a negative aspect.

The negative aspect involves fana, that is, self-abnegation, the death of selfhood, the loss of consciousness. It is voluntary death from which the Sufi can return to consciousness and thus differs from physical death from which there is no such return.

The positive aspect following this negation of the personal or empirical self involves affirmation of the real Self. It involves everlasting life (*baqa*) not as an individual, but as the Universal. It means subsistence in contemplation of God, a life independent of time, and, consequently, exempt from all possibility of change. It is the universal here and the eternal now. It is a spiritual state of liberation from the trammels of self which can be attained while still in the body, except that one must lose oneself before one can attain it. There is no waiting till after death, as in exoteric religion.

The way to *baqa*, to the Unitive Life, lies through the fire of asceticism and mortification. That fire is fire only in appearance and is called so because of the burning pain of dying to self. It should be deemed a divine mercy. To follow Rumi, when 'the provision of unprovidedness' has become one's provision and one has passed through oneself and, having left oneself behind, has become empty of self, that is, empty of Not-being, what remains but Being? (M.II, 1378).[1] What seemed fire at first turns out to be light at the last. It is now refreshing water, a garden of a hundred spring-tides, of a hundred spiritual delights. These are the portion of God's

216

elect. It is like the experience of Abraham who found jasmine and cypress in the fire. The aspirant has become God's elect (M.I, 786–90).

The mystic's life is one of constant death and resurrection. He is ever dying to things of the flesh and ever rising to things of the spirit. His total resurrection is total separation from his individual self and everlasting union with the Universal Self. Being the Universal, his nature comprehends creativity and creatureliness — the outward and the inward. Dead to the universe, which stands dissolved for him, he lives permanently in ecstatic union with the Light of God.

Who or what is it in us that enters the unitive life? The answer is that it is the real 'I'-hood without 'I', that is, without personal or separate selfhood: it is the essence of 'I', all 'I's (M.V, 4139–41). It is only when we have gained knowledge of this essence, of the Real Self, or of the Universal in all things, of the self-less spirit, that we can attain to the unitive life. No external book or tutor can give us this knowledge, nor can discursive intellect. These intellects, according to Rumi, can only land us in the heresy of incarnation (*hulul*) or of absolute union with God (*ittihad*) (M.V, 4147). Union, in keeping with Rumi's pantheistic Monism, can only be with God's Light (*ittihad-i-nur*) which is everywhere, but visible only to the spiritual eye.

For God's lovers, the only book and lesson is the face of the Beloved. Knowledge comes only when He 'expands' the heart, filling it with light which is expansive, as it is the life of all that is in the universe — the light that shineth in darkness, though the darkness comprehendeth it not. God has placed the 'expansion' within our breast. His evidences are within us. Jili speaks of a spirit of God's own Essence, the Holy Spirit (*ruhu'l-quds*), which He puts in man's body (without incarnation) when he has passed away from himself and receives the illumination of a Divine name or attribute, or, as in the rarest of cases, the illumination of the Divine Essence. (This is akin to the Christian mystical doctrine of 'substitution'.) Rumi exhorts us to strive after unitive knowing, so that we can contemplate the 'expansion', the illumination, the whole, within ourselves (M.V, 1065–72).

Rumi likens the journey to the unitive state to a journey to the sea. On dry land, the journey can be performed on horse-back, that is, with the aid of esoteric faith, with instruction from book and tongue. Speech can be an effective guide. But once the edge of the sea is reached, the saddle and horse the conventions of religion, can carry us no further. A 'wooden horse', a boat, has now to be the carrier. Silence is that wooden horse. Speech was for the earlier stages; it is for the uninitiated. Now silence alone avails. Mystical instruction cannot be communicated by tongue, but silently from the gnostic's soul to the soul of the initiated.

Journeying in silence in the sea, when the time is ripe the 'wooden horse' also breaks. When this happens, the seafarer passes away in the Divine Essence. He has lost his separate consciousness. His attributes are no more distinguishable. Silence and speech are identical. He is neither speaking nor silent, and yet is speaking and silent. He has become a 'fish'. His state is ineffable (M.VI, 4622–32).

In this state, the Sufi does not even praise God, for this praise is proof of individual existence, and to consider oneself existing or acting, even as a lover of God, is a duality, a veil that separates one from God. He regards the negation *la* in the Faith formula as the profession of Divine Unity and denial of his individual existence (M.I, 30, 517).

The unitive way is so painful and arduous that, despite his spiritual perfection, Rumi says that a hundred like him would not have the strength to bear the sea. Considering that elsewhere he refers to himself as the Logos (p.35 *supra*), his present reference to his spiritual inadequacy can only be interpreted as a gesture of humility or man's limitation felt by the Sufi when he contemplates the greatness and glory of God. It is not seldom that Sufis adopt the device of what is known as the *tajahul-i-'arif* (pretended ignorance of the gnostic) as an evident mark of humility.

Continuing, Rumi says that regardless of his inadequacy, he

must attempt the journey thus pretending to be a novice,
he was an adept. He just cannot keep away from the dro[
waters. He would march in the sea so long as his feet n
When they cease to function and all his strength is gone, he
would plunge like a duck in the water and let himself be carried
by it. The ring may be crooked, but it is on the door (M.II,
1360). Whether one is straight or crooked, one should keep
crawling towards God, unaffected by thoughts of inadequacy
or of the ultimate result. It is better to be a faithful failure than
a non-starter.

St John of the Cross speaks of 'the dark night of the soul'. It
is the 'Divine Darkness' of self-abnegation, of self-
naughtedness. The night, says Rumi, which the King in His
Wrath makes pitch-dark, scoffs at a hundred worldly delights,
at a thousand days of festival. For it is but a manifestation of
His Grace masquerading as Wrath. The circumambulation
performed by one who sees God transcends the duality of
grace and wrath, of infidelity and faith (M.IV, 2966–7).

The Path to the unitive state is the Path of love which
involves self-giving. In this Path, no one can run with two feet
or play the love game with a single head. Thousands of feet
and heads are needed. The Sufi, of course, does not walk on
his feet, but on his heart. His journey is not in the body, but in
the spirit. He has to cross countless stations and die to self
countless times, metaphorically sacrificing countless feet and
heads in the process, before he can attain to union with God.
Everyone dies but once, but the King sacrifices the lover afresh
at every moment (M.VI, 4602–6). Each time, it is a new
experience, a new life, entailing a new death. Bring 'not-being
as your gift, if you are not a fool', says Rumi (M.I, 3201).

The lover of God does not complain of the Beloved's cruelty
or of the afflictions of love he suffers in his quest of Him. He
loves both His kindness and wrath alike, although they are
contraries. He is a strange nightingale that opens its mouth to
swallow both thorns and roses. No, he is not a nightingale that
loves the rose, and for its sake swallows the thorn, but a fiery
shark to whom love has sweetened all unsweetnesses. In all

His attributes, whether of His Beauty or of His Majesty, in His Wrath no less than in His Grace, he sees the glorious Beauty of His Essence. He is a lover of the Universal and is himself the Universal. Everything is in him and from him. Humility is in him, wrath is in him; good and evil, beauty and ugliness are in him. If he knows himself, he knows God and loves equally all His attributes reflected in him (M.I, 1570-4).

Besides, whatever befalls the lover of God is predestined. How can he be disgruntled with what the Lord has predestined?

Not only is the lover of God full-content with whatever befalls him, but he freely gives his life for His sake, and can bear no intercessor to come between them to save him. In fact, he is delighted to be slain by the Beloved's own hand, because this means that He has emptied him of self and taken him to His bosom. It is a sign of His love for him; otherwise, why should He bother about him? That head, says Rumi, is honoured which the King's own hand severs; shame to that head which looks to another for protection (M.IV, 2959-65).

Hell and Heaven are nothing before the lover. Love dissolves infidelity, which is the brimstone of Hell, and, at the same time, it relegates the delights of Paradise to nothing, as the lover owns the whole stack of corn, while Paradise is only a gleaner. Hell and Paradise tremble with fear of him, and ask him to pass quickly, leaving them alone, lest the former should be quenched and the latter rendered worthless (VI, 4608-14). Love transcends Heaven and Hell, whether of exoteric religion or of esoteric feeling. Being himself the Universal of which he is a lover, he is a seeker of his own love.

There is, however, a distinction in rank between the Sufi who is steeped in the Lord's attributes and the one who is steeped in His Essence. The former, excluded from His Essence and limited to His attributes, sees all action as proceeding from His attributes reflected in him. How should the latter, absorbed in the Divine Essence, look upon His attributes, which are only forms of the Essence? It is the Essence, not the attributes, that is the agent of Divine action. When your head is in the depths of the river, sunk in the Divine Essence, how should your eye fall on the colour of the rippling water — upon the attributes, ignoring the Essence? If it did, it would be a mark of spiritual decline, a relapse from the unitive state into plurality, which veils the Truth (M.II, 2812–15).

In the highest unitive state, the Sufi is veiled neither by the outward world from its inward reality, as in the earlier stages of the Path, nor by its reality from its outward form, as in the state of spiritual intoxication. In this final state, the state of *baqa*, his self knows itself as the Divine Essence manifesting itself to itself and it also sees the Divine Essence in its outwardness. Essence and attributes are combined in him. He is never severed from the Divine Essence.

God's Workshop is Non-existence — a plane of bare potentiality — and there one sees the work and the Worker, i.e. its inward essence, together (M.II, 762). To die to self and to attain to the unitive life is to go back to one's original state of non-existence, when one was a thought, an idea, in God's mind or Nous; it is to realise the Unity of God and His actions. Such a return assumes the pre-existence of all things as ideas in the knowledge of God, which is the source of their origination and their point of return.

To turn to the Sufi gnostic, we may now bring together in brief some of what has already been said about him. Rumi says that, having turned his back on mankind and the world, on all phenomena, the gnostic denies all 'otherness' as false and illusory. He regards God as the sole Agent, and attributes to himself no action, thought or feeling except metaphorically, or as a matter of form, for such attribution would imply the existence of self-consciousness. He does not weep at a loss or rejoice at a gain. He has put behind all secondary causes, every kind of relationship, so that nothing remains but God.

God is eternally revealing Himself to him in an endless variety of forms, and his progress is a perpetual ascension to the throne of God. His vision of Reality is absolute and permanent, as the Lord's epiphanies are countless and without beginning or end (M.V, 2180).

221

The gnostic is in union with God. He may be speaking with others, but, as Noah said of himself, he is really addressing God, the Giver of speech, praying to Him, glorifying Him (M.III, 1343–4). Bayazid is reported to have said: 'For thirty years I have been speaking to God and listening to Him, while people suppose I am speaking to them.' Noah also said to God: 'I look at none and even if I do, it is only a pretext; You alone are the object of my seeing' (M.III, 1359). In the Perfect Man, essence and attributes, subject and object, union and separation are unified.

Rumi tells the story of the person who knocked at a friend's door, and when asked who he was, said: 'I'. The friend turned him away, saying that he knew no friend who was 'I'. The person was spiritually raw. A year later, duly 'cooked', he returned and again knocked at the same door, and when asked who he was, said: ''Tis thou'. The friend said: 'Since you are I, come in, O myself; there is no room for two "I's" in the house' (M.I, 3056 etc.). Compare 'Attar:

> Pilgrim, Pilgrimage and Road
> Was but Myself towards Myself, and Your
> Arrival but Myself at my own Door.
>
> (tr. Fitzgerald)

The gnostic's prayer and petition to God is like God's own petition to Himself, for He has said: 'I am to him an ear and an eye and a tongue and a hand' (M.V, 2242, heading), so that 'By Me he hears and by Me he sees' (M.I, 1938). This means that God has so overpowered his being that his faculties have ceased to function and, when he does seem to will and act, it is not he but God who acts through him.

Of one so overpowered by God, it is improper to say that he possesses the Divine Consciousness. For he is the Divine Consciousness itself. He belongs to God and God belongs to him. Sometimes, God says to him: ''Tis thou', sometimes, ''Tis I'. The Lord sees all His attributes in the Perfect Man and, through his medium, sees the entire creation (M.I, 1938–40).

Although in his ecstatic utterances Rumi gives the impression that the Sufi in the unitive state has lost his personality and become God, or is utterly indistinguishable from Him, on other occasions he says unequivocally that his personality still is intact, with no loss of essence or corporeality, and that the Divine and human natures cannot commingle. Is Rumi being inconsistent?

No, the question whether in the unitive state, or in *Nirvana* in Buddhism, the Sufi exists or ceases to exist cannot be properly answered in the positive or in the negative. The Lord Buddha was asked this question and he would not answer it. The answer is relative and depends on the point from which the question is viewed. In the unitive state, the personal self of the Sufi is united with the Universal Self and so does not exist, except in the body. On the other hand, his real being does not cease merely because it does not stand forth. Affirmation of his existence can, therefore, be as misleading as its denial (Sri Krishna Prem, *The Yoga of the Kathopanishad*, pp.44–5).

In Rumi's story of Buhlul, a saint who lived in the reign of Harun al-Rashid, a dervish, in reply to his question, says that nowhere in earth and Heaven does a leaf drop from a tree or an atom move or a straw turn, except according to what the Lord has predestined and decreed. As no action takes place without His command, a man who lives for God's sake, not for his personal self; who dies happily for His sake, with no fear in his heart; who is faithful for His sake, not for the sake of Paradise; who abandons infidelity for the sake of God, not for fear of Hell; such a person has become a willing slave to His decree, and what God has predestined has become his pleasure. He knows himself as the subject and object of all action, both being the same thing viewed from different aspects. His personal self no more operative as a separate entity, he has become non-existent (*fani fi'llah*). His personal will lost in the Will of the Lord, and his desire in the Desire of the Lord, the world moves, the torrents and rivers flow, the stars move, according to his pleasure, which is the Lord's pleasure. Even life and death are his officers, carrying out his will which is the Lord's Will. Compulsion is non-existent for the non-existent (M.III, 1884–7, 1902, etc.; also, see p.113 *supra*).

In the above story, the non-existent aspect of the Sufi in the unitive state has been stressed. Elsewhere, Rumi speaks of the other aspect. He says that all piebald things become of one colour in the dyeing vat of *Hu* (God). When a Sufi falls into the vat, he exclaims in rapture: 'I am the vat', that is, 'I am God.' What he means is not that he has ceased to be, but that he has received the light from God. It is like iron and fire. The iron loses its colour in the fire, and, becoming red-hot like fire, boasts, 'I am the fire.' The fact is that it is only glorified by the colour and nature of fire (M.II, 1345–50).

Narrating the conversation between David and God, Rumi says that to pass away in God is to be overpowered by Him. The overpowered man is like the non-existent. It is a case of likeness, not identity. His attributes have passed away in the attributes of God, and he has gained everlasting life, being conscious of no separate existence (M.IV, 395–9).

Using an analogy, Rumi explains that the overpowered one is like a drop of water which throws itself into the sea. Its separateness is lost. It has expanded itself into the sea. But its essence is inviolate and permanent. Dead to sense, the overpowered one is free from the destructive influence of lust and corruption, and has become pure, and, in his unsullied purity, triumphant over death. Hence Rumi's exhortation: Sell and buy at once. 'Give a drop and take the Sea, which is full of pearls' (M.IV, 2615–22).

Speaking of *fana* and *baqa*, Rumi says that the essence of the dervish who has naughted himself in His Essence still survives. He is like the candle flame in the sunlight. The sun has naughted it; it gives no light. And yet it exists; the essence of the candle flame exists. If you put some cotton wool upon it, its sparks will burn it (M.III, 3669–73).

To take another analogy, when you dissolve an ounce of vinegar in two hundred maunds of honey, and taste the honey, the flavour of the vinegar will be non-existent, though the ounce of vinegar has not disappeared, but is in it. To say that the vinegar exists or does not exist is misleading. It both exists and does not exist. The lover's pulse is in a similar position. It bounces irreverently and claims equality with the Beloved. But what happens before the Beloved? Both he and his claim are naughted (M.III, 3674–82).

Elsewhere, Rumi says that the Perfect Man is not a congener of the King of kings, but only a recipient of light from Him. His genus is not the genus of God. When his ego passes away for the sake of His Ego, God remains and he is like dust at His feet. The only signs of his individual soul are the marks of His eternal attributes as imprinted on it in pre-existence. He has attained everlasting life not as an individual or as a separate entity, but as the Universal. That is man's flower and crown. He cannot become God (M.II, 1170–6).

Speaking of *fana* in recollection of God (*fana fi'l-dhikr*), Rumi cites the example of a naked man who jumps into the water in order to protect himself from the sting of the hornets. The water is a symbol for the recollection of God, and the hornets for the remembrance of this man or that woman, or of this world or that world. Rumi says: Hold your breath in the water of recollection and exercise patience, so that you may be liberated from the old thought and temptation, and your inmost nature may assume the nature of the water. They whose remembrance of all 'otherness' is annihilated and who recollect nothing but God, attributing everything to Him, nothing to themselves, do not lose their entity. If their normal human attributes have passed away in the Divine attributes, it is just like the stars disappearing in the radiance of the sun. Rumi cites from the Koran: 'All of them shall be brought into Our presence' (Koran, xxxvi,32, 52). One who is non-existent cannot be brought into anyone's presence (M.IV, 435–45).

Rumi also speaks of the *murid*'s passing away in the *murshid*, that is, of the disciple's in the master. The former loses himself in the *murshid*'s universal nature and experiences the joy of union with the Divine Spirit through the medium of the *murshid*. The distinction in rank between the two goes. The *murshid* ceases to be the *murid*'s superior.

In Rumi, every intermediary is a veil, except that the guidance of the *pir* is necessary up to a certain stage on the

Path. The true lover of God seeks direct contemplation of God. As stated earlier, self-knowledge is knowledge of God, and when such knowledge is attained, an external *pir* or intermediary is needed no more (see p.146 *supra*).

But while every form of 'otherness' is disapproved of, God approves of every kind of union, as every union is the death of selfhood or individuality and all 'otherness' and is revelation of God. Romances like *Layla and Majnun*, *Yusuf and Zulaykha* and *Salaman and Absal*[2] are taken to represent the soul's yearning for reunion with God. To take but one of these, that of *Layla and Majnun*, Rumi says that passion for Layla had so utterly overwhelmed Majnun that he saw her image in everything, and had no need to see her in flesh and blood or hear her voice, as that would interrupt his contemplation of her real essence. As he said, Layla was a cup and he drank wine out of it, and he had no eyes for the beaker. He had vision of divine beauty in her, and had no use for its reflection in her physical form.

Speaking of their 'oneness', Rumi says that once, when Majnun's blood boiled up with the fire of longing for Layla and the symptoms of quinsy developed in him, the physician who came to treat him advised blood-letting as the only cure. But Majnun refused the treatment, saying that his whole being was full of Layla and if he let his blood, he was afraid lest the cupper should suddenly wound Layla with his lancet[3] (M.V., 1999 etc.).

Majnun is also said to have freed a gazelle from a hunter, as it looked like his gazelle-eyed Layla, and, on another occasion, to have bought a cypress which was for burning, as it resembled his cypress-statured Layla. To him, the gazelle was Layla, the cypress was Layla; all was Layla; there was nothing but Layla.

Personal deification is a heresy in Islam. How then can we justify Hallaj's 'I am the Truth' or 'I am God'?

Hallaj, as we know, was God-intoxicated, and yet he was cruelly tortured to death in AD 922 for his supposedly heretical utterances, though the real reason for his execution is believed

to be political. Later, not only was his blasphemy forgiv
but he came to be venerated as a martyr-saint. It is said that b
claiming identity with God, he had sinned against the Law,
but as there is an essential kinship between humanity and
divinity — identity-in-difference — and, dead to self, he lived
in the divinely illumined sphere of being, with all 'otherness'
excluded, he had not sinned against the Truth. In the words of
Shabistari:[4]

> Whoever became empty of howness and whyness
> In him 'I am the Truth' became the sound and echo.
> > (*Gulshan-i-Raz*)

In the following verse, Hafiz says that Hallaj's fault was that
he was proclaiming the Divine Mystery — a Mystery reserved
for the elect, not meant for the masses:

He said: that friend [Hallaj] by whom the gibbet's head was exalted
His crime was this — that he was divulging the [Divine] secrets.

Like other Sufis, Rumi believes in 'the doctrine of reserve'
and says that of a hundred esoteric mysteries he speaks only of
one and that, too, not in full, but in hair-fine form, so that the
subject does not reach every ear (M.I, 1762; M.II, 3505).
Those in communion with God must veil their secrets in
reserve and silence, lest their divulgence should destroy the life
and livelihood of men (M.VI, 3527) by making them heedful
of God and heedless of the affairs of the world, the means of
livelihood not excluded. Many, of course, would not
understand or be interested in the subject and may even regard
it as rank nonsense or as effusions of eccentrics.

Explaining Hallaj's 'I am God', Rumi says that Hallaj meant
that his self was dead, and he was a pure non-entity; and that
God alone is, and it was not Hallaj as an individual, but as the
Divine *Huwiya* (He-ness), that is, God Himself who spoke
these words. Rumi also refers to the Koran and says that
though dictated from the lips of the Prophet, it was God that
spoke the Koran (M.IV, 2122). Hallaj would not even call
himself His servant, as that meant that two existed, the Lord
and the servant, which would have been polytheistic. God

227

alone can see God's glory or feel God's love; He alone has the right to say: 'I am'. Hallaj was one of the rarest impersonal monotheists the world has known.

Elsewhere, Rumi explains that Hallaj's 'I am God' was in his inmost consciousness not from a feeling of incarnation, but of oneness with the Light of God — the *ittihad-i-nur* (M.V, 2038). This explanation, however, is more in accord with Rumi's Monistic Pantheism than with the spirit of Hallaj's mystical utterance.

In the story of Bayazid and his disciples to which reference was made earlier (p.119 *supra*), Bayazid would exclaim in moments of ecstasy: 'Glory to me: How very great is my estate'; 'There is no God except I, so worship me'; 'There is nothing within my cloak but God. How long will you seek Him on the earth and in heaven?' (M.IV, 2102, heading; 2103, 2125).

As every one of God's revelations is different, it is a different mystical experience for the Sufi and a different madness seizes him each time, and it may become so intolerable as to attract legal punishment. Thus, Dhu'l-Nun was put in a prison by the people when they could not endure his madness and disregard of formal religion (M.II, 1386–90).

It was the intense, uncontrollable love of God that wrung blasphemous utterances from Dhu'l-Nun, and led Hallaj as well as Bayazid to exclaim that he, a creature, had become the Creator. The drunken lover is guided not by his intellect which in such moments remains in abeyance, but by his inmost feeling. Bayazid himself could not remember on return to sobriety what he had uttered in the drunkenness of love. One 'possessed' or in ecstasy cannot be held responsible for his utterances or actions.

In the unitive state, there is no positive distinction between affirmation and negation. The Perfect Man in this state, dead to self, may negatively exclaim: I am Not-being; I am a non-entity; I am nothing. Or completely overpowered by love of God, sunk in Him, he may exclaim: I am everything; and proclaim rapturously with Rumi:

The Unitive Life

If there be any lover in the world, O Moslems, 'tis I.
If there be any believer, infidel, or Christian hermit, 'tis I.
The wine-dregs, the cup-bearer, the minstrel, the harp and
the music,
The beloved, the candle, the drink and the joy of the
drunken — 'tis I.

(Diwan, tr. Nicholson)

10
Death and After

All major faiths agree that death is not the absolute end of man, and that something subtle in the fleshly body survives. In Islam, it is the *ruh*, in Christianity the soul, in Hinduism the *atman*, and in Buddhism, a continually changing, transforming complex of physical and psychical activities (*skhanda*).

The One Life that is in all and is hidden manifests itself as a duality, as an outbreath followed by inbreath, as life followed by death. Life and death are thus two aspects of the One Life. It is only our ignorance that makes us love life and hate death. Death is as much a part of the One Life as life itself. Death is life's culmination.

It is hence that Rumi says that the next world is not inanimate, but, as will be evident on the Day of Resurrection, it is living and is the spiritual aspect of the outward, phenomenal world. Surely, the last abode is Life, says the Koran, this world being a mere pastime and a game (Koran, xxix,64).

That this world is no more than a pastime will become plain as daylight on Judgement Day, when, as is said in the Koran, the mountain will become soft as wool (Koran, ci,5), and this earth of heat and cold will mightily quake and become naught, and we will see neither the sky, nor the stars, nor existence of any kind, but only God the Living, Loving God (M.II, 1044–5).

Explaining the reference to the rending asunder of heaven and the quaking of this earth on Judgement Day, Rumi says that the reference is to us. The meaning is that while on earth we find pleasure in our parts being gathered together and have forgotten the pleasure of being free in the infinite expanse of the other world, we will again experience the pleasure of these parts being separated and set free from their present straitness (*Discourses*, p.203).

Death and Resurrection are the birth of the soul into the spiritual realm. This present world is the sowing field; whatever we sow here, we reap There. For it is decreed that good will be met with good and evil with evil. How should the All-wise God change that decree and say that good is the reward of evil? Do men gather grapes of thorns or figs of thistles? (Matthew, ch.vii, 16).

Hence, at the Resurrection, we shall be drawn up in ranks before God, and He will ask us how we have used our five senses, our intellect, and the Divine Nature reflected in us, and how we have used our hands and feet which He gave us for sowing good works (M.III, 2151–3). There will be no dearth of witnesses in that Supreme Court. The very earth will bear witness and declare plainly what she knows, and we will be shown every atom's weight of good and evil we have done during our earthly sojourn (Koran, xcix,1–8). Our mouths will be sealed and our limbs, eyes and ears and skin will testify in their own way as to what we did on earth. They can speak, as God has given them speech, as to all things (Koran, xli,20,21).

Worldly wealth and domed and turreted tombs will be of no avail in the other world. We will stand or fall by what we have done here, by how we have lived, whether in spiritual purity or in sin and corruption (M.III, 130–3). There will be no other help. We may seek the intercession of the spirits of prophets and saints, but they will turn away from us, saying that the day for remedy is past; you had your chance on earth to sow righteousness, but you wasted it. We may turn towards our family and relatives, and they also will express their inability to help, and will ask us to answer for ourselves to the Creator (M.III, 2165–70; also, see p.203 *supra*).

Rumi says that dawn is the little Resurrection. Just as everyone's spirit, as the ancients believed, is freed at night, but is made cognisant of its body and returns to it at dawn, similarly, at the Resurrection, when everybody is commanded to arise from the grave, everyone's soul will return to the body — the scholar's to the scholar, the tyrant's to the tyrant — for the Divine Knowledge has made every soul cognisant of the body (M.V, 1772–80).

But what kind of body is it in the next world of which the soul is made cognisant?

It is not the physical body, according to Rumi. The bodily particles are dissipated. It is the spiritual faculties that God gathers together there, and He makes for them another 'bodiless body' or vehicle, homogeneous with the character and essential nature of the spirit. Nothing gross or physical can exist in the spiritual kingdom (M.III, 1613, 1759–60; also, see p.169 *supra*). In St Paul, it is the spiritual body.

According to Ibnu'l-'Arabi, after death the spirit receives an immortal body homogeneous with the new environment. In Jili, the spirit bears the same corporeal aspect as before (*Islamic Mysticism*, 134).

In Northern Buddhism, the *Bardo* or after-death body is formed of matter in an invisible or ethereal-like state and is an exact duplicate of the previous human body (*The Tibetan Book of the Dead*, p.92, footnote 4).

In this world, we may not be aware of our good and evil, but at the Resurrection, every good and evil will not only be made manifest to us, but also given a visible form. The most concealed thought will appear in the body. As a result of this manifestation, the devout will look fresh and joyous, with the scroll of their noble deeds coming to them from the right, while the unrighteous will look miserable and despairing, with the scroll headed with black and full of crime and sin coming to them from the left. (In Plato's *Republic*, the *Karmic* record boards are affixed to the souls that have been judged.) The guardian angels who were hiddenly following them as custodians on earth, now become visible like policemen (corresponding to Plato's demons), and goad the unrighteous towards Hell.

The Judgement of the dead is one of the most ancient beliefs almost universally held. In most versions, the conscience of the deceased is his judge, and his memory the mirror reflecting his entire past. What is called the Book of Judgement corresponds to Plato's record boards, and is an objective symbol of the Memory Book.

According to the Koran, as already mentioned, God is the Judge — the voice of conscience also is the Voice of God or inspiration from God — and the scroll of noble deeds or of crime and sin comes to the deceased, depending on whether his life on earth has been righteous or sinful.

This takes us to the question of recompense or retribution.

If one sheds another's blood in this world of probation, the blood that is shed will not rest unavenged. An immediate penalty is imposed here. But that is a mere make-shift, compared with the blow of retaliation suffered in the other world (M.IV, 3664–5).

Speaking of the penalty for murder, Rumi says that it is like a castration in the other world, while in this world which the Prophet called a 'play', it is only like a circumcision (M.IV, 3666–7).

The immediate sufferance of penalty for anti-social acts is understandable. For the entire universe, permeated unbrokenly by the Divine Essence, is hiddenly interlinked, so that any disturbance anywhere must disturb the whole, setting up an equal and opposite reaction. We cannot 'stir a flower without troubling of a star'. The Law of Retribution operates unerringly. It is God's eternal Justice.

But will the envious be resurrected and brought to judgement in the shape of wolves, and the greedy in the shape of hogs? (M.II, 1412–13). Does Rumi believe in metempsychosis?

METEMPSYCHOSIS

The Koran says that God said to the Jews who broke the Sabbath: 'Be ye apes, despised and hated.' They underwent outward metamorphosis, so that they would be an example to others (Koran, ii, 65–6; M.V, 2598).

Rumi says that there never has been metamorphosis of the body among the Moslems, but only metamorphosis of the spirit (M.V, 2594). It is our evil dispositions that will arise as so many wolves and tear our limbs in anger (M.IV, 3663–4). A hundred thousand have become hogs and asses inwardly through violating vows of repentance (M.V, 2599). The sensual soul will arise in the shape of an ass, reflecting its foul interior (M.V, 1394–5).

Thus in Rumi, as in Plato and oriental philosophy, the reference to these animal forms in the present context is allegorical, not literal; they reflect the predominant animal passions and propensities of man.

In any case, the human form has taken aeons to develop from the lowest forms and it cannot at one stride migrate into the form of an animal. If there were to be any retrogression, it must, like progression, and for the same reason, be equally gradual and take countless ages. But the question of retrogression does not arise. The entire purpose of evolution is progression, not retrogression.

The rationalists may reject Resurrection or any form of after-death life, as its existence cannot be established by logic or discursive reason. But did we believe in existence when we were in non-existence? There is no material proof we did. And, yet, we came into existence, and went through different states of being of which we had no prior thought, and of which, currently also, we have no remembrance. Is it then too fanciful to believe that when we die and become non-existent, another existence will arise out of this non-existence? (M.I, 3678–81). As Rumi says:

> Which seed went into the earth and did not grow again?
> Why should you have this doubt about the seed of man?

Nature furnishes us with another analogy. Is not spring-time a new birth for things that had died in winter? The earth shows up what it has eaten, that is, what has gone or been cast into it; its secrets are revealed through its mouth and lips; its interior becomes manifest. The secret of every bush and tree and of the food it has consumed shows up on its leafy top (M.V, 3971–4). We see the recurrence of this resurrection every spring.

IS DEATH AN OCCASION FOR SORROW OR JOY?

Most people fear death, because it means severance from this world which they cherish and is the only world they know. Death means the end of everything for them. Even if they have some belief in after-life, they are haunted by fear of the dark and uncertain intermediate states between death and the Resurrection, and of the possibility that their portion in the next world may be the torments of Hell.

To the Sufi, everyone's death is of the same quality as himself: a friend to the friend of God, an enemy to the enemy of God. It is like a mirror in which everyone sees the reflection of his own nature, of all his thoughts, words and deeds. If they have been evil, one will find death terrible; if they have been good, he will see the reflection of that goodness and find death lovely and will love it. Both our love and fear of death have grown from us, and reflect our inner hue (M.III, 3438–43).

With Rumi and his Mevlevi Order of Dervishes, death was no occasion for sorrow, but an occasion for rejoicing, for it meant the Homeward flight of the human spirit, freed from the trammels of matter. Hence, they viewed the death of their friends with delight, and carried their coffins for burial to the accompaniment of joyous singing and dancing (see p.194 *supra*).

Some holy men actually long for and love physical death. Rumi cites the instance of 'Ali, the prince of the Faithful, who was destined to be slain by his stirrup-holder. The servant falls before 'Ali and begs him to slay him, so that such a horrible crime does not issue from him. 'Ali says to him: 'How can I seek to escape destiny? God is the real Agent of action; you are only His instrument. I long for death. Dagger and sword have become my sweet basil; death has become my banquet and beds of narcissi. Slay me, O youth. In my death is my life.

How long shall I remain parted from God?' (M.I, 3844 etc.).

Again, when the Negro *muezzin* Bilal was dying, he told his sorrowing wife at his bedside that death is a joy. And as he said this, as if in confirmation, his eyes became radiant with light, and his face bloomed with rose-petals and anemones. His spirit was coming Home from a strange country, he said. This was not parting, but union with God (M.III, 3517 etc.).

In Tibet, the great Yogi Milarepa, poisoned by an envious lama through the evil offices of a concubine, welcomed death, and singing hymns, preaching the *Dharma* (the Law; the Truth), passed into eternal rest.[1]

REINCARNATION AND RESURRECTION

What is regarded as a major difference between Islam, Christianity and the Jewish faith on the one hand and Hinduism and Buddhism on the other is that while the former three believe in Resurrection, the latter two believe in Reincarnation. It may be mentioned in passing that the Pythagoreans and the Gnostics and also some of the early Christians, including the learned Father Origen and Father Clemens Alexandrinus, believed in Reincarnation and that in Christianity it was in AD 553 that the Second Council of Constantinople repudiated Reincarnation as anathema or heresy. In Sufism also, of the twelve Sufi Orders mentioned by Hujwiri, two — the Hululis and the Hallajis — stood condemned because of their belief in heresies like Reincarnation (*hulul*) and transmigration of souls (*naskh-i-arwah*) (*Kashf*, p.131).

A brief indication of the difference between Reincarnation and Resurrection may be relevant in this context, especially as some scholars — an insignificant minority — have equated Rumi's theory of psycho-spiritual evolution with Reincarnation, though most scholars have rejected the existence of any basis for associating this heresy with him.

The concept of Reincarnation is highly complex and it has no agreed definition. The common belief is that people will exist in their next birth as they exist now and their permanent self will also be the same as in this birth. But, as explained by Sir John Woodroffe, an eminent Sanskrit scholar, there is an infinite series of universes, the 'sparks of eternity' (Blavatsky), beginningless and endless, though each appears and disappears; and man has successive lives in these universes, until he has fitted himself for entry into the Sorrowless State of Liberation from the turning wheel of life and death.[2]

Resurrection, on the other hand, believes in one universe only, the one we live in, and in two lives, one here in the earthly body and the other in the resurrected body in the next world. Till the Resurrection, the dead remain in the tomb, some enjoying 'a sweet repose and drunken sleep', and some suffering pain and agony (*Discourses*, pp.175–6).

According to both, there is an appropriate body to enjoy Paradise or suffer Hell, but in Reincarnation it is not a resurrected body as in Resurrection.

In Resurrection, the character of the first life determines the character of the second for all eternity, giving some the eternal joys of Paradise and others the eternal torments of Hell. In Reincarnation, there is no such eternity of enjoyment or suffering. (In Rumi also, as will be seen later, 'Hell for ever' is not literally true.) According to the Reincarnationist, when the disincarnated soul or the soul complex has expiated the sins or completed its term of enjoyment, it is ready for rebirth. The same soul serves for more than one life.

Rumi's belief in Resurrection is above question. He flatly rejects Reincarnation. He says:

> Like a child in the womb, I receive nourishment from God,
> Man is born once, but I have been born many times.
>
> (*Diwan*)

Rumi means that man as such is born only once on this earth-plane. The case of a Sufi like him is however different; he has repeated births — but spiritual, not physical. Subject to alternating states of spiritual expansion or rapture (*bast*) and spiritual contraction or occultation (*qabd*), the Sufi is spiritually born each time God irradiates his consciousness or illumines his heart. The verse can also mean that the World-Spirit evolving through countless lower forms of soul-life, thus being 'born many times', finds its ultimate and fullest manifestation in man who 'is born once' and has no second birth on earth.[3]

In another ode, referring to the Essence that reveals itself in different prophets and saints, now as Adam, now as Noah, now as Abraham, now as Jesus, and finally as Muhammad (not to count the other prophets in between), Rumi says that 'there is no transmigration, nothing is transferred' (Nicholson, *Rumi, Poet and Mystic*, p.142). It is the One playing the Many. 'The white radiance of Eternity' remains; only the forms change and pass. Individuals do not reincarnate.

THE SPIRITUAL WORLD

At times, Rumi may appear inconsistent, but generally this is so because meaning has many levels, and when he is concerned with more than one level, he changes his speech to accord with the level concerned. If any inconsistency arises in the process, it is only apparent, not real.

Thus, while he speaks of Resurrection, the Judgement of the Dead, and of Paradise for the righteous and Hell for the wicked, in the manner of the orthodox, he also says that there is no earthly spatiality, nothing gross or physical in the spiritual realm; that Heaven and Hell are spiritual states, and Hell is purifying; and that, eventually, the Mercy of the All-merciful will save us all.

Rumi says that our present station is not the last. Many loftier stations lie ahead, 'from man to angel and so *ad infinitum*' (*Discourses*, p.32) the *Mathnawi* mentions 18,000 worlds and more (M.I, 3756) — and we will escape from the present self-seeking intelligence and behold 'a hundred thousand most wonderful intelligences' (M.IV, 3649; also, see pp.65 *supra*).

Here, the reference may be to the countless spiritual states or worlds of consciousness which the Sufi must pass before he can attain to *fana* (self-abnegation) and, with it, to *baqa* (life everlasting).[4]

But we are not all Sufis or Perfect Men, but common mortals, with common frailties, or sinners marked for Hell. Perfection is not our portion. How and where should we then hope to see these myriads of different worlds and most wonderful intelligences which the elect see on this side of the veil?

We shall see these countless wondrous forms of spiritual life, the ones we have not seen here, on the other side of the veil, where we saw them during our descent. The ascent is by the same route by which we came, for the way up is the same as the way down.

According to Rumi, he who goes to Hell will suffer and his suffering will bring him remembrance of God, and this remembrance will make him repent and purify him and give him experience of wonderful spiritual states.

'Hell for ever' is not literally true with Rumi. All are saved in the end. As he says, the Lord's eternal Mercy will deliver the infidel from the thorn-field of unbelief and make him blossom like a rose in the cypress-garden of God (M.I, 3828).

HEAVEN AND HELL

According to the Koran, it is a fixed ordinance of the Lord that at the Congregation for Judgement, the believers and the infidels will be brought crouching around Hell and there the righteous will be rescued and the evil-doers left crouching (Koran, xix,68, 71–2).

On the spiritual level, Rumi describes Heaven and Hell as non-spatial; they are spiritual states. They are the effects of our actions and attributes exhibited in this life. As what is Below is in accordance with what is Above, and what is not Below is nowhere at all, Heaven and Hell exist not only in the other world, but also in this world. The criteria of judgement also is the same in both cases. None of us is wholly good or wholly evil, wholly white or wholly black. We are shades of grey. Now to our delight, an angel raises its head within us; now to our anguish a devil; now to our lustful unease, a beast.

It is the preponderating quality that determines our inner state and worth both in this world and the next. If there is more of gold than copper in us, we shall be reckoned as of gold both Here and There (M.II, 1417–19; 1426). In the words of Abu Sa'id ibn Abi'l-Khayr, 'Hell is where thou art, and Paradise, where thou art not', that is where thou art naughted. Hell is selfhood, Paradise is selflessness (*Islamic Mysticism*, p.64).

Rumi says that Hell has seven gates, symbolising seven vices or capital sins. Every vice issues from our carnal soul which is of the nature of Hell.

Not that we are not warned against the machinations of the carnal soul. When we do wrong, our conscience stings us, and that sting is God's warning and corrective action. But if we ignore the small still voice of conscience, its stings will appear to take material form and become chains of torment in the next world (M.III, 348–54).[5]

According to *The Tibetan Book of the Dead*, the body there will be repeatedly hacked, causing intense pain, but, being a mental body, it will be incapable of dying (p.166).

These torments need not be taken in the physical sense. They are meant to symbolise the intense pangs of the deceased's conscience, compared with which the pangs suffered in this world are 'a mere play'.

While the evil-doers will be left burning in the flames of their lust, the righteous, according to Rumi, will have no awareness of the existence of Hell or of its smoke or fire. For in their earth-life, they conquered their appetitive soul, quenched the flaming fire of lust and transformed it into the garden of piety; they killed all envy and turned their anger to forbearance, ignorance to knowledge, greed to unselfishness. They extinguished these inner fires for God's sake and made their fiery soul like an orchard sown with fidelity. They brought water into the blazing Hell of their soul. No wonder that Hell also has changed its aspect and become greenery and roses to them — a fit return for a goodly life (M.II, 255468).

Speaking of Paradise and Hell in the context of his Monistic Pantheism, Rumi says that they are but the reflections of the

Divine attributes. They are aspects in which God presents Himself to our consciousness. Our attributes, like love and righteousness, anger and lust, thoughts and actions, all come from Him, and when the soul leaves the body, they ultimately return to Him. The four fountains or rivers of Paradise *Kawthar*, *Salsabil*, *Zanjabil* and *Tasnim* — which are the fountains of pure water, wine, honey and milk, symbolise His beautiful attributes, while the adamantine chains and penal fires represent His wrathful attributes. They are, as mentioned earlier, the reflections or effects of the nature and actions of the righteous and the unrighteous. Just as spiritual men living in heedfulness of Him in Paradise display His Beauty, the wicked in Hell display His Majesty, His Terror and Wrath. Nothing is good or evil in itself. It is the religious commands and prohibitions (*amr-i-taklifi*) that qualify some actions as good and others as evil, and test the faith of each one of us, as we are free to obey or disobey them. They are a cohering influence in society.

As sin and righteousness are relative and spring from a single source, they are interchangeable. They are like the Peaceful and Wrathful Deities of Northern Buddhism that also are from a single source and are interchangeable. It was because Pharaoh could visualise this possibility of interchange, if God so willed, that he hoped that the honey of *Zanjabil* might change the poison of hatred in him to sweetness of love and faith; or, from the reflection of the fountain of milk (*Tasnim*), his imprisoned reason might receive nourishment for a while; or, from the reflection of wine (*Salsabil*), he might get intoxicated and savour the delight of bowing to His command; or, from the pure water of *Kawthar*, his barren body might be spiritually refreshed and regenerated and become a veritable garden villa; or, in brief, from the reflection of Paradise and its four fountains, his soul might become the seeker of God. But that was not Pharaoh's portion on earth. God had willed otherwise. At times, from the reflection of the snake of Hell, he would be dropping poison on those destined for Paradise; sometimes, from the reflection of the scalding water of Hell, he would putrefy the bones of good people; or, from the reflection of the freezing cold of Hell or of its burning flames, he would freeze or burn people to death. He was the Hell of the poor and oppressed. Both Moses and Pharaoh reflected God's attributes, the former His beautiful attributes and the latter His wrathful ones. The reflection of the former constituted the ingredients of Paradise and that of the latter those of Hell (M.IV, 2517–27).

EVENTUAL SALVATION AND PARADISE FOR ALL

Rumi does not interpret the doctrine of 'Hell for ever' for the damned in the literal sense. Just as God's universal Mercy gave existence to us as a free robe of honour, it will eventually tear aside the veils of ignorance and infidelity, which are the constituents of the torments of Hell and bar to the damned entry into Paradise. Like Jili and Ibnu'l-'Arabi, Rumi believes that there is no soul, howsoever devoid of merit, that will not be ultimately saved. Different people have different forms of worship, but as everyone worships according to God's Will — even Satan's disobedience was according to His Will — all will be saved in the end.

God says in the Koran that He will adjust our works, and forgive us our trespasses (Koran, xxxiii,71). The reference is to this act of mercy, when He says:

> I will kindle such a fire of Grace that the
> least spark thereof consumes all sin and
> necessity and freewill.
> I will set fire to the tenement of Man and
> make its thorns a bower of roses.

(M.V, 1848–50, tr. Dr Nicholson, *Rumi, Poet and Mystic*, p.57)

The idea of the ultimate salvation of all souls is found in other faiths also. In Hinduism, Vishnu, in his tenth *avatar* (incarnation), will throw the wicked into the infernal abodes where they will be purified and then pardoned. In Zoroastrianism, at the general Resurrection, Ahriman (Darkness) and his followers will be immersed and purified in a lake of molten metal. Father Origen, among the early Christians, believed that the doctrine of eternal punishment was wrong, and that at the second advent of Christ, even the devils among the damned would be forgiven and saved (Blavatsky, *Isis Unveiled*, Vol.II, p.238).[6]

Rumi describes Hell as the mosque for the infidel, where the resurrected counterpart of his earthly body will be consumed in the flames of Hell, and, in his suffering, he will become aware of God, and, as a result of his remembrance of Him, his soul will emerge purified. Ultimately, when we reach Him, the Supreme Deity, all souls will be concerned with Him alone, and, purged of all taint of sin and 'otherness', they will become 'one of eye and tongue and ear and understanding' (*Discourses*, p.40), with all dualities absorbed in their source, the undivided Unity.

Why, then, keep harping on God's wrathful attributes? They only belong to His Justice. God is All-forgiving and All-merciful. His Wrath is only Mercy in disguise. It corrects the erring individual and brings him back on the right path. His Mercy is eternally prior to His Wrath and prevails over it. Human clemency is but an oyster-shell before the pearl of Divine Clemency (M.I, 2677). God's worst cruelty is better than the clemency of both worlds (M.V, 1667). An unrighteous person may be weaving his way crookedly, but, in the end, God will purge him of his folly, and His Mercy will cleanse him of its pollution, bestowing on him a light which even the full moon does not possess. God is not really wrathful. With Him, Mercy and Wrath are not a duality. All the Divine attributes are eternal and identical with each other, distinguishable only by their effects on manifestation in this universe.

According to Rumi, man sins because of His forbearance, because He has called Himself All-forgiving and makes every ugliness beautiful; otherwise, none would dare sin (M.II, 336; M.V, 2100).

The Prophet has said that on the Day of Resurrection, he will not leave the sinners to shed tears, but intercede on their behalf with all his soul and deliver them from the torments of Hell (M.III,1783–5).

Nor, according to Rumi, should Hell-dwellers be thought to be unhappier than they were in this world, as there they are aware of God, which they were not in this world, and awareness of God is sweeter than awareness of any otherness (see p.51 *supra*).

According to a Holy Tradition — on which Rumi bases a long and moving passage (M.V, 1806–46) — on the Day of Resurrection, when God has finished judging mankind, two men will remain, both for Hell. As they are being taken to Hell, one of them will turn round, and, with streaming eyes, look expectantly towards God. God will ask him why he turned round and looked at Him, and, being full of sin and crime and utterly devoid of merit, what did he hope for?

He will answer: 'I am hundreds of times worse than You have declared. But You, in Your forbearance, have thrown a veil over even worse things. I was not looking towards my own actions; I was looking towards hope in Your Bounty and Grace; or, in the words of the Tradition, "I was hoping You would let me enter Paradise".'

As he recounts his sins and never lost hope in His Mercy and Bounty, God will order that he be taken to Paradise (Nicholson, *Commentary*, M.V, 1818).

The fate of the other man in the Tradition can be no different, as the Lord's infinite Mercy will save him also.

According to Rumi, Paradise, like sun and rain, is for all — not only for the righteous, but also for the sinners (M.I, 2739). The Lord's Wrath, which is His Justice, is born of His eternally precedent Mercy and sinks back into it.

Why, then, dread death? Holy men welcome it. Death is not the end; it is life's culmination; it is the entrance to a new life; a life, mystic, wonderful, leading us through countless realms into the Presence of the Judge of judges, the King of kings, enabling us to say at the last: Lo unto Him, we have returned!

Notes

INTRODUCTION

1 Another old source which gives a detailed account of Rumi and his predecessors and successors, and was written under the express orders of Sultan Walad's son Chelebi Amir Arif, is Aflaki's *Manaqibu'l-'Arifin*. Parts of this work have been translated into English and prefixed as *The Acts of the Adepts* to Sir James Redhouse's verse-rendering of Book I of Rumi's monumental work, the *Mathnawi*. Unfortunately, Aflaki's work suffers from grave inconsistencies, and also, the miraculous attainments of Rumi and other adepts which he narrates are well past belief.

2 Redhouse, *The Acts of the Adepts*, Preface, p.x; chapter 3, p.24. Also, see Dr E.G. Browne, *A Literary History of Persia*, Vol. II, p.517.

3 Abu Yazid Taifur al-Bastami (died AD 874) and Abu'l-Qasim al-Junayd (died AD 910) were the most eminent Sufis of their time.

4 M: the *Mathnawi*
I: Book I
1727–30: the verse numbers, according to Dr Nicholson's edited Text.

5 Rumi's other two prose works are the *Majalis-i-Sab'a* ('Seven Sessions'), which consists of sermons, and the *Maktubat* ('Letters').

6 The reference is to E.H. Whinfield whose *Masnavi-i-Ma'navi*, the Spiritual Couplets of Rumi, containing a translation of passages selected from the entire *Mathnawi*, and valuable introductory and other notes, was the first work in English (London, 1887) to give an analysis of its contents and illustrate its qualitative excellence.

7 This Commentary is appended to *The Secret of the Golden Flower*, translated and explained by Richard Wilhelm, and translated into English by Cary F. Baynes.

CHAPTER 1

1 Plotinus (AD 205–70), the author of the *Enneads*, was the chief philosopher of the Alexandrian School of Neo-Platonism.

2 The concept of Primal Light or Fire as the source of life and light figures in practically all faiths. Thus, in Genesis, the Lord first creates light; our visible sun is created three days later. In Zoroastrianism, Ormuzd is light, the life-giver. In Hinduism, Agni, the Divine Fire, with its undecaying radiance, is the source of all life, 'a born master of the life that shall be born'. The throne of the Ancient of Days — the Kabalistic En Soph — was like the fiery flame, and his wheels as burning fire (Daniel, vii, 9), and light is his first emanation. The first light is Sephira or Divine Intelligence of the Kabalists; it is Sophia, the Wisdom principle of the Gnostics.

3 The Mu'tazilites, one of the early sects that arose in the eighth century and called themselves 'Partisans of the Divine Justice and Unity', deny that God has any eternal attributes. Rumi rejects this view. The Divine Essence comprises both names and attributes. They inhere in the Essence and become manifest when God descends into manifestation. As forms of the Essence, they belong to Him. Their creation means manifestation, not origination in time.

4 The reference is to Jili's illuminating work, *al-insanu'l-kamil fi ma'rifatu'l-awakhir w'al-awa'il* ('The man perfect in knowledge of the last and the first things'), which is comprehensively treated in Dr Nicholson's *Studies in Islamic Mysticism*.

5 To cite an anecdote, the most eminent Persian poet Hafiz (fourteenth century) was initially only a poetaster, a public laughing stock. When he realised that he was no poet, it was to the tomb of this very dervish poet Baba Kuhi that he went and wept bitterly there till deep sleep fell upon him. A holy figure appeared to him in a dream, gave him a morsel of food to eat and said: 'Go, all the doors of knowledge are open to you.' As if in confirmation, the Muse of poetry took Hafiz to her bosom and crowned him king of poets.

6 As the Vedas have it, 'In the beginning was Brahman; with whom was *Vak* or the Word; and the Word is Brahman.' St John's Gospel has a similar opening: 'In the beginning was the Word, and the Word was with God, and the Word was God.'

Hinduism mentions *Vak* subsequent to God, as *Vak* exists because God exists and it issues from Him. Similarly, in Islam,

God is prior to His creative Word 'Be'. The priority, of course, is logical, not temporal; while the Word was with God, that is, before its issue, it was God. Time was not yet born.

7 It may be recalled that 'desire' is a cosmological concept. The early Vedic character Kama, for example, and also the Greek Eros personified 'desire', which is the feeling that propels to creation and is the bond connecting Entity with Non-entity (Blavatsky, *The Secret Doctrine*, Vol. II, 176). Without it, there would have been no creation.

8 This 'breaking' of one Thought into many forms of thought, this 'Self-sundering' or 'Self-diremption', is 'the Mystic Sacrifice' mentioned in ancient cosmogonies. 'The sacrifice is the sacrificial self-limitation by which the Many issue from the One.' It is the breaking forth in 'sacrifice' of the One Life or Light and uniting with the world of forms that are of darkness. In the Rig-Veda, it is the sacrificial streaming forth of the life-blood of the supreme *Purusha* into all quarters of the globe, forming and sustaining the manifest creation. In Egypt, it is the Divine Osiris whose limbs are scattered in space. In Plotinus, the One Existent is the Good, and 'it is of the essence of things that each gives of its being to another; else, the Good would not be Good' (*Enneads*, ii, 9, 3).

(For a fuller description of the 'Mystic Sacrifice', reference may be made to Sri Krishna Prem's illuminating work, *The Yoga of the Bhagavat Gita*, 1948, pp.69–70).

9 According to Plotinus, the planes of descent from the One or First Existent are emanations arising out of the contemplation of its prior. The first emanation of the One is the Nous, variously translated as Divine Mind, Divine Thought, Spirit or Intelligence. It is a unity of the archetypes of the present, past and future, or what Plato calls the 'Ideas', which are constituted by the Essence of God and are the total content of the creative Divine Mind, and the ultimate cause of the manifested universe. There 'light runs through light', and each is all and all is each, and no distinctions exist. In Rumi also, the Divine attributes inhering in the Essence are neither mutually joined, nor mutually separate, and yet are one with it and with one another.

From the Divine Mind emanates another being, the Universal Soul (*nafs-i-kull*), and from the Universal or All-Soul emanates its image, 'Nature' which 'possesses the last of the Reason-principle', and from Nature emanates the sensible universe (*'alam-i-nasut*), patterned on the eternal Original in the Divine Mind. There is no incarnation (*hulul*) or entry at any stage. It is just gazing or contemplation.

The reader may refer to Dr Nicholson's classical work, *Selected Poems from the Diwan-i-Shams-i-Tabriz*, edited and translated with an Introduction, Notes and Appendices (Cambridge, 1898), which discusses this similarity in the Introduction.

10 Cf. Ruysbroeck: 'Through the eternal Birth all creatures have come forth in eternity before they were created in time. So God has seen and known them in Himself ... in living ideas, and in an otherness from Himelf, but not as something other in all ways, for all that is in God is God.'

11 Mansur, the name of Hallaj's father, here refers to the martyr-saint Hallaj himself.

12 In the West also, execution used to be the punishment even for petty thefts in the not very distant past, when property was treated as a part of one's person, a projection of one's personality.

13 The reference is to some young believers, generally identified with the Seven Sleepers of Ephesus, who with their dog took shelter from persecution in a cave where God kept them secure for a number of years.

14 The romance of Layla (night) and Majnun (mad) whose original name was Qays but who came to be known as Majnun when the love of Layla had robbed him of his senses, is well known in the East. It has been narrated by more than one writer, and it occurs as the third poem of the Quintet (*khamsa*), written by an eminent poet Nizami of Ganja in AD 1188–9. Though generally known to be night-black (as the name indicates) and short-statured, Nizami paints her as one with a beautiful complexion and graceful stature. In Rumi, she is not superior to other good lookers (M.I, 408).

CHAPTER 2

1 Creative evolution 'typifies the movement of the World-Spirit, evolving through lower forms of soul-life and manifesting itself finally and completely in the Perfect Man' (Nicholson).

2 Of these nine, seven pertain to the seven planets; the eighth is the Sphere of the Fixed Stars, the habitation of the spiritual angels; and the ninth, the 'Starless Sphere', with beings of light, is the all-encircling sphere that divides our manifest cosmos from the unmanifest 'Spiritual Cosmos'. (Also, see p.251, nn. 6 and 7.)

3 Rumi also speaks of 18,000 worlds or more which the spirit has to

traverse both in its ascent and descent. In Sufism, these worlds
and celestial spheres, each with many worlds, represent the
countless spiritual stations that the Sufi has to ascend on his Way
to Reality. (See p.238 *infra*.)

4 In the Gospel of St John, Jesus draws a distinction between
ordinary water of which 'whoever drinketh ... shall thirst again'
and the water he would give which would be to him who drinks 'a
well of water springing into lasting life' (ch. 4, 13–14).

5 *The Tibetan Book of the Dead*, Foreword by Sir John
Woodroffe, p.lxxxii, footnote.

6 *The Secret Doctrine*, Book 2, Part I, pp.148–9.

7 According to ancient philosophy, the first divine conception of
man is formed in slow degrees in several departments of the
universal workshop, and even after the descent of the soul into
matter, there are countless worlds in space through which it
travels as 'an embryonic being ... ever-living, dying, sustaining a
flitting spiritual existence as rudimental as the material shape
from whence it emerged'. It is only on reaching the earth —
which confers self-consciousness on him — that man evolves as
man (Blavatsky, *Isis Unveiled*, Vol.I, pp.345,368).

CHAPTER 3

1 To the Stoics, only the virtuous will, that is, the will exercised by
our Divine part is free.

In Plotinus, the will is free, if it acts according to right
reasoning and complete knowledge. If a killer is ignorant of his
father's being the victim, his killing is not really voluntary. 'Our
freedom of act must be referred not to ... the external thing done
... but to ... virtue's own vision' (*Enneads*, VI,viii,1 and 6).

According to St Paul, the spiritual law makes us feel the
bondage of flesh; for it is the flesh which prevents our will from
obeying the law, thus giving us the knowledge of sin. Freedom
comes, when we 'walk not after the flesh but after the spirit',
when the law becomes our principle of action, the very 'law of
life' (Epistle to the Romans, viii,I-4).

2 The reference is to the Battle of Badr in which a handful of gravel
thrown by the Prophet at the heathen — the army of Quraysh —
caused their rout.

3 Spinoza's view is similar. God knows no evil, as there is no evil to
know; evil appears to arise through regarding parts of the
universe as separate and self-subsistent. If we envision the world
as God envisions it, we will see the interconnectedness of the

parts of the Whole, and every part as necessary to its goodness. Evil is thus born of ignorance or inadequate knowledge.

Or we may liken the Whole to a perfect crystal — not a flaw anywhere. But if it is broken, its pieces come apart as different — some beautiful, some ugly, some smooth, some jagged. But this difference is only relative to the parts as parts. When rejoined to the Whole, they complete the unity of the perfect crystal.

CHAPTER 4

1 According to some Sufis, by disobeying the Lord's command to bow to Adam, Satan gave preference to His eternal Will over His command, and proved himself a greater monotheist than God Himself; he would rather suffer the torments of Hell than compromise the Divine Unity. But no less a Sufi than Junayd rejects this view as utterly false.

2 The reference is to Mu'awia, who, after the assassination of the fourth and last orthodox Caliph Ali in AD 661 and the abdication of his son al-Hasan (by the Prophet's daughter Fatima) assumed the throne of the mighty Moslem empire.

3 B. Furuzanfarr's Persian Commentary (*Sharh*) on the *Mathnawi*, p.458.

4 In ancient philosophy, dragons and serpents are a dual symbol. Among the Ophite gnostics, for example, Ennoia or the Divine Mind and the serpent, the Ophis, the Shadow of the Light, were the Logos as a Unity, manifesting itself as a double principle of good and evil.

Shadow is no evil, but the inevitable corollary that completes light; it is that which enables light to manifest itself, and gives it objective reality; 'it is its creator on earth'.

While as a Unity, Ennoia and Ophis are the Logos, when separated, 'one is the Tree of Life (spiritual), the other the Tree of Knowledge of Good and Evil' (Blavatsky, *The Secret Doctrine*, Vol.2, 214–15).

The early Christians also had their dual Logos — the Good and the bad Serpent (ibid. Vol.I, 410).

Lucifer of Genesis also is dual. The equivalent of Satan, he is the Logos in his highest aspect, being the Light-Bringer, and after his 'fall', he is the Logos in his lowest aspect.

5 Although the devil is generally presented as if it were a distinct entity from the angel in man, ancient philosophy stressed the dual nature of Satan as a single concept. The duality of the serpent symbolising Satan is expressed by De Chateaubriand

thus: 'Object of horror or of admiration ... Lie calls it, Prudence claims it, Envy carries it in its heart, and Eloquence in its caduceus. In hell, it arms the whip of the Furies; in heaven, Eternity makes of it its symbol (Blavatsky, *The Secret Doctrine*, Vol.I, 403).

Satan is not a person, says the nineteenth century Kabalist Eliphas Levi, but a creative force for good and evil. The Red Dragon and the Light-bearer is in us; it is our mind, our tempter or redeemer; it can save us or destroy us, depending on us.

6 Mt *Qaf* is a fabulous mountain imagined to be surrounding the whole earth and binding the horizon on all sides. It is the ninth Heaven of ancient legends surrounding the other eight. In Sufism, it is the psycho-spiritual mountain in whose emerald cities dwell beings of light, and which the Sufi must cross on his way to Reality (see p.60 *supra*).

7 The *'Anqa* (Arabic) or *Simurgh* (Persian) is a fabulous bird whose name is known but whose body is unknown. It symbolises something unknowable, the transcendental Spirit, God 'the Truth'. Its abode can be sighted from the cosmic Mt *Qaf*.

8 *Nirvana* is not a state of simple vacuity, as is often supposed. 'If any teach *Nirvana* is to cease, Say unto such they lie.' It is a state 'where the Silence lives', and in which the Buddhist saint 'is one with life, and yet lives not', and is 'blest ceasing to be' (Sir Edwin Arnold, *The Light of Asia*).

9 The Tradition concerning these veils is explained in Ghazali's *Mishkat al-anwar* ('A Niche of Lights'). Born around AD 1060, Ghazali was the author of *Ihya'u 'ulumi'd-Din* ('Revivification of the Religious Sciences'), and several other valuable works. Because of his services to religion, he was given the title of 'The Proof of Islam'. Ghazali died in AD 1111.

10 The reference is to the wandering dervish Abu Ishaq Ibrahim b. Adham, who figures as a prince of Balkh in Moslem legend, and who, like the Buddha, abandoned his kingdom and took to a life of seclusion and devotion to God.

11 For a detailed description of the organisational aspect of Sufism, reference may be made to Spencer Trimingham's *Sufi Orders in Islam* (Oxford University Press).

12 Esoterically, both these 'falls' were an essential part of the creative process which God initiated in order that He might be known (see p.99 *supra*).

13 Sri Krishna Prem, *The Yoga of the Kathopanishad*, ed. 1955, p.99, footnote.

CHAPTER 5

1 According to one of its descriptions in Sufism, good behaviour is to carry out the Lord's commands; to be just and comradely to one's equals, without expecting justice or anything in return; to be kind and generous to one's inferiors; not to speak ill of anyone, for to do so is to criticise the Creator; and to be good to oneself by following the rules of good behaviour, and ignoring the call of the flesh and the devil.

CHAPTER 6

1 The idea of the soul's being the spouse of the spirit is also found in the Cairo-born Ibnu'l-Farid, the greatest mystical Arab poet (AD 1182–1235).

   Explaining his verses 669–71 from the Odes, Dr Nicholson says that, in pre-existence, the soul was 'one with the Being, which is the subject and object of all knowledge, and *qua* Universal Spirit (the father) eternally begets in itself, *qua* Universal Soul (the mother), the ideal, i.e., non-externalised essences of things' (*Islamic Mysticism*, pp. 258–9, footnote).

2 In the *Kathopanishad*, the one Inner Atman of all beings corresponds to, and is, yet, outside every form.

3 In some descriptions, the soul's progress is extended to seven stages by adding the following three as separate stages to the above four: (i) 'the contented soul' (*nafs-i-radiya*), i.e. content in the Lord's good pleasure; (ii) 'the approved soul' (*nafs-i-mardiya*), so called as it satisfies and pleases the Lord; and (iii) 'the perfect soul' (*nafs-i-kamila*), which is entirely purified or sanctified.

   For an English rendering of one of the formalised accounts of the seven-staged purgation of the soul, the reader may refer to Trimingham's *The Sufi Orders in Islam*, pp.155–7.

4 Also, see the description of the four 'worlds' in *The Sufi Orders in Islam*, pp.159–61.

CHAPTER 7

1 According to one of the descriptions of the three stages of certainty, in the first stage, the seeker knows that the object of his quest is within him; in the second stage, he sees the object with the eye of spiritual intuition or mystical contemplation; in the third stage, the illusion of subject and object, seeker and sought, vanishes and he attains to absolute unity. (See *Islamic Mysticism*, p.247.)

2 This anecdote is quoted from Aflaki by Furuzanfarr in his *Commentary (sharh)* on the *Mathnawi*, p.703.

CHAPTER 8

1 The bridge across Hell, thinner than a hair and sharper than the edge of a sword (Tradition).

2 There are two 'h's in the Arabic alphabet, *hawwaz* (pronounced as English 'h') and *hutti* (throaty 'h'). The latter is followed by the letter *kha* (pronounced as in Scottish 'ch' in loch). Bilal could not pronounce the throaty 'h'.

As is aptly said: 'The worship of words is more pernicious than the worship of images. Grammatolatory is the worst species of idolatory' (Robert Dale Owen, *The debatable Land*, p.145, quoted in *Isis Unveiled*, Vol.II, p.560).

3 Junayd invests the various rites with the significance given against each below:

i) Journeying from home for the pilgrimage is to journey away from all sins;

ii) At every night-halt en route, one must traverse a 'station' (*maqam*) on the Way to God;

iii) When putting on the pilgrim's garb at the proper place, discard the attributes of humanity;

iv) When standing on Arafat, stand one instant in contemplation of God (it is the Arafat of *ma'rifat* — Hujwiri);

v) When you go to Muzdalifa and achieve your desire, renounce all sensual desires (it is the Muzdalifa of *ulfat*, that is amity — Hujwiri);

vi) While circumambulating the *Ka'ba*, behold the immaterial beauty of God (it is the temple of *tanzih*, that is, of Divine purification — Hujwiri);

vii) When you run between Safa and Marwa (two hillocks at Mecca), attain to the rank of purity (*safa*) and virtue (*muruwwat*);

viii) When you come to the valley of Mina, all your wishes must cease (it is the Mina of faith — Hujwiri);

ix) When you reach the slaughter-place and offer sacrifice, sacrifice the objects of sensual desire; and

x) When you throw the stones as prescribed, throw away whatever sensual thoughts were accompanying you.

If the pilgrim does not perform the pilgrimage in this spirit, he cannot enter the station of Abraham which the sacred territory contains and because of which it is called *haram* (sanctuary).

(Summarised from the *Kashf*, pp.326–8.)

4 Some Sufis disregard the need for pilgrimage to Mecca, as they believe that their pilgrimage takes place within themselves. Thus Abu Sa'id ibn Abi'l-Khayr, a famous eleventh-century Persian mystic, says: 'Why walk thousands of miles to visit a stone house? The true man of God sits where he is, and the *Bayt al-Ma'mur* [the celestial archetype of the *Ka'ba*] comes several times a day and night to visit him and perform the circumambulation above his head' (*Islamic Mysticism*, p.62).

CHAPTER 9

1 Cf. Ibnu'l-Farid: 'When I died of his love, I lived by him, through the wealth of my self-denial and the abundance of my poverty.'

2 Both *Yusuf and Zulaykha* and *Salaman and Absal* are *mathnawi* poems written by an eminent fifteenth-century poet and mystic Jami (AD 1414–92) and included in his *Haft Awrang* ('Seven Thrones'), comprised of seven poems. *Layla and Majnun*, to whose earlier version by Nizami reference was made at p.248 *supra*, n.14, is also included in this septet.

3 According to the popular version, Layla's vein is incised and, simultaneously, a bleeding wound appears on Majnun's arm.

4 The *Gulshan-i-Raz* ('Rose-garden of Mystery') is a symbolistic, mystical poem written by the Sufi poet Sa'du'd-Din Mahmud Shabistari (born around AD 1250), of which more than one translation exists, the one by E.H. Whinfield being the best known.

CHAPTER 10

1 Dr Evans-Wentz, *Tibet's Great Yogi Milarepa*, ch.xii, p.244 etc.

2 *The Tibetan Book of the Dead*, Foreword by Sir John Woodroffe, pp.lxvii,lxviii.

It may be of interest to note that, instead of an infinite series of universes, Northern Buddhism speaks of seven worlds, constituting seven globes of a planetary chain; and on each globe, according to it, there are seven rounds of evolution, so that there are forty-nine stations of active existence, also referred to as Forty-nine Days.

The Forty-nine Days also symbolise the Forty-nine Powers of the Seven Vowels, which in India were the Mystery of the Seven Fires or the consciousness principles and their forty-nine sub-fires. In Hermetic writings, it is on each of the sevenfold seven zones of after-death 'ascent' that the deceased leaves one of his principles, until he arrives on the plane above all zones and remains as 'the great Formless Serpent of Absolute Wisdom, or the Deity itself' (*The Secret Doctrine*, Vol.I, 411).

The reader may recall our earlier reference to the Prophet's Tradition concerning the 700 or 70,000 veils of light and darkness between man and God which in Sufism the soul or spirit has to rend both on its way up and down (p.166 *supra*); and also to nine celestial spheres through which the spirit has to descend and ascend (pp.59–60 *supra*).

3 As stated earlier, according to the popular interpretation of Reincarnation, successive rebirths of the same individual (or of his 'astral monad') take place on this very plane, either immediately or after enjoying Paradise or suffering Hell for a time, according to his performance on earth. But on the basis of some authoritative fragments, Blavatsky says that rebirth on the same planet is not a rule in nature, but an exception prevailing only where the original purpose of man's physical and spiritual development in his earthly existence is frustrated by lunacy, idiocy, abortion, death at birth or by accident. In such cases, the astral monad is violently thrown back into earth-life, simply because he 'cannot skip over the physical and intellectual sphere of the terrestrial man, and be suddenly ushered into the spiritual sphere above' (*Isis Unveiled*, Vol.I, pp.351–2).

In Rumi, man makes the spiritual 'ascent' through nine celestial spheres, and these have countless worlds symbolising spiritual states or stations, but in no case does he reincarnate or take rebirth on earth.

4 It is interesting to compare Rumi's account of the spiritual ascent — through 700 (or 70,000) veils of light and 18,000 worlds and more, and nine celestial spheres, which also have countless worlds — with what was said about the infinite series of universes, the Forty-nine Days and the Mystery of the Seven Fires (see n.3 *supra*), and note the similarity amid dissimilarity.

5 There is no rigid dualism of spirit and matter. Matter is but spirit in 'ex-istence'; it is spirit's exterior.

6 In Dante's *Divine Comedy*, the *Inferno*, the *Purgatorio* ('Mountain of Purification') and the *Paradiso* are a beautiful embodiment of this noble conception.